A Preface to
MARKETING
MANAGEMENT

Consulting Editors in Marketing

ROBERT E. WITT
MARK I. ALPERT

both of The University of Texas at Austin

A Preface to
MARKETING
MANAGEMENT

LAWRENCE X. TARPEY
University of Kentucky

JAMES H. DONNELLY, JR.
University of Kentucky

J. PAUL PETER
Washington University

 1979

BUSINESS PUBLICATIONS, INC.   Dallas, Texas   75243
Irwin-Dorsey Limited   Georgetown, Ontario   L7G 4B3

ISBN 0-256-02207-0
Library of Congress Catalog Card No. 78–70019

Printed in the United States of America

3 4 5 6 7 8 9 0 ML 6 5 4 3 2 1 0

PREFACE

As the title suggests, this book is intended to serve as a relatively brief overview of the critical aspects of marketing management. Since it was developed with a variety of uses in mind, one of our major concerns was to achieve a balance between theory and practice. Through the use of chapter materials, additional sections, and "highlights," we believe this balance has been achieved.

Preliminary drafts of this book have been used successfully in advanced undergraduate and MBA-level marketing management courses where case problems have been the focus of the course. The three major sections of the book have been used as a resource supplement in these courses to enable students to gain more meaningful experience from the use of case problems.

Preliminary drafts of this book have also been used successfully in short courses, executive training, and continuing education seminars. The content and structure of the book have proven to be very useful for these purposes.

The book has three major sections:

Section I. *Essentials of Marketing Management*

This section contains the essentials of marketing management in 13 chapters. The objective here is to present only that material which might be useful in analyzing a marketing problem. While the chapters are necessarily broad in scope, relevant research and review literature serves as the bases for the concepts presented. Whenever possible the reader is directed to relevant research literature and also provided with additional sources at the end of each chapter.

Section II.   *Analyzing Marketing Problems and Cases*

This section presents an approach to analyzing, writing, and presenting case analyses. It has been utilized successfully by the authors and has been thoroughly tested in the classroom. It could have been presented as the first section of the book since it it designed to be read at the start of a case course. However, since it is usually referred to throughout the semester, it was placed after the text material for convenience. Also, for those executive training and short courses that do not employ cases, the text may be used without reference to the case analysis section.

Section III.   *Selected Reference Tools for Marketing Management*

This section contains an annotated bibliography of numerous relevant secondary sources which can be used as a resource for the analysis of many types of marketing problems. We have found that this section has been extremely valuable. Thus, this section should also increase the depth of analysis as well as expose readers to important secondary sources that will be useful to them in their careers. Five classifications of secondary sources are presented: marketing sources, financial information sources, basic U.S. statistical sources, general business and industry sources, and indexes and abstracts.

Since this book is designed to serve as a handbook or sourcebook, we have also included occasional "Highlights," which we have found are useful as handy references when analyzing cases and problems. They are not a part of the regular chapter material but are placed at appropriate points in the flow of material.

We would like to acknowledge the contributions of the reviewers whose detailed reviews and numerous suggestions are reflected throughout this book. We are indebted to Bob Witt and Mark Alpert of the University of Texas and Michael J. Houston of the University of Wisconsin.

Finally, we acknowledge Robert L. Virgil, Dean of the School of Business, Washington University, and William W. Ecton, Dean of the College of Business and Economics, University of Kentucky, for their support of our efforts. The excellent secretarial assistance of Ruth Scheetz is also gratefully acknowledged.

December 1978   **Lawrence X. Tarpey**
                                   James H. Donnelly, Jr.
                                   J. Paul Peter

CONTENTS

Section I
ESSENTIALS OF MARKETING MANAGEMENT, 1

A. Introduction, 3

Chapter 1
AN OVERVIEW OF THE MARKETING
MANAGEMENT PROCESS   5

The Marketing Concept. What Is Marketing? What Is Marketing Man-
agement? *Organizational Mission and Objectives. Situation Analysis.
Marketing Planning. Implementation and Control of the Marketing
Plan. Marketing Information Systems and Marketing Research.*

B. Marketing Information, Research, and
Understanding the Target Market, 17

Chapter 2
MARKETING INFORMATION SYSTEMS AND
MARKETING RESEARCH   19

Marketing Information Systems: *Information Flows in the Marketing
System. The Marketing Information Center.* Marketing Research: *The
Research Process. Problems in the Research Process.*

Chapter 3
CONSUMER BEHAVIOR   40

The Buying Process: *Felt Need. Alternative Search. Alternative Evaluation. Purchase Decision. Postpurchase Feelings.* Group Influences on Consumer Behavior: *Cultural and Subcultural Influences. Social Class. Reference Groups.* Product Class Influences. Situational Influences.

Chapter 4
INDUSTRIAL BUYER BEHAVIOR   56

Product Influences on Industrial Buying. Organizational Influences on
Industrial Buying: *Multiple Buying Influence or Joint Decision Making.
Diffusion of Buying Authority. Company-Specific Factors.* Behavioral
Influences on Industrial Buying: *Nonpersonal Motivations. Personal
Motivations. Role Perception.* Stages in the Buying Process: *Problem
Recognition. Assignment of Buying Authority. Search Procedures. Choice
Procedures.*

C. The Marketing Mix, 71

Chapter 5
PRODUCT STRATEGY   73

Product Definition. Product Classification. Product Life Cycle. Product
Policy Considerations: *Product Mix and Product Line. Market Segmentation. Private Brands. Distinctive Packaging.* Product Management Concept: *Organizing for Product Management.* The Product Audit: *Dele-
tions. Product Improvement.*

Chapter 6
NEW PRODUCT PLANNING AND
DEVELOPMENT   94

New Product Policy. New Product Planning and Development Process:
*Idea Generation. Idea Screening. Project Planning. Product Development.
Test Marketing. Commercialization.* Profit Planning for New Products:
Estimating Investment Worth. Causes of New Product Failure: *Need for
Research.* Organizing for New Product Development.

Chapter 7
PROMOTION STRATEGY: ADVERTISING AND
SALES PROMOTION   108

The Promotion Mix. Advertising: Planning and Strategy: *Objectives of
Advertising. Specific Tasks of Advertising.* Advertising Decisions: *The
Expenditure Question. The Allocation Question.* Sales Promotion.

Chapter 8
PROMOTION STRATEGY: PERSONAL SELLING   126

Importance of Personal Selling. The Sales Process: *Selling Fundamentals.*
Managing the Sales Process: *The Sales Management Task. Controlling
the Sales Force.*

Chapter 9
DISTRIBUTION STRATEGY   142

The Need for Marketing Intermediaries. Classification of Marketing
Intermediaries and Functions. Channels of Distribution. Selecting Chan-
nels of Distribution: *General Considerations. Specific Considerations.*
Managing a Channel of Distribution: *A Channel Leader.*

Chapter 10
PRICING STRATEGY   155

Demand Influences on Pricing Decisions. Supply Influences on Pricing
Decisions: *Pricing Objectives. Cost Considerations in Pricing. Product
Consideration in Pricing.* Environmental Influences on Pricing Decisions:
Competition. Government Regulations. A General Pricing Decision
Model.

D. Marketing in Special Fields, 167

Chapter 11
THE MARKETING OF SERVICES   169

Important Characteristics of Services: *Intangibility. Inseparability.
Perishability and Fluctuating Demand. Highly Differentiated Marketing
Systems. Client Relationship.* Roadblocks to Innovation in Service
Marketing: *Limited View of Marketing. Limited Competition. Noncrea-
tive Management. No Obsolescence.* Innovations in the Distribution of
Services: *Marketing Intermediaries in the Distribution of Services. Impli-
cations for Service Marketers.*

Chapter 12
INTERNATIONAL MARKETING   181

Organizing for International Marketing: *Problem Conditions: External.
Problem Conditions: Internal.* Programming for International Market-
ing: *International Marketing Research. Product Planning for Interna-
tional Markets. International Distribution System. Pricing for Interna-
tional Marketing. International Advertising.* Strategies for International
Marketing: *Strategy One: Same Product, Same Message Worldwide.
Strategy Two: Same Product, Different Communications. Strategy
Three: Different Product, Same Communications. Strategy Four: Dif-*

ferent Product, Different Communications. Strategy Five: Product Invention.

E. Marketing Response to a Changing Society, 197

Chapter 13
MARKETING AND SOCIETY   199

Marketing's Social Responsibility: *Societal Concept. Marketing Ethics. Consumerism. Recent Efforts.* Broadening the Concept of Marketing.

Section II
ANALYZING MARKETING PROBLEMS AND CASES, 209

A Case Analysis Framework: *1. Analyze and Record the Current Situation. 2. Analyze and Record Problems and Their Core Elements. 3. Formulate, Evaluate, and Record Alternative Courses of Action. 4. Select, Implement, and Record the Chosen Alternative Course of Action.* Pitfalls to Avoid in Case Analysis. Communicating Case Analyses: *The Written Report. The Oral Presentation.*

Section III
SELECTED REFERENCE TOOLS FOR MARKETING MANAGEMENT, 225

SECONDARY DATA SOURCES   227

Marketing Sources. Financial Information Sources. Basic U.S. Statistical Sources. General Business and Industry Sources. Indexes and Abstracts.

NAME INDEX, 235
SUBJECT INDEX, 241

Section I

ESSENTIALS OF MARKETING MANAGEMENT

Introduction

Chapter 1
An Overview of the Marketing Management Process

1

AN OVERVIEW OF THE MARKETING MANAGEMENT PROCESS

The purpose of this introductory chapter is to present the marketing management process and outline what marketing managers do. As such, *it will present the framework around which the remaining chapters are organized.* Our first task is to review the organizational philosophy known as the marketing concept, since it underlies much of the thinking presented in this book.

THE MARKETING CONCEPT

Simply stated, the marketing concept means that *an organization should seek to make a profit by serving the needs of customer groups.* It is very straightforward and has a great deal of common-sense validity. Perhaps this is why it is often misunderstood, forgotten, or overlooked.

The purpose of the marketing concept is to rivet the attention of marketing managers on serving broad classes of customer needs (customer orientation), rather than on the firm's current products (production orientation) or on devising methods to attract customers to current products (selling orientation). Thus, effective marketing starts with the recognition of customer needs and then works backward to devise products and services to satisfy these needs. In this way, marketing managers can satisfy customers more efficiently in the present and anticipate changes in customer needs more accurately in the future. Hopefully, the end result is a more efficient market in which the customer is better satisfied and the firm is more profitable.

5

HIGHLIGHT 1–1

Basic Elements of the Marketing Concept

1. Company-wide managerial awareness and appreciation of the consumer's role as it is related to the firm's existence, growth, and stability. As Drucker has noted, business enterprise is an organ of society; thus, its basic purpose lies outside the business itself. And the valid definition of business purpose is the creation of customers.

2. Active company-wide managerial awareness of, and concern with interdepartmental implications of decisions and actions of an individual department. That is, the firm is viewed as a network of forces focused on meeting defined customer needs, and comprising a system within which actions taken in one department or area frequently result in significant repercussions in other areas of the firm. Also, it is recognized that such actions may affect the company's equilibrium with its external environment, for example, its consumers, its competitors.

3. Active company-wide managerial concern with innovation of products and services designed to solve selected consumer problems.

4. General managerial concern with the effect of new products and service introduction on the firm's profit position, both present and future, and recognition of the potential rewards which may accrue from new product planning, including profits and profit stability.

5. General managerial appreciation of the role of marketing intelligence and other fact-finding and reporting units within, and adjacent to the firm, in translating the general statements presented above into detailed statements of profitable market potentials, targets, and action. Implicit in this statement is not only an expansion of the traditional function and scope of formal marketing research, but also assimilation of other sources of marketing data, such as the firm's distribution system and its advertising agency counsel, into a potential marketing intelligence service.

6. Company-wide managerial effort, based upon participation and interaction of company officers, in establishing corporate and departmental objectives, which are understood by, and acceptable to these officers, and which are consistent with enhancement of the firm's profit position.

Source: Robert L. King. "The Marketing Concept: Fact or Intelligent Platitude," *The Marketing Concept in Action*, Proceedings of the 47th National Conference (Chicago: American Marketing Assn., 1964), p. 657.

The principle task of the marketing function operating under the marketing concept is not to manipulate customers to do what suits the interests of the firm, but rather to find effective and efficient means of making the business do what suits the interests of customers. This is not to say that all firms practice marketing in this way. Clearly, many firms still emphasize only production and sales. However, effective marketing, as defined in this text, requires that consumer needs come first in organizational decision making.

One qualification to this statement deals with the question of a conflict between consumer wants and societal needs and wants. For example, if society deems clean air and water as necessary for survival, then this need may well take precedent over a consumer's want for goods and services that pollute the environment.

WHAT IS MARKETING?

One of the most persistent conceptual problems in marketing is its definition.[1] For the purposes of this text, the following general definition by Professor Philip Kotler will be used: "Marketing is human activity directed at satisfying needs and wants through exchange processes."[2] Although this broad definition allows the inclusion of nonbusiness exchange processes (that is, persons, places, organizations, ideas) as part of marketing, the primary emphasis in this test is on marketing in the business environment. However, this emphasis is not meant to imply that marketing concepts, principles, and techniques cannot be fruitfully employed in other areas of exchange. In fact, some discussions of nonbusiness marketing take place later in the text.

WHAT IS MARKETING MANAGEMENT?

Marketing management can be defined as "the analysis, planning, implementation, and control of programs designed to bring about desired exchanges with target markets for the purpose of achieving organizational objectives. It relies heavily on designing the organization's offering in terms of the target market's needs and desires and using effective pricing, communication, and distribution to inform, motivate, and service the market."[3] It should be noted that this definition is entirely consistent with the marketing concept, since it emphasizes the serving of target market needs as the key to achieving organizational objectives. The remainder of this section will be devoted to a discussion of the marketing management process in terms of the model in Figure 1–1.

---

[1] See Reinhard Angelmar and Christian Pinson, "The Meaning of Marketing," *Philosophy of Science* 24 (June 1975), pp. 208–14.

[2] Philip Kotler, *Marketing Management: Analysis Planning and Control*, 3d ed. (Englewood Cliffs: Prentice-Hall, Inc., 1976), p. 5.

[3] Ibid., p. 7.

FIGURE 1–1
The Marketing Management Process

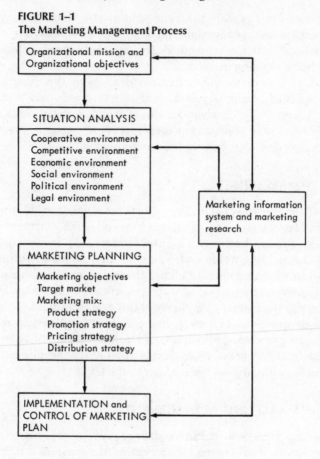

Organizational Mission and Objectives

Marketing activities should start with a clear understanding of the organization's mission and objectives. These factors provide marketing management with direction by specifying the industry, the desired role of the firm in the industry, such as research-oriented innovator, custom-batch specialist, or mass producer, and hopefully, a precise statement of what the firm is trying to accomplish. However, since written mission statements and objectives are often ambiguous or ill-defined, the marketing manager may have to consult with other members of upper management to determine precisely what the firm is trying to accomplish, both overall and during a specific planning period. For example, a commonly stated organizational objective is "growth." Obviously, this objective is so general that it is practically useless. On the other hand, a statement such as "sustained growth in profits before taxes of 14 percent" provides a quantitative goal which the marketing manager can use for determining desired sales levels and the marketing strategies to achieve them. In addition, the marketing manager must monitor any changes in mission or objectives and adapt marketing strategies to meet them.

Situation Analysis

With a clear understanding of organizational objectives and mission, the marketing manager must then analyze and monitor the position of the firm, and specifically the marketing department, in terms of its past, present, and future situation. Of course, the future situation is of primary concern. However, an analysis of past trends and current situation are most useful for predicting the future situation.

The situation analysis can be divided into six major areas of concern: (1) the cooperative environment, (2) the competitive environment, (3) the economic environment, (4) the social environment, (5) the political environment, and (6) the legal environment. In analyzing each of these environments, the marketing executive must search both for opportunities and for constraints or threats to achieving objectives. Opportunities for profitable marketing often arise from changes in these environments which bring about new sets of needs to be satisfied. Constraints on marketing activities, such as limited supplies of scarce resources, also arise from these environments.

The Cooperative Environment. The cooperative environment includes all firms and individuals who have a vested interest in the firm's accomplishing its objectives. Parties of primary interest to the marketing executive in this environment are (1) suppliers (2) resellers (3) other departments in the firm and (4) subdepartments and employees of the marketing department. Opportunities in this environment are primarily related to methods of increasing efficiency, while constraints consist of such things as unresolved conflicts and shortages of materials.

The Competitive Environment. The competitive environment includes primarily other firms in the industry which rival the organization for both resources and sales. Opportunities in this environment include such things as (1) acquiring competing firms, (2) offering demonstrably better value to consumers and attracting them away from competitors, and (3) in some cases, driving competitors out of the industry. The primary constraints in this environment are demand stimulation activities of competing firms and the number of consumers who cannot be lured away from competition.

The Economic Environment. The state of the macro-economy and changes in it also bring about marketing opportunities and constraints. For example, such factors as high inflation and unemployment levels can limit the size of the market that can afford to purchase a firm's top-of-the-line product. At the same time, these factors may offer a profitable opportunity to develop rental services for such products or to develop less expensive models of the product. In addition, changes in technology can provide significant threats and opportunities. For example, in the communication industry technology has developed to a level where, in the not too distant future, it may be possible to have totally wireless communication anywhere in the world. Obviously, such a system poses a severe threat to the existence of telephone and telegraph industries as they are today.

The Social Environment.   This environment includes general cultural and social traditions, norms, and attitudes. While these values change slowly, such changes often bring about the need for new products and services. For example, a change in values concerning the desirability of large families brought about an opportunity to market better methods of birth control. On the other hand, cultural and social values also place constraints on marketing activities. As a rule, business practices that are contrary to social values become political issues, which are often resolved by legal constraints.

Political Environment.   The political environment includes the attitudes and reactions of the general public, social and business critics, and other organizations such as the Better Business Bureau. Dissatisfaction with such business and marketing practices as unsafe products, products that waste resources, and unethical sales procedures can have adverse effects on corporation image and customer loyalty. On the other hand, adapting business and marketing practices to these attitudes can be an opportunity. For example, these attitudes have brought about markets for such products as unbreakable children's toys, high efficiency air conditioners, and more economical automobiles.

The Legal Environment.   This environment includes a host of federal, state, and local legislation directed at protecting both business competition and consumer rights. In recent years legislation has reflected social and political attitudes and has been primarily directed at constraining business practices. Examples of such recent legislation are:

Drug Abuse Control Amendments (1965).

Fair Packing and Labeling Act (1965).

National Traffic and Motor Vehicle Safety Act (1966).

Child Safety Act (1966).

Cigarette Labeling Act (1966).

Wholesale Meat Act (1967).

National Commission on Product Safety Act (1967).

Consumer Credit Protecting Act (1968).

Wholesome Poultry Products Act (1968).

Hazardous Radiation Act (1968).

Child Protection and Toy Safety Act (1969).

Public Health Smoking Cigarette Act (1969).

Fair Credit Reporting Act (1970).

Council on Environmental Quality (1970).

Federal Boat Safety Act (1971).

Consumer Product Safety Act (1972).

Motor Vehicle Information and Cost Savings Act (1974).

Magnuson-Moss Warranty—Federal Trade Commission Act (1974).

Transportation Safety Act (1974).

Consumer Product Warranty Act (1975).

Such legislation usually acts as a constraint on business behavior, but again can be viewed as providing opportunities for marketing safer and more efficient products.

Marketing Planning

In the previous sections it was emphasized that (1) marketing activities must be aligned with organizational objectives and (2) marketing opportunities are often found by systematically analyzing situational environments. Once an opportunity is recognized, the marketing executive must then plan an appropriate strategy for taking advantage of the opportunity. This process can be viewed in terms of three interrelated tasks: (1) establishing marketing objectives, (2) selecting the target market, and (3) developing the marketing mix.

Establishing Objectives. Marketing objectives are usually derived from organizational objectives; in some cases where the firm is totally marketing-oriented, the two are identical. In either case objectives must be specified and performance in achieving them should be measurable. Marketing objectives are usually stated as standards of performance (for example, a certain percentage of market share or sales volume) or as tasks to be achieved by given dates. While such objectives are useful, the marketing concept emphasizes that profits rather than sales should be the overriding objective of the firm and marketing department. In any case, these objectives provide the framework for the marketing plan.

Selecting the Target Markets. The success of any marketing plan hinges on how well it can identify consumer needs and organize its resources to satisfy them profitably. Thus, a crucial element of the marketing plan is selecting the group or segments of potential con-

HIGHLIGHT 1-2

Military Commander's Planning Model

1. Mission

    A statement of the task and its purpose. If the mission is general in nature, determine by analysis what task must be performed to insure that the mission is accomplished. State multiple tasks in the sequence in which they are to be accomplished.

2. The Situation and Courses of Action

    a. Determine all facts or in the absence of facts logical assumptions which have a bearing on the situation and which contribute to or influence the ultimate choice or a course of action. Analyze available facts and/or assumptions and arrive at deduction from these as to their favorable or adverse influence or effect on the accomplishment of the mission.

    b. Determine and list significant difficulties or difficulty patterns which are anticipated and which could adversely affect the accomplishment of the mission.

    c. Determine and list all feasible courses of action which will accomplish the mission if successful.

3. Analysis of Opposing Courses of Action

    Determine through analysis the probable outcome of each course of action listed in paragraph 2c when opposed by each significant difficulty enumerated in paragraph 2b. This may be done in two steps—

    a. Determine and state those anticipated difficulties or difficulty patterns which have approximately equal effect on all courses of action.

    b. Analyze each course of action against each significant difficulty or difficulty pattern (except those stated in paragraph 3a above) to determine strength and weakness inherent in each course of action.

4. Comparison of Own Courses of Action

    Compare courses of action in terms of the significant advantages and disadvantages which emerged during analysis (par. 3 above). Decide which course of action promises to be most successful in accomplishing the mission.

5. Decision

    Translate the course of action selected into a complete statement, showing *who, what, when, where, how,* and *why* as appropriate.

Source: War Department, *Staff Officers' Field Manual*, FM 101-5, U.S. Department of Defense (Washington, D.C.: U.S. Government Printing Office).

sumers the firm is going to serve with its particular products. Four important questions must be answered:

1.   What do consumers need?
2.   What must be done to satisfy these needs?
3.   What is the size of the market?
4.   What is its growth profile?[4]

Present target markets and potential target markets are then ranked according to (*a*) profitability, (*b*) present and future sales volume, and (*c*) the match between what it takes to appeal successfully to the segment and the organization's capabilities. Those that appear to offer the greatest potential are selected. Chapters 3 and 4 are devoted to discussing consumer and industrial buyers.

Developing the Marketing Mix.   The marketing mix is the set of controllable variables that must be managed to satisfy the target market and achieve organizational objectives. These controllable variables are usually classified according to four major decision areas: product, price, promotion, and place (or channels of distribution). The importance of these decision areas cannot be overstated and in fact, the major portion of this text is devoted to analyzing them. Chapters 5 and 6 are devoted to product and new product strategies; Chapters 7 and 8 to promotion strategies in terms of both nonpersonal and personal selling; Chapter 9 to distribution strategies and Chapter 10 to pricing strategies. In addition, marketing mix variables are the focus of analysis in two chapters on marketing in special fields, that is, the marketing of services (Chapter 11) and international marketing (Chapter 12). Thus, it should be clear to the reader that the marketing mix is the core of the marketing management process.

The output of the foregoing process is the marketing plan. It is a formal statement of decisions which have been made in regard to marketing activities; a blueprint of the objectives, strategies, and tasks to be performed.

Implementation and Control of the Marketing Plan

Implementing the marketing plan involves putting the plan into action and performing marketing tasks according to the predefined schedule. Even the most carefully developed plans often cannot be executed with perfect timing. Thus, the marketing executive must closely monitor and coordinate implementation of the plan. In some cases adjustments may have to be made in the basic plan because of

---

[4] David T. Kollat, Roger D. Blackwell, and James F. Robeson, *Strategic Marketing* (New York: Holt, Rinehart and Winston, Inc., 1972), chap. 2.

HIGHLIGHT 1–3

Key Elements in the Marketing Plan

People   —What is the target market for the firm's product(s)? What is its size and growth potential?

Profit   —What is the expected profit from implementing the marketing plan? What are the other objectives of the marketing plan and how will their achievement be evaluated?

Personnel —What personnel will be involved in implementing the marketing plan? Will only intrafirm personnel be involved or will other firms such as advertising agenices or marketing research firms also be employed?

Product   —What product(s) will be offered? What variations in the product will be offered in terms of style, features, quality, branding, packaging, and terms of sale and service? How should products be positioned in the market?

Price   —What price or prices will products be sold for?

Promotion—How will information about the firm's offerings be communicated to the target market?

Place   —How, when and where will the firm's offerings be delivered for sale to the target market?

Policy   —What is the overall marketing policy for dealing with anticipated problems in the marketing plan? How will unanticipated problems be handled?

Period   —For how long a time period is the marketing plan to be in effect? When should the plan be implemented and what is the schedule for executing and evaluating marketing activities?

---

changes in any of the situational environments. For example, competitors may introduce a new product, which may make it desirable to speed up or delay implementation of the plan. In almost all cases, some minor adjustments or "fine tuning" will be necessary in implementation.

Controlling the marketing plan involves three basic steps. First, the results of the implemented marketing plan are measured. Second, these results are compared with objectives. Third, decisions are made as to whether the plan is achieving objectives. If serious deviations exist between actual and planned results, then adjustments may have to be made to redirect the plan toward achieving objectives.

Marketing Information Systems and Marketing Research

Throughout the marketing management process current, reliable, and valid information is needed to make effective marketing decisions. Providing this information is the task of the marketing information system (MIS) and marketing research. These topics will be discussed in detail in Chapter 2.

CONCLUSION

This chapter has described the marketing management process and provided an outline for many of the remaining chapters in this text. At this point it would be useful for the reader to review Figure 1–1 as well as the Table of Contents. This will enable you to relate the content and progression of material to the marketing management process.

ADDITIONAL READINGS

Adler, Lee. "Systems Approach to Marketing," *Harvard Business Review* 45 (May–June 1967), pp. 105–18.

Ansoff, H. Igor. *Corporate Strategy.* New York: McGraw-Hill, Inc., 1965.

Cohen, J. Kalman; and Cyert, Richard M. "Strategy: Formulation, Implementation, and Monitoring." *Journal of Business* 46 (1973), pp. 349–67.

Kotler, Philip. "The Major Tasks of Marketing Management," *Journal of Marketing* 37 (October 1973), pp. 42–49.

McCaskey, Michael B. "A Contingency Approach to Planning: Planning with Goals and Planning without Goals." *Journal of the Academy of Management* 17 (June 1974), pp. 281–91.

Mintzberg, Henry. "Strategy-Making in Three Modes." *California Management Review* 16 (Winter 1973), pp. 44–53.

Schoeffler, Sidney; Buzzell, Robert D.; and Heany, Donald F. "Impact of Strategic Planning on Profit Performance." *Harvard Business Review* 52 (March–April 1974), pp. 136–45.

Winer, Leon. "Are You Really Planning Your Marketing?" *Journal of Marketing* 29 (January 1965), pp. 1–8.

Marketing Information, Research, and Understanding the Target Market

Chapter 2
Marketing Information Systems and
Marketing Research

Chapter 3
Consumer Behavior

Chapter 4
Industrial Buyer Behavior

2

MARKETING INFORMATION SYSTEMS AND MARKETING RESEARCH

It is obvious that the American business system has been capable of producing a vast quantity of goods and services. However, in the past two decades the American business system has also become extremely capable of producing massive amounts of information and data. In fact, the last decade has often been referred to as the "Information Era" and the "Age of Information."

This situation is a complete reverse from what previously existed. In the past, marketing executives did not have to deal with an over-supply of information for decision-making purposes. In most cases they gathered what little data they could and hoped that their decisions would be reasonably good. In fact, it was for this reason that marketing research came to be recognized as an extremely valuable staff function in the 1930s and 1940s. It provided marketing management with information where previously there had been little or none and thereby alleviated to a great extent the paucity of information for marketing decision making. However, marketing management in many companies has failed to store marketing information, and much valuable marketing information is lost when marketing personnel change jobs or companies.

Today marketing managers often feel buried by the deluge of information and data that comes across their desks. How can it be, then, that so many marketing managers complain that they have insufficient or inappropriate information on which to base their everyday operating decisions? Professor Kotler has classified these complaints into the following categories:

1. There is too much marketing information of the wrong kind, and not enough of the right kind.
2. Marketing information is so dispersed throughout the company that great effort is usually needed to locate simple facts.
3. Important information is sometimes suppressed by other executives or subordinates, for personal reasons.
4. Important information often arrives too late to be useful.
5. Information often arrives in a form that provides no idea of its accuracy, and there is no one to turn to for confirmation.[1]

Marketing management requires current, reliable information before it can function efficiently. Because of this need and the information explosion of the past decade, many large corporations have banked their total marketing knowledge in computers. Well-designed marketing information systems can eliminate corporate losses of millions of dollars from lost information and lost opportunities.

This chapter is concerned with marketing information systems and marketing research. Since the two concepts are easily confused, it is important initially to distinguish one from the other. In general terms, a marketing information system (MIS) is concerned with the continuous gathering, processing, and utilization of pertinent information for decision-making purposes. The primary objective of a MIS is to get the right information to the right decision maker at the right time. Marketing research, on the other hand, usually focuses on a specific marketing problem with the objective of providing information for a particular decision. As such, marketing research is an integral part of the overall marketing information system but is usually project oriented rather than a continuous process.

MARKETING INFORMATION SYSTEMS

Many types of information systems are required to manage a firm efficiently. For example, there is an accounting information system, a personnel information system, and a financial information system. The primary concern in this section is with only one of these information systems, the marketing information system, which can be formally defined as:

> A structured, interacting complex of persons, machines and procedures designed to generate an orderly flow of pertinent information, collected from both intra- and extra-firm sources, for use as the basis for decision-making in specified responsibility areas of marketing management.[2]

---

[1] Philip Kotler, "A Design for the Firm's Marketing Nerve Center," *Business Horizons* 9 (Fall 1966), pp. 63–74.

[2] Richard H. Brien and James E. Stafford, "Marketing Information Systems: A New Dimension for Marketing Research," *Journal of Marketing* 32 (July 1968), p. 21.

From the beginning, the reader should be informed that many United States firms have not yet established any kind of formal marketing information system. The term *formal* describes a carefully developed plan for information flows, with stated objectives and a place in the formal organization structure. Dun and Bradstreet is an example of a formal marketing information system. This firm has established a computerized data bank designed to be the world's largest single source of marketing information on virtually every U.S. commercial business firm. For example, the data bank includes market profiles on approximately 500,000 business organizations in the Eastern part of the U.S. This service is known as Dun's Market Identifiers (DMI) and is useful to manufacturers, banks, wholesalers, and any other enterprise requiring up-to-date information on members of the business community.

As more and more managers realize the gains that result from a well-planned marketing information system, the number of firms that have such systems will increase. These managers will realize that obtaining the information needed to manage the marketing mix in the most effective way can only be achieved through a well-planned information system.

Information Flows in the Marketing System

Information flows in a marketing information system can be categorized into two basic types. First, there are *external information flows,* which include (1) intelligence information (information from the environment that flows to the firm) and (2) marketing communication (information that flows from the firm to the environment). Second, there are *internal* or *intrafirm information flows* (information that flows within the internal boundaries of the organizational system).[3] The major types of information flows are illustrated in Figure 2–1.

External Information Flows. As has been indicated, the external flow proceeds from the firm to the market and from the market to the firm. The flow of information from the environment to the firm is often described as marketing intelligence. Traditionally, the marketing research department has had exclusive responsibility for collecting this data.

Marketing intelligence information includes data on the elements in the company's operating environment, such as competitors, channel numbers, and consumers, for use in evaluating short-run trends in the immediate environment. In addition, it includes long-run information

---

[3] For comprehensive discussions of marketing information flows, consult William T. Kelley, "Marketing Intelligence for Management," *Journal of Marketing* 29 (October 1965), pp. 19–24, and Kotler, "Firm's Marketing Nerve Center," pp. 66–68.

HIGHLIGHT 2–1

The Marketing Information System

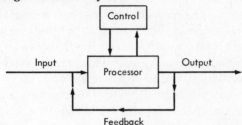

Invoice

price
quantity purchased
customer name
customer location
credit terms
method of delivery
date of order

Annual Reports

of customers
of competitors
of suppliers

Trade Association Data
Payroll
Departmental Budgets
Manufacturing Cost
   Reports
Accounts Receivable
Accounts Payable
Inventory Reports
Trade Journals
Sales Call Reports
Manning Tables
Personnel Department
   Reports
Census Data
Marketing Cost Reports

Market Research Inputs, e.g.,

audit and panel data
special projects
customer demand schedules
questionnaire replies

Sales

by product
by product line
by customer class
by cost center
by region
by salesman
by competitors

Market Share
Inventory
Forecasts
Technical Service

Marketing Personnel

turnover ratio
hiring ratio
transfers
promotions
absenteeism

Financial

credit
discount analysis
   (by customer,
    region, etc.)
promotional
   allowances
budgets

Customer List
New Accounts
Etc.

Profitability

by product
by product line
by customer class
by salesman

Life Cycle
Analysis

Source: Conrad Berenson, "Marketing Information Systems," *Journal of Marketing* 33 (October 1969), p. 19.

FIGURE 2–1
Marketing Information Flows

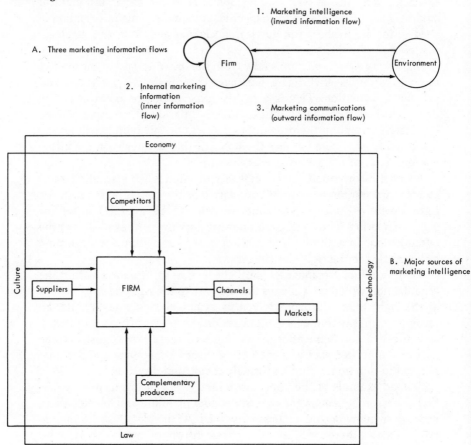

A. Three marketing information flows

1. Marketing intelligence
   (inward information flow)

2. Internal marketing
   information
   (inner information
   flow)

3. Marketing communications
   (outward information flow)

B. Major sources of
   marketing intelligence

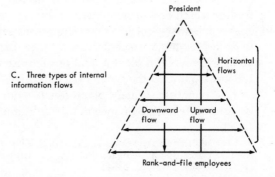

C. Three types of internal
   information flows

Source: Philip Kotler, "A Design for the Firm's Marketing Nerve Center," *Business Horizons* 9 (Fall 1966), p. 65.

on the economic environment, such as consumer income trends and spending patterns, as well as developments in the social and cultural environment of buyers and prospective customers. This information is needed for both short-run tactical decisions and long-run strategic planning.

Marketing communications flow from the firm outward to the market in such forms as advertising messages, personal selling efforts, and product information. This is a highly important type of information flow, which is directed at influencing the market. This topic will be discussed in detail in the promotion chapters of this text. It will not be discussed further here because the focus of this chapter is on the information needs of marketing management.[4]

Internal Information Flows.   It is obvious that when marketing intelligence information enters the boundaries of the firm it must reach the right executive at the right time in order to be a useful input for decision making. Thus, information must flow *through* as well as *to* the organization. In addition, information generated within the firm must be channeled to the right decision maker.

There are many managers who believe that information within the organization will almost always find its way to the right decision maker at the right time. Unfortunately, this is not always true. It must be recognized that within every organization there are vertical, horizontal, and informal communication flows. Each of these flows must become part of the master plan of a marketing information system and not be allowed to function without a formal scheme and direction.[5]

A good example of the importance (and need) of intrafirm information flows can be seen in the case of product planning and development, because so many departments are involved. At the idea stage (origins of product ideas) there are at least four basic information sources: (1) sales force, (2) research and engineering, (3) other company personnel, and (4) outside sources. At the screening stage information is usually needed from research and development and from the legal department, which does a patent search. The marketing research department will be asked to do a preliminary technical, consumer, competitor, and general economic survey. Pilot plant operations require information from research and development, the technical laboratory, production engineers and cost accountants. If new plant construction is involved, information is required from the finance department and plant engineers. This list

---

[4] For additional discussion, see William R. King and David I. Cleland, "Environmental Information Systems for Strategic Marketing Planning," *Journal of Marketing* 38 (October 1974), pp. 35–40.

[5] For an account of what happens to internal information in an unmanaged system, see Gerald S. Albaum, "Horizontal Information Flow: An Exploratory Study," *Journal of the Academy of Management* 7 (March 1964), pp. 21–33.

is not exhaustive but is intended as an example to show how many different intrafirm sources of information are vital to a specific type of marketing decision.

The Marketing Information Center

Although the growth of the concept of a marketing information system has been fairly recent, most experts agree that a single, separate marketing information center must exist in order to centralize responsibility for marketing information within the firm.[6] This is necessary because both the users and suppliers of such information are widely scattered throughout the organization and some unit is needed to oversee the entire operation.

The purpose or objective of such an organizational unit is to improve and upgrade the accuracy, completeness, and timeliness of information for marketing management decisions. Kotler describes this entity as the "marketing nerve center" for the firm, which provides instantaneous information and develops analytical and decision aids for marketing management. Specifically, he sees this new organizational unit providing marketing management with three major information services—gathering, processing, and utilization—in addition to numerous constituent services.[7]

1. *Information gathering* is concerned with locating information that is needed by or is relevant to the tasks of marketing management. It consists of three constituent services.

The first is *search* activity, which is based upon management's requests for certain types of marketing information and data. Search activities can range from locating already published data to conducting full-scale marketing studies.

Scanning is the second information gathering service. This relates to the responsibility of the marketing information unit to assemble general marketing intelligence data. This involves scanning trade journals, reports, magazines, newspapers, and any other source that may provide useful information pertinent to the executive's task. This also relieves executives from this time-consuming activity.

The third information gathering service is *retrieval*. This involves storing and retrieving information when it is needed. Many of the modern computerized information retrieval techniques can be used here.

2. *Information processing* is designed to improve the overall quality

---

[6] Kenneth P. Uhl, "Better Management of Market Information," *Business Horizons* 9 (Spring 1966), pp. 75–82; Kotler, "Firm's Marketing Nerve Center," pp. 70–74, and Kelley, "Marketing Intelligence," pp. 21–22.

[7] Kotler, "Firm's Marketing Nerve Center, pp. 71–74.

HIGHLIGHT 2–2

Company Organization Structure Showing Centralized Information System

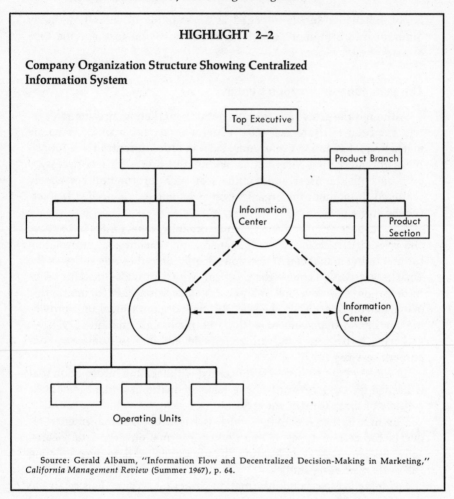

Source: Gerald Albaum, "Information Flow and Decentralized Decision-Making in Marketing," *California Management Review* (Summer 1967), p. 64.

of marketing information. Here there are five supporting services.

The first is *evaluation*, which involves determining how much confidence can be placed in a particular piece of information. Such factors as source credibility, and reliability and validity of the data must be determined.

The second information processing service is that of *abstraction*. This involves editing and condensing incoming information in order to provide the executive with only that information relevant to a particular task.

Once information has been gathered, the service of *indexing* is very important. The purpose of indexing is to provide classification for storage and retrieval purposes.

The fourth information processing service is that of *dissemination*, which entails getting the right information to the right marketing decision maker at the right time. Indeed, this is the overriding purpose of an information system.

The final information processing service is that of *storage*. Every information system must provide efficient storage of data so that it can be used again if needed. Many of the modern computerized information storage techniques can be used here.

3. *Information utilization* dictates that the marketing information unit must assist in more than just information gathering and processing. It must provide additional support in aiding the executive in utilizing the information. This means that the marketing information unit must include specialists in statistics, psychology, econometrics, and operations research in order to determine executive needs and interpret research results.

In summary, many experts feel there is a need for a centralized marketing information unit within the business organization. The basic purpose of this unit is to coordinate the flow of information to ensure that decision makers receive timely, pertinent information. The marketing information unit within the organization does not focus on specific problems. Instead, it acts as a thermostat that monitors the external operating environment and facilitates intrafirm information flows so that the firm can better adjust itself to changes that occur in its operating environment. Specifically, this unit must be responsible as a consultant, coordinator, and controller for the three basic marketing information activities: *gathering, processing,* and *utilization.* In order to justify its existence it must facilitate better management through more and better information availability and use. This can only be achieved through company-wide management of all the various marketing information components.

MARKETING RESEARCH

Marketing research should be an integral part of the marketing information system. In essence, marketing research combines insight and intuition with the research process to provide information for making marketing decisions.[8] In general, it can be defined as "the systematic and objective search for an analysis of information relevant to the iden-

---

[8] Our discussion of marketing research will be in terms of the business firm. However, marketing research has also been found useful in the public sector. For discussions, see William L. Wilkie and David M. Gardner, "The Role of Marketing Research in Public Policy Making," *Journal of Marketing* 38 (January 1974), pp. 38–47; J. R. Brent Richie and Roger J. LaBreque, "Marketing Research and Public Policy: A Functional Perspective," *Journal of Marketing* 39 (July 1975), pp. 12–19.

tification and solution of any problem in the field of marketing."[9]

Today's marketing managers should understand the role of research in decision making. It cannot be overstated that *marketing research is an aid to decision making and not a substitute for it.* In other words, marketing research does not make decisions but it can substantially increase the probability that the best decision will be made. Unfortunately, too often marketing managers view marketing research reports as the final answer to their problems. Instead, marketing managers should recognize that (1) even the most carefully controlled research projects can be fraught with pitfalls and (2) decisions should be made in the light of their own knowledge and experience and other factors that are not explicitly considered in the research project. The introduction and subsequent failure of the Edsel automobile is a classic example of the use of marketing research findings that were not properly tempered with sound executive judgment.[10]

Although marketing research does not make decisions, it is a direct means of reducing risks associated with managing the marketing mix and long term marketing planning. In fact, a company's return on investment from marketing research is a function of the extent to which research output reduces the risk inherent in decision making. For example, marketing research can play an important role in reducing new product failure costs by evaluating consumer acceptance of a product prior to full-scale introduction.

In a highly competitive economy a firm's survival depends on the marketing manager's ability to make sound decisions, to outguess competitors, to anticipate consumer needs, to forecast business conditions, and to plan generally for company growth. Marketing research is one tool to help accomplish these tasks. Research is also vital for managerial control, because without appropriate data the validity of past decisions on the performance of certain elements in the marketing system (for example, the performance of the sales force or advertising) cannot be evaluated reliably.

Although many of the technical aspects of marketing research such as sampling design or statistical analysis can be delegated to experts, the process of marketing research begins and ends with the marketing manager. In the beginning of a research project it is the marketing manager's responsibility to work with researchers to define the problem carefully. When the research project is completed the application of the results in

[9] Paul E. Green and Donald S. Tull, *Research for Marketing Decisions*, 4th ed. (Englewood Cliffs, N.J.: Prentice-Hall, Inc., 1978), p. 4.

[10] For an excellent discussion of this classic failure, see Robert J. Hartley, "The Edsel: Marketing Planning and Research Gone Awry," *Marketing Mistakes* (Columbus, Ohio: Grid, Inc., 1976), pp. 59–70.

HIGHLIGHT 2–3

The Teflon Case

Teflon, that magic nonstick finish for cookware was an overnight success for DuPont a few years ago—but it was only a success for a little while before running into big problems in the marketplace. Teflon (Tetrafluoroethylene) was first marketed as a coating for cookware. Because food would not stick to it, promotion was based on the idea of "fat-free frying." But just as the full production of pans hit the market, demand dried up. Dealers became overloaded with thousands of dollars of inventory.

DuPont knew some of the reasons for this product failing—some manufacturers were not applying Teflon properly. DuPont was faced with a serious marketing problem: scuttle the whole idea of nonstick cookware or find a way to salvage it. It decided to invest some funds in research and hired N. W. Ayer, one of its ad agencies, to conduct a series of market studies. This research effort between Ayer and DuPont produced these results:

A plan for strict quality control on proper application of Teflon by cookware manufacturers.

A new selling approach based on convenience (nonstick cooking with nonscour clean up) rather than fat-free frying.

Agreement to concentrate all advertising on the job of convincing housewives (via TV commercials) that Teflon would make life in the kitchen much easier.

Extensive testing in 13 cities of the creative components of the TV ads.

Six months after the four-part plan was launched, sales were up 50 percent, one out of three metal pans sold was Teflon coated, and the total sales of cookware were up 21 percent. Here is an example of how marketing research and creative marketing saved a product.

---

terms of decision alternatives rests primarily with the marketing manager.[11] For these reasons, and since the marketing manager must be able to communicate with researchers throughout the course of the project, it is vital for managers to understand the research process from the researcher's point of view.

---

[11] For a discussion of the researcher's role in decision making, see Robert J. Small and Larry J. Rosenberg, "The Marketing Researcher as a Decision Maker: Myth or Reality?" *Journal of Marketing* 39 (January 1975), pp. 2–7.

The Research Process

Marketing research can be viewed as a systematic process for obtaining information to aid in decision making. Although there are many different types of marketing research, the framework illustrated in Figure 2–2 represents a general approach to defining the research process. Each element of this process will be briefly discussed.

FIGURE 2–2
The Five Ps of the Research Process

Purpose of the Research.   The first step in the research process is to determine explicitly the purpose of the research. This may well be much more difficult than it sounds. Quite often a situation or problem is recognized as needing research, yet the nature of the problem is not clear or well defined. Thus, an investigation is required to clarify the problem or situation. This investigation includes such things as interviewing corporate executives, reviewing records, and studying existing information related to the problem. At the end of this stage the researcher should know (1) the current situation, (2) the nature of the problem, and (3) the specific question or questions the research is to find answers to, that is, why the research is being conducted.

Plan of the Research.   The first step in the research plan is to formalize the specific purpose of the study. Once this is accomplished, the sequencing of tasks and responsibilities for accomplishing the research are spelled out in detail. This stage is critical since decisions are made that determine the who, what, when, where, and how of the research study.

An initial decision in this stage of the process is the type of data that

The Channel Selection Decision:
How Marketing Research Can Help

Marketing research can assist marketing managers in selecting a channel of distribution by supplying them with information concerning the following items in several major areas of consideration.

Analyzing the product
1. The product's potential market.
2. The channels necessary to reach this market, that is, classification of the product as an industrial or consumer good, etc.
3. Frequency of purchase.
4. Influence of fashion.
5. Necessity of repair parts and service.
6. Seasonal character of sales, if any.
7. Price.

Determining the nature and extent of the market
1. Who the potential buyers and users of the product are.
2. How many there are.
3. Where they live.
4. How they satisfy the wants that the product satisfies.
5. What their likes, dislikes, and so forth are.
6. What the buying motives and habits of the buyers are.

Reviewing existing channels of distribution for comparable products
1. What channels of distribution other manufacturers of similar products use and why.
2. What each channel represents in relation to the objective the manufacturer is seeking to attain.

Appraising sales, cost, and profit possibilities of each channel
1. Volume of sales of each channel.
2. Profit levels for each channel.
3. Costs of each channel.

Conducting a marketing survey
1. Actually conduct the survey.
2. Ascertain opinions of potential buyers regarding their previous experiences with this or similar products.
3. Determining what competitors' outlets' opinions are.

Defining the cooperation expected from the distribution channel
1. Promotional assistance.
2. Servicing of goods after the sale.
3. Financial aid.
4. Displays.

Determining the forms of assistance to be given the channel
1. Advertising and sales promotional aids.
2. Training programs for distributors and other personnel.
3. Use of missionary salespeople, if any.

Highlight 2–4 (continued)

Frequent review and appraisal of channels chosen
1. Determine changes in the market structure, if any.
2. Conduct the review and appraisal.
3. Analyze how well the company is meeting its objectives.
4. Assess performance of the channel used.

---

will be required. The two major types of data are primary and secondary. Primary data is data that must be collected from original sources for the purposes of the study. Secondary data is information which has been previously collected for some other purpose but can be used for the purposes of the study.

If the research project requires primary data, decisions have to be made as to:

1. How will the data be collected? Personal interviews? Mail questionnaires? Telephone interviews?
2. How much data is needed?
3. What questions will be asked and how many?
4. Who will design the questions and collect the data?
5. Where will the data be collected? Nationally? Regionally? Locally? At home? At work?
6. When and for how long will data be collected?

If secondary data will suffice for the research question(s), similar decisions have to be made. However, since the data is already in existence, the task is much simpler (and cheaper). For example, most of the sources of secondary data listed in Section III of this text are available in a public or university library.

In addition to determining data requirements, the research plan also specifies the method of data analysis, procedures for processing and interpreting the data, and the structure of the final report. In other words, the entire research project is sequenced, and responsibility for the various tasks is assigned. Thus, the research plan provides the framework for the coordination and control of the entire project.

When the research plan is fully specified the time and money costs of the project are estimated. If management views the benefits of the research as worth the costs, the project proceeds to the next phase. A sample research plan is presented in Figure 2–3.

Performance of the Research. *Performance* is used here in the narrow sense of preparing for data collection and actually collecting the data. It is at this point that the research plan is put into action.

FIGURE 2–3
Sample Research Plan

   I.   Tentative project title.
  II.   Statement of the problem.
        One or two sentences to outline or to describe the general problem under consideration.
 III.   Define and delimit the problem.
        Here the writer states the purpose(s) and scope of the problem. *Purpose* refers to goals or objectives. Closely related to this is *justification*. Sometimes this is a separate step, depending upon the urgency of the task. *Scope* refers to the actual limitations of the research effort, in other words, what is *not* going to be investigated. Here is the point where the writer spells out the various hypotheses to be investigated or the questions to be answered.
  IV.   Outline.
        Generally this is a tentative framework for the entire project by topics. It should be flexible enough to accommodate unforeseen difficulties. Show statistical tables in outline form and also show graphs planned. Tables should reflect the hypotheses.
   V.   Method and data sources.
        The types of data to be sought (primary, secondary) are briefly identified. A brief explanation of how the necessary information or data will be gathered (for example, surveys, experiments, library sources) is given. *Sources* refer to the actual depositories for the information, whether from government publications, company records, actual people, and so forth. If measurements are involved, such as consumers' attitudes, the techniques for making such measurements are stated. All of the techniques (statistical and nonstatistical) should be mentioned and discussed as to their relevance for the task at hand. The nature of the problem will probably indicate the types of techniques to be employed, such as factor analysis, depth interviews, or focus groups.
  VI.   Sample design.
        This provides the limits of the universe or population to be studied and how it will be listed (or prepared). The writer specifies the population, states the sample size, whether sample stratification will be employed, and how. If a nonrandom sample is to be used, the justification and the type of sampling strategy to be employed, such as a convenience sample, are stated.
 VII.   Data collection forms.
        The forms to be employed in gathering the data should be discussed and, if possible, included in the plan. For surveys this will involve either a questionnaire or an interview schedule. For other types of methods the forms could include IBM cards, inventory forms, psychological tests, and so forth. The plan should state how these instruments have been or will be validated and the reader should be given some indication of their reliability.

Figure 2–3 (continued)

VIII. Personnel requirements.

This provides a complete list of all personnel who will be required, indicating exact jobs, time duration, and expected rate of pay. Assignments should be made indicating each person's responsibility and authority.

IX. Phases of the study with a time schedule.

This is a detailed outline of the plan to complete the study. The entire study should be broken down into workable pieces. Then, considering the person who will be employed in each phase, their qualifications and experience, and so forth, the time in months for the job is estimated. Some jobs may overlap. This will help in estimating the work months required. The overall time for the project should allow for time overlaps on some jobs.

Illustration:

1. Preliminary investigation—two months.
2. Final test of questionnaire—one month.
3. Sample selection—one month.
4. Mail questionnaires, field follow-up, and so forth—four months.
5. Additional phases . . .

X. Tabulation plans.

This is a discussion of editing and proof of questionnaires, card punching, and the type of computer analysis. An outline of some of the major tables required is very important.

XI. Cost estimate for doing the study.

Personnel requirements are combined with time on different phases to estimate total personnel costs. Estimates on travel, materials, supplies, drafting, computer charges, and printing and mailing costs must also be included. If an overhead charge is required by the administration, it should be calculated and added to the subtotal of the above items.

The preparations obviously depend on the type of data desired and method of data collection. For primary research, questions and questionnaire items must be pretested and validated. In addition, preparations for mail surveys include such things as sample selection, questionnaire printing, and envelope and postage considerations. For telephone or personal interviews, such things as interviewer scoring forms, instructions, and scheduling must be taken care of. For secondary data, such things as data recording procedures and instructions need attention.

In terms of actual data collection, a cardinal rule is to obtain and record the maximal amount of useful information subject to the constraints of time, money, and interviewee privacy. Failure to obtain and record data clearly can obviously lead to a poor research study, while failure to consider the rights of subjects or interviewees raises both ethical and practical questions. Tybout and Zaltman have observed that "if subjects' rights are continually violated, they may exercise their right to be heard in the form of protest against abusive researchers. Protests may involve boycotting marketing research or lobbying for legislation restricting marketing researchers."[12] Thus, both the objectives and constraints of data collection must be closely monitored.

Processing Research Data. Processing research data includes the preparation of data for analysis and the actual analysis of the data. Preparations include such things as editing and structuring the data and perhaps coding and punching it on computer cards. Data sets should be

---

HIGHLIGHT 2–5

Techniques of Collecting Primary Data

Personal Interview	*Mail*	*Telephone*
Advantages		
Most flexible means of obtaining data	Wider and more representative distribution of sample possible	Representative and wider distribution of sample possible
Identity of respondent known	No field staff	No field staff
Nonresponse generally very low	Cost per questionnaire relatively low	Cost per response relatively low
Distribution of sample controllable in all respects	People may be more frank on certain issues, e.g., sex	Control over interviewer bias easier; supervisor present essentially at interview
	No interviewer bias; answers in respondent's own words	Quick way of obtaining information
	Respondent can answer at his leisure, has time to "think things over"	Nonresponse generally very low
	Certain segents of population more easily approachable	Callbacks simple and economical

---

[12] Alice M. Tybout and Gerald Zaltman, "Ethics in Marketing Research: Their Practical Relevance," *Journal of Marketing Research* 11 (November 1974), p. 367. For additional discussions and viewpoints see Robert L. Day, "A Comment on Tybout and Zaltman's Ethics in Marketing Research," *Journal of Marketing Research* 12 (May 1975), pp. 232–33; Alice M. Tybout and Gerald Zaltman, "A Reply to Comments on Ethics in Marketing: Their Practical Relevance," *Journal of Marketing Research* 12 (May 1975), pp. 234–37; George S. Day, "The Threats to Marketing Research," *Journal of Marketing Research* 12 (November 1975), pp. 462–67.

Highlight 2–5 (continued)

Disadvantages

Likely to be most expensive of all	Bias due to nonresponse often indeterminate	Interview period not likely to exceed five minutes
Headaches of interviewer supervision and control	Control over questionnaire may be lost	Questions must be short and to the point; probes difficult to handle
Dangers of interviewer bias and cheating	Interpretation of omissions difficult	Certain types of questions cannot be used
	Cost per return may be high if nonresponse very large	Nontelephone owners as well as those without listed numbers cannot be reached
	Certain questions, such as extensive probes, cannot be asked	
	Only those interested in the subject may reply	
	Not always clear who replies	
	Certain segments of population not approachable, e.g., illiterates	
	Likely to be slowest of all	

Source: Robert Ferber and P. J. Verdoorn, *Research Methods in Economics and Business* (New York: The Macmillan Co., 1962), p. 210.

---

clearly labeled to ensure that they are not misinterpreted or misplaced. The data is then analyzed according to the procedure specified in the research plan and is interpreted according to standard norms of the analysis.

Preparation of Research Report.   The research report is a complete statement of everything accomplished relative to the research project and includes a writeup of each of the previous stages. Figure 2–4 illustrates the types of questions the researcher should ask prior to submitting the report to the appropriate decision maker.

The importance of clear and unambiguous report writing cannot be overstressed since the research is meaningless if it cannot be communicated. Often the researcher must trade off the apparent precision of scientific jargon for everyday language that the decision maker can understand. It should always be remembered that research is an aid for decision making and not a substitute for it.

FIGURE 2–4
Six Criteria for Evaluating Marketing Research Reports

1. Under what conditions was the study made? The report should provide:
   a. Full statement of the problems to be resolved by the study.
   b. Source of financing for the study.
   c. Names of organizations participating in the study, together with their qualifications and vested interests.
   d. Exact time period covered in data collection.
   e. Definitions of terms employed.
   f. Copies of data collection instruments.
   g. Source of collateral data.
   h. Complete statement of method.
2. Has the questionnaire been well designed?
3. Has the interviewing been adequately and reliably done?
4. Has the best sampling plan been followed or has the best experimental design been used?
5. Was there adequate supervision and control over the editing, coding, and tabulating?
6. Have the conclusions been drawn in a logical and forthright manner?

Problems in the Research Process

Although the foregoing discussion presented the research process in a simplified framework, this does not mean that conducting research is a simple task. There are many problems and difficulties that must be overcome if a research study is to be of value. For example, consider the difficulties in one type of marketing research, *test marketing*.

The major goal of most test marketing is to measure new product sales on a limited basis where competitive retaliation and other factors are allowed to operate freely. In this way future sales potential can be estimated. Test market research is a vital element in all new product marketing. Listed below are a number of problem areas that can invalidate test market study results.[14]

1. Representative test areas are improperly selected from the standpoint of size, geographical location, population characteristics, and promotional facilities.

2. Sample size and design are incorrectly formulated because of ignorance, budget constraints, or an improper understanding of the test problem.

---

[14] For a discussion of some general problems in marketing research, see John A. Martilla and Davis W. Carvey, "Four Subtle Sins in Marketing Research," *Journal of Marketing* 39 (January 1975), pp. 8–15.

3. Pretest measurements of competitive brand's sales are not made, which means that the researcher has no realistic base to use for comparison purposes.

4. Attempts are not made to control the cooperation and support of test stores. Consequently, certain package sizes might not be carried or pricing policies might not be adhered to.

5. Test market products are overadvertised or overpromoted during the test.

6. The full effect of sales-influencing factors such as sales force, season, weather conditions, competitive retaliation, shelf space, and so forth are not fully evaluated.

7. Market test periods are too short to determine whether the product is fully accepted by consumers or only tried on a limited basis.

Similar problems could be listed for almost any type of marketing research. However, the important point to be recognized is that careful planning, coordination, and control are imperative if the research study is to accomplish its objective.

CONCLUSION

This chapter has been concerned with marketing information systems, and marketing research. In terms of marketing information systems, one of the major reasons for increased interest has been the rapid growth in information-handling technology. However, as we have seen in this chapter, the study of information systems is not the study of computers. The study of marketing information systems is part of a much larger task, the study of more efficient methods for marketing management.

In terms of marketing research, this chapter has emphasized the importance of research as an aid for marketing decision making. Just as planning is integral for marketing management, the research plan is critical for marketing research. A research plan not only formalizes the objectives of the study but also details the tasks and responsibilities of the research team as well as cost estimates. Conducting research is a matter of following the research plan and reporting the events of each stage clearly and unambiguously. Finally, emphasis was placed on the extreme care that must be taken to avoid research difficulties and pitfalls.

ADDITIONAL READINGS

Boyd, Harper W., Jr.; Westfall, Ralph; and Stasch, Stanley F. *Marketing Research: Text and Cases*, 4th ed. Homewood, Ill.: Richard D. Irwin, Inc., 1977.

Buzzell, Robert D.; Cox, Donald F.; and Brown, Rex V. *Marketing Research and Information Systems.* New York: McGraw-Hill, Inc., 1969.

Churchill, Gilbert A., Jr. *Marketing Research.* Hinsdale, Ill.: The Dryden Press, 1976.

Deardon, John. "How to Organize Information Systems." *Harvard Business Review,* March–April 1965, pp. 65–73.

Emory, C. William. *Business Research Methods.* Homewood, Ill.: Richard D. Irwin, Inc., 1976.

Evans, Marshall K.; and Hague, Lou R. "Master Plan for Information Systems," *Harvard Business Review* 40 (January–February 1962), pp. 92–103.

Gibson, Lawrence D.; Mayer, Charles S.; Nugent, Christopher E.; and Vollmann, Thomas E. "An Evolutionary Approach to Marketing Information Systems." *Journal of Marketing* 37 (April 1973), pp. 2–6.

Johnson, Richard A.; Kast, Fremont E.; and Rozenzweig, James E. *The Theory and Management of Systems.* New York: McGraw-Hill, Inc., 1973.

Luck, David J.; Wales, Hugh G.; and Taylor, Donald A. *Marketing Research,* 4th ed. Englewood Cliffs, N.J.: Prentice Hall, Inc., 1974.

Montgomery, David B.; and Urban, Glen L. "Marketing Decision–Information Systems: An Emerging View." *Journal of Marketing Research* 7 (May 1970), pp. 226–34.

Runkel, Philip J.; and McGrath, Joseph E. *Research on Human Behavior: A Systematic Guide to Method.* New York: Holt, Rinehart and Winston, Inc., 1972.

Smith, Samuel V.; Brien, Richard H.; and Stafford, James E. *Readings in Marketing Information Systems.* New York: Houghton-Mifflin Co., 1968.

Tull, Donald S.; and Hawkins, Del L. *Marketing Research.* New York: Macmillan Publishing Co., Inc., 1976.

3

CONSUMER BEHAVIOR

The marketing concept emphasizes that profitable marketing begins with the discovery and understanding of consumer needs and then develops a marketing mix to satisfy these needs. Thus, an understanding of consumers and their needs and purchasing behavior is integral to successful marketing.

Unfortunately, there is no single theory of consumer behavior that can totally explain why consumers behave as they do. Instead, there are numerous theories, models, and concepts making up the field. In addition, the majority of these notions have been borrowed from a variety of other disciplines such as sociology, psychology, social psychology, and economics and must be integrated to understand consumer behavior.

In this chapter some of the many influences on consumer behavior will be examined in terms of the buying process. The reader may wish to examine Figure 3–1 closely since it provides the basis for this discussion.

The chapter will proceed by first examining the buying process and then discussing the group, product class, and situational influences on this process.

THE BUYING PROCESS

The buying process can be viewed as a series of five stages: felt need, alternative search, alternative evaluation, purchase decision, and post-

FIGURE 3–1
An Overview of the Buying Process

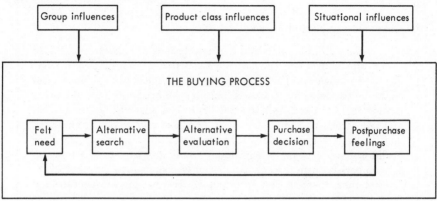

purchase feelings. In this section each of these stages will be discussed. It should be noted at the outset that this is a general model for depicting a logical sequence of buying behavior. Clearly, individuals will vary from this model because of personal differences in such things as personality, self-concept, subjective perceptions of information, the product, and the purchasing situation. However, the model provides a useful framework for organizing our discussion of consumer behavior.

Felt Need

The starting point for any type of behavior is the recognition of an unsatisfied need. It is no different for consumer behavior since the purchase and use of products and services are one means of satisfying needs. A need can be activated either internally (for example, a person feels hungry) or externally (as when a person sees a McDonald's sign and then feels hungry).

It is the task of marketing management to discover the needs that operate in a particular market or the needs that a particular product can satisfy. This includes not only being aware of currently operating needs (that is, what buyers are really seeking when they purchase a particular product), but also identifying insufficiently developed or unsatisfied needs (that is, what needs consumers have that current market offerings are not fully satisfying). Thus, an understanding of basic human needs is important for adapting marketing strategies to the consumer.

A widely adopted classification of needs was developed some years ago by A. H. Maslow.[1] The basic tenets of this framework are that:

---

[1] A. H. Maslow, *Motivation and Personality* (New York: Harper and Brothers, 1954).

HIGHLIGHT 3–1

Personality and Brand Images

Consider Virginia Slims and Eve, two brands of cigarettes marketed specifically for women. They are obviously marketed for different kinds of women, however. The Virginia Slims package is plain, almost masculine in its simplicity, enhanced only by the product name and edged on one side by a series of straight lines. The advertising is impudent and self-assertive. The model wears a tailored suit, exudes confidence, and is attractively audacious. The copy and illustrations compare the traditional role of women with today's liberated woman and sums up the comparison with the headline, "You've come a long way, baby."

And then there is Eve—pretty Eve. The package is delicate and feminine, covered with frills of interwoven vines and leaves. The advertising carries out the feminine theme, characterizing feminity as soft, desirable, dependent, and unique.

The choice is clear. Virginia Slims is for the liberated woman; Eve is for the woman who likes things the way they are. Virginia Slims and Eve represent two different kinds of women, dramatically different in personality.

Source: Kenneth E. Runyon, *Consumer Behavior and the Practice of Marketing* (Columbus, Ohio: Charles E. Merrill Publishing Co., 1977), p. 218.

---

1. Humans are wanting animals whose needs depend on what they already have. Only needs not yet satisfied can influence behavior; a satisfied need is not a motivator.
2. Human needs are arranged in a hierarchy of importance. Once one need is satisfied, another higher level need emerges and demands satisfaction.

Maslow hypothesized five classes of needs. In the order of their importance, these are: (1) physiological, (2) safety, (3) belongingness, (4) esteem, (5) self-actualization. He placed them in a formal framework referred to as the *hierarchy of needs* because of the different levels of importance indicated. This framework is presented in Figure 3–2. Less described, and hence, not as well known are the cognitive and aesthetic needs hypothesized by Maslow. Cognitive needs relate to the need to know or to understand and aesthetic needs are satisfied by moving from ugliness to beauty. Maslow did not include them in the formal hierarchy framework.

Maslow states that if all a person's needs are unsatisfied at a particular time, satisfaction of the most prepotent needs will be more pressing

FIGURE 3–2
Hierarchy of Needs

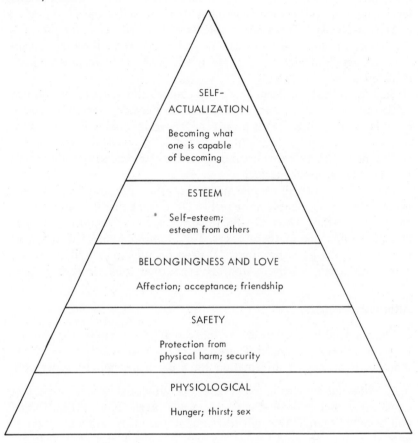

SELF-
ACTUALIZATION

Becoming what
one is capable
of becoming

ESTEEM

Self-esteem;
esteem from others

BELONGINGNESS AND LOVE

Affection; acceptance; friendship

SAFETY

Protection from
physical harm; security

PHYSIOLOGICAL

Hunger; thirst; sex

than the others. Those that come first must be satisfied before a higher-level need comes into play, and only when they are satisfied are the next ones in line significant. Each level will now be briefly examined.

Physiological Needs.   This category consists of the primary needs of the human body such as food, water, and sex. Physiological needs will dominate when all needs are unsatisfied. In such a case, none of the other needs will serve as a basis for motivation.

Safety Needs.   With the physiological needs met, the next higher level assumes importance. Safety needs consist of such things as protection from physical harm, ill health, economic disaster and avoidance of the unexpected.

Belongingness and Love Needs.   These needs are related to the social and gregarious nature of humans and the need for companionship. This level in the hierarchy is the point of departure from the physical or quasi-physical needs of the two previous levels. Nonsatisfaction of this level of need may affect the mental health of the individual.

Esteem Needs.   These needs consist of both the need for the self-awareness of importance to others (self-esteem) and actual esteem from others. Satisfaction of these needs leads to a feeling of self-confidence and prestige.

Self-Actualization Needs.   Maslow defines this need as the "desire to become more and more what one is, to become everything one is capable of becoming."[2] This means that the individual will fully realize the potentialities of given talents and capabilities. Maslow assumes that satisfaction of these needs are only possible after the satisfaction of all the needs lower in the hierarchy.

While the hierarchy arrangement of Maslow presents a convenient explanation, it is probably more realistic to assume that the various need categories overlap. Thus, in affluent societies, many products may satisfy more than one of these needs. For example, gourmet foods may satisfy both the basic physiological need of hunger as well as esteem and status needs for those who serve gourmet foods to their guests.

Alternative Search

Once a need is recognized, the individual then searches for alternatives for satisfying the need. There are five basic sources from which the individual can collect information for a particular purchase decision.

1.   *Internal Sources.* In most cases the individual has had some previous experience in dealing with a particular need. Thus, the individual will usually "search" through whatever stored information and experience is in his/her mind for dealing with the need. If a previously acceptable product for satisfying the need is remembered, the individual may purchase with little or no additional information search or evaluation. This is quite common for routine or habitual purchases.

2.   *Group Sources.* A common source of information for purchase decisions comes from communication with other people such as family, friends, neighbors, and acquaintances. Generally, some of these (that is, relevant others) are selected which the individual views as having particular expertise for the purchase decision. Although it may be quite difficult for the marketing manager to determine the exact nature of this source of information, group sources of information are often considered to be the most powerful influence on purchase decisions.

3.   *Marketing Sources.* Marketing sources of information include

---

[2] Ibid., p. 92.

such factors as advertising, salespeople, dealers, packaging, and displays. Generally this is the primary source of information about a particular product. These sources of information will be discussed in detail in the promotion chapters of this text.

4. *Public Sources*. Public sources of information include publicity such as a newspaper article about the product and independent ratings of the product such as *Consumer Reports*. Here product quality is a highly important marketing management consideration since such articles and reports often discuss such features as dependability and service requirements.

5. *Experiential Sources*. Experiential sources refer to handling, examining, and perhaps trying the product while shopping. This usually requires an actual shopping trip by the individual and may be the final source consulted before purchase.[3]

Information collected from these sources is then processed by the consumer. However, the exact nature of how individuals process information to form evaluations of products is not fully understood. In general, information processing is viewed as a four-step process in which the individual is (1) exposed to information, (2) becomes attentive to the information, (3) understands the information, and (4) retains the information.[4]

Alternative Evaluation

During the process of collecting information or, in some cases, after information is acquired, the consumer then evaluates alternatives based on what has been learned. One approach to describing the evaluation process can be found in the logic of attitude modeling.[5] This basic logic can be described as follows:

1. The consumer has information about a number of brands in a product class.

---

[3] This framework is based in part on Philip Kotler, *Marketing Management: Analysis Planning and Control*, 3d ed. (Englewood Cliffs, N.J.: Prentice-Hall, Inc., 1976), p. 88.

[4] For recent reviews of information processing see William L. Wilkie *How Consumers Use Product Information* (Washington, D.C.: National Science Foundation); Robert W. Chestnut and Jacob Jacoby, "Consumer Information Processing: Emerging Theory and Findings," *Purdue Papers in Consumer Psychology*, No. 158, Purdue University, 1976.

[5] For excellent reviews and insights into attitude modeling see William L. Wilkie and Edgar A. Pessemier, "Issues in Marketing's Use of Multi-Attribute Attitude Models," *Journal of Marketing Research* 10 (November 1973), pp. 428–41; Michael J. Ryan and E. H. Bonfield, "The Fishbein Extended Model and Consumer Behavior," *Journal of Consumer Research* 2 (September 1975), pp. 118–36.

2. The consumer perceives that at least some of the brands in a product class are viable alternatives for satisfying a felt need.

3. Each of these brands has a set of attributes (color, quality, size, and so forth).

4. A set of these attributes are relevant to the consumer, and the consumer perceives that different brands vary in terms of how much of each attribute they possess.

5. The brand that is perceived as offering the greatest number of desired attributes in the desired amounts and desired order will be the brand the consumer will like best.

6. The brand the consumer likes best is the brand the consumer will intend to purchase.

Purchase Decision

If no other factors intervene after the consumer has decided on the brand that is intended for purchase, then actual purchase is a common result of search and evaluation. Actually, a purchase involves many decisions, which include product type, brand, model, dealer selection, and method of payment among other factors. In addition, rather than purchasing, the consumer may make a decision to modify, postpone, or avoid purchase based on an inhibitor to purchase, or a perceived risk.

Traditional risk theorists believe that consumers tend to make risk-minimizing decisions based on their *perceived* definition of the particular purchase. The perception of risk is based upon the possible consequences and uncertainties involved. Consequences may range from economic loss, to embarrassment if a new food product does not turn out well, to actual physical harm. Perceived risk may be either functional (related to financial and performance considerations) or psychosocial (related to whether the product will further one's self- or reference group image). The amount of risk a consumer perceives in a particular product depends on such things as the price of the product and whether or not other people will see the individual using the product.[6]

The perceived risk literature emphasizes that consumers generally try to reduce risk in their decision making.[7] This can be done by either reducing the possible consequences or by reducing the uncertainty. The possible consequences of a purchase might be minimized by purchasing

---

[6] For a review see Ivan Ross, "Perceived Risk and Consumer Behavior: A Critical Review," in M. J. Schlinger, ed., *Advances in Consumer Research*, vol. 2 (Chicago: Association for Consumer Research, 1975), pp. 1–19.

[7] J. Paul Peter and Lawrence X. Tarpey, "A Comparative Analysis of Three Consumer Decision Strategies," *Journal of Consumer Research* 2 (June 1975), pp. 29–37; J. Paul Peter and Michael J. Ryan, "An Investigation of Perceived Risk at the Brand Level," *Journal of Marketing Research* 13 (May 1976), pp. 184–88.

in small quantities or by lowering the individual's aspiration level to expect less in the way of results from the product. However, this cannot always be done. Thus, reducing risk by attempting to increase the certainty of the purchase outcome is the more widely used strategy. This can be done by seeking additional information regarding the proposed purchase. In general, the more information the consumer collects prior to purchase, the less likely postpurchase dissonance is to occur.

Postpurchase Feelings

In a general behavioral sense, if the individual finds that a certain response achieves a desired goal or satisfies a need, the success of this cue-response pattern will be remembered. The probability of responding in a like manner to the same or similar situation in the future is positively reinforced. In other words, the response has a higher probability of being repeated when the need and cue appear together again, and thus it can be said that learning has taken place. Frequent reinforcement increases the habit potential of the particular response. Likewise, if a response does not satisfy adequately the need, the probability that the same response will be repeated is reduced as a result of negative reinforcement.

For some marketers this means that if an individual finds that a particular product fulfills the need for which it was purchased then the probability is high that the product will be repurchased the next time the need arises. The firm's promotional efforts often act as the cue. If an individual repeatedly purchases a product with favorable results, then loyalty may result toward the particular product or brand. This loyalty can result in habitual purchases and such habits are often extremely difficult for competing firms to alter.

Although many studies in the area of buyer behavior center around the buyer's attitudes, motives, and behavior before and during the purchase decision, emphasis has also been given to study of behavior after the purchase. Specifically, studies have been undertaken to investigate postpurchase dissonance.[8]

The occurrence of postdecision dissonance is related to what Festinger calls "cognitive dissonance."[9] His theory states that there is often a lack of consistency or harmony among an individual's various cogni-

---

[8] For a review of the literature on dissonance research in consumer behavior, see William H. Cummings and M. VenKatesan, "Cognitive Dissonance and Consumer Behavior: A Review of the Evidence," in Mary Jane Schlinger, ed., *Advances in Consumer Research*, vol. 2 (Chicago: Association for Consumer Research, 1975), pp. 21–32.

[9] Leon Festinger, *A Theory of Cognitive Dissonance* (New York: Harper and Row, Inc., 1957), chap. 1.

tions, or attitudes and beliefs, after a decision has been made. That is, the individual has doubts and second thoughts about the choice made. Further, it is more likely that the intensity of the anxiety will be greater when any of the following conditions exist:[10]

1. The decision is an important one psychologically and/or financially.
2. There are a number of foregone alternatives.
3. The foregone alternatives have many favorable features.

These factors can relate to many buying decisions. For example, post-purchase dissonance might be expected to be present among many purchasers of such products as automobiles, major appliances, and homes. In these cases the decision to purchase is usually an important one both financially and psychologically and there are usually a number of favorable alternatives available.

When dissonance occurs after a decision has been made, the individual may attempt to reduce it by one or more of the following methods:[11]

1. By seeking information that supports the wisdom of the decision.
2. By perceiving information in a way to support the decision.
3. By changing attitudes to a less favorable view of the foregone alternatives.
4. By avoiding the importance of the negative aspects of the decision and enhancing the positive elements.

Dissonance could, of course, be reduced by admitting that a mistake had been made. However, most individuals are reluctant to admit that a wrong decision has been made. Thus, it is more likely that a person will seek out supportive information in order to reduce dissonance.[12]

These findings have much relevance for the marketer. In a buying situation, when a purchaser becomes dissonant it is reasonable to predict that such a person would be highly receptive to advertising and sales promotion which supports the purchase decision. Such communication presents favorable aspects of the product and can be useful in reinforcing the buyer's wish to believe that a wise purchase decision was made. For example, one study found that recent appliance purchasers who

---

[10] Ibid.

[11] W. J. McGuire, "Cognitive Consistency and Attitude Change," *Journal of Abnormal and Social Psychology* 61 (1960), pp. 345–53. This is a classic study of dissonance.

[12] See J. S. Adams, "Reduction of Cognitive Dissonance by Seeking Consonant Information," *Journal of Abnormal and Social Psychology* 62 (1961), pp. 74–78; and J. Mills, E. Aronson, and H. Robinson, "Selectivity in Exposure to Information," *Journal of Abnormal and Social Psychology* 60 (1959), pp. 250–53.

received a post-transaction letter expressing the appreciation of the store and reassurance that a wise decision had been made showed more favorable attitudes toward the store and had higher intentions of future purchases than buyers who did not receive the letter.[13] In another study it was found that automobile buyers who received favorable information regarding their choice after the purchase had been made but prior to delivery showed less tendency to back out of the purchase.[14]

GROUP INFLUENCES ON CONSUMER BEHAVIOR

Behavioral scientists have become increasingly aware of the powerful effects of the social environment and personal interactions on human behavior. In terms of consumer behavior, culture, social class, and reference group influences have been related to purchase and consumption decisions. It should be noted that these influences can have both direct and indirect effects on the buying process. By direct effects we mean direct communication between the individual and other members of society concerning a particular purchase decision. By indirect effects we mean the influence of society on an individual's basic values and attitudes as well as the important role that groups play in structuring an individual's personality.

Cultural and Subcultural Influences

Culture is one of the most basic influences on an individual's needs, wants, and behavior since all facets of life are carried out against the background of the society in which an individual lives. Cultural antecedents affect everyday behavior and there is empirical support for the notion that culture is a determinant of certain aspects of consumer behavior.[15]

Cultural values are transmitted through three basic organizations: the family, religious organizations, and educational institutions, and in today's society educational institutions are playing an increasingly greater role in this regard. Marketing managers should adapt the marketing mix to cultural values and constantly monitor value changes and differences in both domestic and international markets. For example, one of the changing values in America is the increasing emphasis upon

---

[13] Shelby D. Hunt, "Post-Transaction Communications and Dissonance Reduction," *Journal of Marketing* 34 (July 1970), pp. 46–51.

[14] James H. Donnelly, Jr., and John M. Ivancevich, "Post-Purchase Reinforcement, and Back-out Behavior," *Journal of Marketing Research* 7 (August 1970), pp. 399–401.

[15] Walter A. Henry, "Cultural Values Do Correlate with Consumer Behavior," *Journal of Marketing Research* 13 (May 1976), pp. 121–27.

leisure, replacing the values of hard work and long hours.[16] This change in values has been recognized by many business firms which have expanded their emphasis on providing entertainment and recreational services.[17]

HIGHLIGHT 3–2

Some Basic Changes in American Core Values

From	To
Self-reliance ⟶	Government reliance
"Hard work" ⟶	The "easy life"
Religious convictions ⟶	Secular convictions
Husband-dominated home ⟶	Wife-dominated home
Parent-centered household ⟶	Child-centered household
Respect for individual ⟶	Dislike of individual differences
Postponed gratification ⟶	Immediate gratification
Saving ⟶	Spending
Sexual chastity ⟶	Sexual freedom
Parental values ⟶	Peer-group values
Independence ⟶	Security

Source: Philip Kotler, *Marketing Management: Analysis Planning and Control,* 3d ed. (Englewood Cliffs, N.J.: Prentice-Hall, Inc., 1976), p. 43.

In a nation as large as the United States the population is bound to lose a significant amount of its homogeniety, and thus subcultures arise. In other words, there are subcultures in the American culture where people have more frequent interactions than with the population at large and thus tend to think and act alike in some respects. Subcultures are based on such things as geographic areas, religions, nationalities, and ethnic groups. While many subcultural barriers are decreasing because of mass communication, mass transit, and a decline in religious influences, ethnic influences such as the black subculture have considerable effect on purchase behavior.[18]

Social Class

While one likes to think of America as a land of equality, a class structure does exist. Social classes develop on the basis of such things as

---

[16] James E. Engel, David T. Kollat, and Roger D. Blackwell, *Consumer Behavior,* 2d ed. (New York: Holt, Rinehart and Winston, Inc., 1973), pp. 104–5.

[17] Ibid.

[18] See Engel, Kollat, and Blackwell, *Consumer Behavior,* pp. 178–88.

HIGHLIGHT 3–3

The Warner Social Class Hierarchy

Social Class	Membership	Population Percentage
Upper-upper	Locally prominent families, third- or fourth-generation wealth. Merchants, financiers or higher professionals. Wealth is inherited. Do a great amount of traveling.	1.5
Lower-upper	Newly arrived in upper class, "nouveau riche." Not accepted by upper-upper class. Executive elite, founders of large businesses, doctors, lawyers.	1.5
Upper-middle	Moderately successful professionals, owners of medium-sized businesses, and middle management. Status conscious. Child- and home-centered.	10.0
Lower-middle	Top of the average-person world. Non-managerial office workers, small-business owners, and blue-collar families. Described as "striving and respectable." Conservative.	33.0
Upper-lower	Ordinary working class. Semiskilled workers. Income often as high as the next two classes above. Enjoy life. Live from day to day.	38.0
Lower-lower	Unskilled, unemployed, and unassimilated ethnic groups. Fatalistic. Apathetic.	16.0
Total —		100.0

Source: Louis E. Boone and David L. Kurtz, *Foundations of Marketing* (Hinsdale, Ill.: The Dryden Press, 1977), p. 143.

---

wealth, skill, and power. The single best indicator of social class is occupation. However, interest at this point is in the influence of social class on the individual's behavior. What is important here is that different social classes tend to have different attitudinal configurations and values, which influence the behavior of individual members. Examples of some important attitudinal differences between the lower and middle classes are shown in Figure 3–3.

For the marketing manager, social class offers some insights into consumer behavior and is potentially useful as a market segmentation

FIGURE 3–3
Attitudinal Differences between Two Social Classes

Middle	Lower
Pointed to the future.	Pointed to the present.
Viewpoint embraces a long expanse of time.	Lives and thinks in a short expanse of time.
Stresses rationality.	Nonrational essentially.
Horizons vastly extended or not limited.	Horizons sharply defined and limited.
Greater sense of choice making.	Limited sense of choice making.
Self-confident, willing to take risks.	Very concerned with security.

Source: P. Martineau, "The Pattern of Social Class," in R. L. Clewett, ed., *Marketing's Role in Scientific Management* (Chicago: American Marketing Association, 1957), pp. 246–47. Although this study was conducted over 20 years ago, these results still appear valid today.

variable. However, there is considerable controversy as to whether social class is superior to income for the purpose of market segmentation.[19]

Reference Groups

Groups that an individual looks to (uses as a reference) when forming attitudes and opinions are described as reference groups. Primary reference groups are such groups as family and close friends, while secondary reference groups include such groups as fraternal organizations and professional associations. A buyer may also consult a single individual about various decisions and this individual would be considered a reference individual.

A person normally has several reference groups or reference individuals for various subjects or different decisions. For example, a woman may have one reference group when she is purchasing a car and a different reference group for lingerie. In other words, the nature of the product and the role the individual is playing during the purchasing process influences which reference group will be consulted. Reference group influence is generally considered to be stronger for products that are "public" or conspicuous, that is, products that other people see the individual using such as clothes or automobiles.

As noted, the family is generally recognized to be an important reference group and it has been suggested that the household, rather than the individual, is the relevant unit for studying consumer behavior.[20] This is because within a household the purchaser of goods and services is not

---

[19] For example, see James H. Myers, Roger R. Stanton, and Arne F. Haug, "Correlates of Buying Behavior: Social Class versus Income," *Journal of Marketing* 35 (October 1971), pp. 8–15. For a recent discussion of social class, see Arun K. Jain, "A Method of Investigating and Representing Implicit Social Class Theory," *Journal of Consumer Research* 2 (June 1975), pp. 53–59.

[20] See Harry L. Davis "Decision Making within the Household," *Journal of Consumer Research* 2 (March 1976), pp. 241–60.

always the user of these goods and services. Thus, it is important for marketing managers to determine not only who makes the actual purchase, but also who makes the decision to purchase. In addition, it has been recognized that the needs, income, assets, debts, and expenditure patterns change over the course of what is called the *family life cycle.* Basic stages in the family life cycle include:

1. Bachelor stage, young single people not living at home.
2. Newly married couples, young, no children.
3. Full nest I; young married couples with youngest child under six.
4. Full nest II; young married couples with youngest child six or over.
5. Full nest III; older married couples with dependent children.
6. Empty nest I; older married couples, no children living with them, household head(s) in labor force.
7. Empty nest II; older married couples, no children living at home, household head(s) retired.
8. Solitary survivor in labor force.
9. Solitary survivor, retired.

Because the life cycle combines trends in earning power with demands placed on income, it has been called one of the most powerful ways of classifying and segmenting individuals and families.[21]

PRODUCT CLASS INFLUENCES

The nature of the product class selected by the consumer to satisfy an aroused need plays an important role in the decision-making process. Basically, the nature of the product class and the brands within it determine (1) the amount of information the consumer will require before making a decision and consequently (2) the time it takes to move through the buying process. In general, product classes in which there are many alternatives that are expensive, complex, or new will require the consumer to collect more information and take longer to make a purchase decision. For example, buying an automobile is probably one of the most difficult purchase decisions most consumers make. An automobile is expensive, complex, and there are many new styles and models to choose from. Such a decision will usually require extensive information search and time before a decision is made.

A second possibility is referred to as limited decision making. For these purchases a lesser amount of information is collected and less time is devoted to shopping. For example, in purchasing a new pair of jeans the consumer may already have considerable experience, and price and complexity are somewhat limited. However, since there are many alter-

---

[21] Engel, Kollat, and Blackwell, *Consumer Behavior,* p. 194.

native styles and brands, some information processing and decision making is generally needed.

Finally, some product classes require what is called routinized decision making. For these product classes, such as cigarettes or some food products, the consumer has faced the decision many times before and has found an acceptable alternative. Thus, little or no information is collected and the consumer purchases in an habitual, automatic manner.[22]

SITUATIONAL INFLUENCES

Situational influences can be defined as "all those factors particular to a time and place of observation which do not follow from a knowledge of personal and stimulus attributes and which have a demonstrable and systematic effect on current behavior."[23] In terms of purchasing situations, five groups of situational influences have been identified.[24] These influences may be perceived either consciously or subconsciously and may have considerable effect on product and brand choice.

1. *Physical surroundings* are the most readily apparent features of a situation. These features include geographical and institutional location, decor, sounds, aromas, lighting, weather, and visible configurations of merchandise or other material surrounding the stimulus object.

2. *Social surroundings* provide additional depth to a description of a situation. Other persons present, their characteristics, their apparent roles and interpersonal interactions are potentially relevant examples.

3. *Temporal perspective* is a dimension of situations that may be specified in units ranging from time of day to season of the year. Time may also be measured relative to some past or future event for the situational participant. This allows conceptions such as time since last purchase, time since or until meals or paydays, and time constraints imposed by prior or standing commitments.

4. *Task definition* features of a situation include an intent or requirement to select, shop for, or obtain information about a general or specific purchase. In addition, task may reflect different buyer and user roles anticipated by the individual. For instance, a person shopping for a small appliance as a wedding gift for a friend is in a different situation than when shopping for a small appliance for personal use.

5. *Antecedent states* make up a final feature that characterizes a

---

[22] This discussion is based in part on John A. Howard, *Consumer Behavior: Application of Theory* (New York: McGraw-Hill, Inc., 1977), p. 9.

[23] Russell W. Belk, "An Exploratory Assessment of Situational Effects in Buyer Behavior," *Journal of Marketing Research* 11 (May 1974), pp. 156–63.

[24] Russell W. Belk, "Situational Variables and Consumer Behavior," *Journal of Consumer Research* 2 (December 1975), pp. 156–64.

situation. These are momentary moods (such as acute anxiety, pleasantness, hostility, and excitation) or momentary conditions (such as cash on hand, fatigue, and illness) rather than chronic individual traits. These conditions are further stipulated to be immediately antecedent to the current situation in order to distinguish the states the individual brings to the situation from states of the individual resulting from the situation. For instance, people may select a certain motion picture because they feel depressed (an antecedent state and a part of the choice situation), but the fact that the movie causes them to feel happier is a response to the consumption situation. This altered state may then become antecedent for behavior in the next choice situation encountered, such as passing a street vendor on the way out of the theater.[25]

CONCLUSION

The purpose of this chapter was to present an overview of consumer behavior in terms of an analysis of the buying process. The buying process is viewed as a series of five stages: felt need, alternative search, alternative evaluation, purchase decision and postpurchase feelings. This process is influenced by group, product class and situational factors. Clearly, the marketing manager must understand the buying process in order to formulate effective marketing strategies.

ADDITIONAL READINGS

Block, Carl E., and Roering, Kenneth J. *Essentials of Consumer Behavior.* Hinsdale, Ill.: The Dryden Press, 1976.

Hansen, Flemming. *Consumer Choice Behavior.* New York: The Free Press, 1972.

Kerby, Joe Kent. *Consumer Behavior.* New York: Dun-Donnelley Publishing Corp., 1975.

Markin, Rom J., Jr. *Consumer Behavior: A Cognitive Orientation.* New York: Macmillan Publishing Co., Inc., 1974.

Reynolds, Fred D., and Wells, William D. *Consumer Behavior.* New York: McGraw-Hill, Inc., 1977.

Walters, C. Glenn. *Consumer Behavior: Theory and Practice.* 3d ed. Homewood, Ill.: Richard D. Irwin, Inc., 1974.

Wasson, Chester R. *Consumer Behavior.* Austin, Tex.: Austin Press, 1975.

---

[25] Russell W. Belk, "Situational Variables and Consumer Behavior," *Journal of Consumer Research* 2 (December 1975), p. 159.

4

INDUSTRIAL BUYER BEHAVIOR

In recent years the individuals who purchase goods and services for organizations and institutions, industrial buyers, have been examined from a behavioral science perspective. Traditionally, the industrial buying situation was usually described as more "rational" or economic in nature than consumer buying. The implicit assumption was that the psycho-social factors that operate in consumer buying situations were not present or at least did not significantly influence the industrial buyer. This viewpoint has changed over the years as marketers have come to realize that while industrial and institutional markets are composed of organizations of many types, sales are not made to organizations, sales are made to individuals (or groups of individuals) within organizations. Thus, in addition to economic factors, behavior influences have been recognized as important influences on industrial purchasing.

The purpose of this chapter is to examine the industrial buying process and the factors which influence it. Figure 4–1 provides the framework for the discussion in this chapter. It presents a model of the industrial buying process.

PRODUCT INFLUENCES ON INDUSTRIAL BUYING

A major consideration that affects the industrial buying process is the nature of the product itself. Such factors as the price, riskiness, and technical complexity of the product affect the process in three ways.

56

FIGURE 4-1
A Simplified Model of the Industrial Buying Process

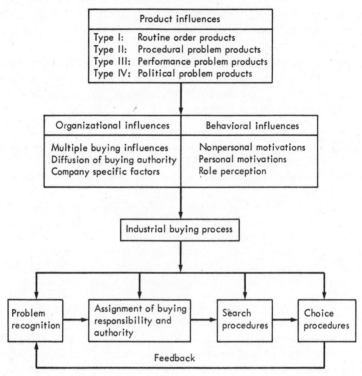

HIGHLIGHT 4-1

The Industrial Buyer versus the Consumer Buyer

Industrial customers, like household consumers, must often act on impressions, on feelings, and on attitudes, the origins of which they cannot entirely explain. He is no more irrational than the housewife is irrational for selecting and sticking with Betty Crocker Cake Mix without trying all the other brands. There is just not the time either for her or for the industrial purchasing agent to try everything.

Source: J. Edward Shrawder, "Popular Misconceptions about Industrial Marketing Research," John S. Wright and Jac L. Goldstucker, eds., *New Ideas for Successful Marketing* (Chicago: American Marketing Association, 1966), pp. 487–98.

First, they affect how long it will take for the firm to make a purchasing decision. Second, they have an effect on how many individuals will be involved in the purchasing process. Last, these factors may affect whether organizational or behavioral influences play the major role in the purchasing process.

A useful classification for examining product influences was developed by Professors Lehmann and O'Shaughnessy.[1] In their approach, products are classified on the basis of problems inherent in their adoption. They identify four basic types:

> *Type I: Routine order products.* A Type I product is frequently ordered and used. There is no problem in learning how to use such products, nor is there any question about whether the product will do the job. In short, this type of product is expected to cause no significant problems in use.
>
> *Type II: Procedural problem products.* For Type II products the buyer is also confident the product will do the job. However, problems are likely because personnel must be taught how to use the product. A buyer intent on minimizing problems associated with such a product will favor the supplier whose total offering is perceived as likely to reduce to a minimum the time and difficulty required to learn the product's operation.
>
> *Type III: Performance problem products.* With Type III products, there is doubt as to whether the product will perform satisfactorily in the application for which it is being considered. Here the problem concerns the technical outcomes of using the product. There is likely to be no firm buying commitment until this problem has been resolved. It is argued that the buyer will favor the supplier who can offer appropriate technical service, providing a free trial period, and who appears flexible enough to adjust to the demands of the buyer's company.
>
> *Type IV: Political problem products.* Type IV products give rise to "political" problems in that there is likely to be difficulty in reaching agreement among those affected if the product is adopted. "Political" problems occur when products necessitate large capital outlays, since there are always allocational rivals for funds. More frequently, political problems arise when the product is an input to several departments whose requirements may not be congruent.[2]

There are two important implications of this classification for industrial marketers. First, in a study of purchasing agents in both the United

---

[1] Donald R. Lehmann and John O'Shaughnessy, "Difference in Attribute Importance for Different Industrial Products," *Journal of Marketing* 38 (April 1974), pp. 36–42. The reader should also see Thomas T. Semon, "A Cautionary Note on 'Differences in Attribute Importance for Different Industrial Products,'" *Journal of Marketing* 39 (January 1975), p. 79; John O'Shaughnessy and Donald R. Lehmann, "A Reply to 'A Cautionary Note on Difference in Attribute Importance for Different Industrial Products,'" *Journal of Marketing* 39 (January 1975), p. 80.

[2] Lehmann and O'Shaughnessy, "Difference in Attribute Importance, p. 37.

States and Great Britain, it was found that different product attributes were rated as relatively more important depending on the type of product.[3] For example, the most important attributes for Type I products were the reliability of delivery and price; for Type II products the most important attributes were technical service offered, ease of operation or use, and training offered by supplier; for Type III products the technical service offered, flexibility of supplier, and product reliability were rated as most important; for Type IV products the price, reputation of supplier, data on product reliability, reliability of delivery and flexibility of supplier were rated as most important. Thus, marketing strategy for industrial products should be adapted to variations in buyer perceptions of problems in selection, introduction, and performance.[4]

Second, the type of product may influence whether organizational or behavioral factors are relatively more important in the industrial purchasing process. For example, behavioral influences may decrease from Type I to Type IV products while organizational influences may increase. A routine order product is most probably the sole responsibility of the purchasing agent. Here organizational influences such as joint decision making are minimal and the purchasing agent may well be more strongly influenced by behavioral influences such as a personal friendship with the supplier. On the other hand, Type IV product decisions may require considerable joint decision making (such as a purchasing committee) and thus be more influenced by organizational factors.

ORGANIZATIONAL INFLUENCES ON INDUSTRIAL BUYING

As was noted previously, sales are not made to organizations but to individuals within organizations. Thus, in order to gain an understanding of industrial buyers it is necessary to examine the environment in which they exist. Since they must function within an organizational setting there are organizationally-determined factors that will influence their buying behavior.

Multiple Buying Influence or Joint Decision Making

This refers to situations where more than one person influences the purchase of a particular product. Such a situation is common in industrial buying. The problem for the seller is to determine which individuals hold the decisive influence for purchasing the product. Obviously, where several persons influence the decision, the marketer may need to

---

[3] Ibid.

[4] Ibid., p. 42.

use a variety of means to reach each individual or group since each must be convinced of the product's worth before a buying decision is reached. Fortunately, it is often easy to find out characteristics related to purchasing by industrial companies because many such companies provide this type of information to their suppliers. They do this because it makes the suppliers more knowledgeable about their purchasing practices and this saves time and effort by the company's purchasing people.[5]

Diffusion of Buying Authority

Placing the actual order is usually the responsibility of a purchasing agent, regardless of who influences the decision. Also, the purchasing department usually has the authority on standardized, established products that involve no great technical or commercial uncertainty.

However, because of the factor of multiple buying influence, more and more industrial marketers appear to be centering attention on the buying function rather than on the specific individual who places the order. Apparently they realize that functional responsibilities and job titles are not always perfectly matched and that buying responsibility is diffused throughout the firm. Thus, it is important to study how the buying function is discharged rather than investigating the specific responsibilities of the purchasing agent or buyer. In some cases the seller may be misled into thinking that the firm's purhcasing power lies in one individual or department, when in reality the purchasing agent may be only one of a group of people who influence the purchasing decisions or may only be carrying out someone else's purchasing decision.

Company-Specific Factors

There are three primary organization-specific factors that influence the industrial purchasing process: company orientation, company size, and degree of centralization. First, if the company is technology oriented it is likely to be dominated by the engineering people and the buying decisions will, in essence, be made by them. Similarly, if the company is production oriented the buying decision will be made by the production personnel. Second, if the company is a large corporation decision making will tend to be joint. Finally, the greater the degree of centralization, the less likely it is that the decisions will be joint. Thus, a privately owned small company with technology or production orientation will

---

[5] Robert Haas, *Industrial Marketing Management* (New York: Petrocelli Books, 1976), p. 52.

HIGHLIGHT 4-2

An Operational View of the Industrial Buying Process

Although there is no single format dictating how industrial companies actually purchase goods and services, there is a relatively standard process that is followed in most cases. This process is as follows: (1) a department discovers or anticipates a problem in its operation that it believes can be overcome with the addition of a certain product or service; (2) the department head then draws up a requisition form describing the desired specifications he feels the product or service must have to solve his problem; (3) the requisition form is then sent by the department head to the firm's purchasing department; (4) based on the specifications required, the purchasing department then conducts a search for qualified sources of supply (5) once sources have been located, proposals based on the specifications are solicited, received, and analyzed for price, delivery, service, and so on; (6) proposals are then compared with the cost of producing the product in-house in a make or buy decisions: if it is decided that the buying firm can produce the product more economically, the buying process for the product in question is terminated; however, if the inverse is true, the process continues; (7) a source or sources of supply is selected from those who have submitted proposals; (8) the order is placed, and copies of the purchase order are sent to the originating department, accounting, credit, and any other interested departments within the company; and (9) after the product is shipped, received, and used, a followup with the originating department is conducted to determine that department's level of satisfaction or dissatisfaction with the purchased product in terms of the problem faced for which the product was purchased.

Although there are many variations of this process in actual operation, this is typical of the process by which industrial goods and services are purchased. It must be understood that in actual practice these are not separate steps, but, in fact, are often combined. Nevertheless, the process described in the preceding section is probably a good illustration of the operation of the industrial purchasing process.

Source: From *Industrial Marketing Management* by Robert Haas. © 1976 Litton Educational Publishing, Inc. Reprinted by permission of Van Nostrand Reinhold Company.

tend toward autonomous decision making and a large-scale public corporation with considerable decentralization will tend to have greater joint decision making.[6]

---

[6] This section is from Jagdish N. Sheth, "A Model of Industrial Buyer Behavior," *Journal of Marketing* 37 (October 1973), p. 54.

BEHAVIORAL INFLUENCES ON INDUSTRIAL BUYING

Much has been written on the rationality of industrial buying decisions and most psychologists agree that human behavior is "goal directed." That is, individuals establish behavior patterns in order to achieve some previously established goal. Therefore, to avoid making value judgments on the rationality or irrationality of an individual's behavior, a two-way classification of motivations influencing the industrial buyer will be examined: nonpersonal motivations and personal motivations.

Nonpersonal Motivations

Traditionally, industrial purchases have been viewed from a normative standpoint as methodical, objective, preplanned undertakings.[7] Thus, industrial buyers are viewed as basing purchase decisions on such factors as quality of product, cost of product, delivery reliability, technical ability and reliability of the supplier, information and market services provided by suppliers, general reputation of suppliers, geographical location of suppliers, and the suppliers' technical innovativeness.[8] By considering these factors, industrial buyers are assumed to make their decisions in such a way as to maximize the profit obtained through their purchases.

Personal Motivations

Industrial buyers are of course, subject to the same personal motives or motivational forces as other individuals. Although it is hoped that industrial buyers emphasize nonpersonal motives in their buying activities, it has been found that industrial buyers often are influenced by such personal factors as friendship, professional pride, fear and uncertainty (risk), and personal ambitions in their buying activities.[9]

For example, professional pride often expresses itself through efforts to attain status in the firm. One way to achieve this might be to initiate or influence the purchase of goods that will demonstrate their value to the company. If new materials, equipment, or components result in cost savings or increased profits, the individuals initiating the changes have demonstrated their value to the company at the same time. Fear and

---

[7] William J. Stanton, *Fundamentals of Marketing* (New York: McGraw-Hill, Inc., 1978), chap. 7.

[8] Ibid.

[9] See Raymond E. Corey, *Industrial Marketing: Cases and Concepts* (Englewood Cliffs, N.J.: Prentice-Hall, Inc., 1965). Also see David T. Wilson, "Industrial Buyers' Decision-Making Styles." *Journal of Marketing* 35 (November 1971), pp. 433–36.

HIGHLIGHT 4–3

Nonpersonal Buying Motives*

I. Heavy machinery.
   A. "Product" motives.
      1. Economy.
      2. Productivity.
      3. Dependability.
      4. Time or labor saving.
      5. Durability.
   B. "Patronage" motives.
      1. Reliability of seller.
      2. Cooperation.
      3. Low prices.
      4. Quick repair service.
      5. Past services rendered; satisfactory relationships.

II. Raw materials.
   A. "Product" motives.
      1. Right quality.
      2. Uniformity.
      3. Dependability.
      4. Purity.
      5. Ability to increase salability of user's product.
   B. "Patronage" motives.
      1. Reliability of seller.
      2. Continuous supply under all conditions.
      3. Accessibility of seller.
      4. Low prices.
      5. Quick and reliable delivery of product.

III. Supplies.
   A. "Product" motives.
      1. Right quality.
      2. Dependability.
      3. Uniformity.
      4. Economy.
      5. Durability.
   B. "Patronage" motives.
      1. Reliability of seller.
      2. Continuous supply under all conditions.
      3. Accessibility of seller.
      4. Low prices.
      5. Quick and reliable delivery of product.

* Based on a sample of National Association of Purchasing Agents conducted by Delbert F. Duncan.

uncertainty are strong motivational forces on industrial buyers and reduction of risk is often important to them. This can have a strong influence on purchase behavior.[10] Industrial marketers should understand the relative strength of personal gain versus risk-reducing motives and emphasize the more important motives when dealing with buyers.

HIGHLIGHT 4–4

The Industrial Buyer

The typical buyer is a man past middle-life, wrinkled, intelligent, cold, passive, noncommittal with eyes like a codfish, polite in contact, but at the same time, unresponsive, cool, calm, and damnably composed as a concrete post or a plaster of Paris cat; a human petrification with a heart of feldspar and without charm; or the friendly germ, minus bowels, passions, or a sense of humor. Happily they never reproduce, and all of them finally go to Hell.

Source: Louis E. Boone and Robert E. Stevens, "Emotional Motives in the Purchase of Industrial Goods: Historically Considered," *Purchasing* 6 (August 1970), p. 48.

Thus, in examining industrial buyer motivations, it is necessary to consider both personal and nonpersonal motivational forces and recognize that the relative importance of each is not a fixed quantity. It will very with the nature of the product, the climate within the organization, and the relative strength of the two forces in the particular buyer.[11]

Role Perception

A final factor that influences industrial buyers is their own perception of their role. The manner in which individuals perform their roles depends on their perception of it, their commitment to what they believe is expected of their role, the "maturity" of the role type and the extent to which the institution is committed to the role type.[12]

---

[10] See Thomas P. Copley and Frank L. Callom, "Industrial Search Behavior and Perceived Risk," Daniel M. Gardner, ed., *Proceedings of the Second Annual Conference of the Association for Consumer Research*, 1971, pp. 208–23.

[11] For representative examples of research concerned with industrial buyer behavior, see Jerome B. Kernan and Montrose S. Sommers, "Role Theory and Behavioral Style," *Journal of Purchasing* 3 (November 1967), pp. 27–38; George M. Robertson, "Motives in Industrial Buying," Marcus Alexis, Robert J. Holloway, and Robert S. Hancock, eds., *Empirical Foundations of Marketing* (Chicago: Markham Publishing Co., 1969), pp. 64–70.

[12] Kernan and Sommers, *Role Theory.*

Different industrial buyers will have different degrees of commitment to their buying role which will cause variations in role behavior from one buyer to the next. By commitment we mean willingness to perform their job according to the manner in which the organization expects them to perform. For example, some buyers seek to take charge in their role as buyer and have little commitment to company expectations. The implication for the industrial marketer is that such buyers expect, even demand, that they be kept constantly advised of all new developments in order to enable them to more effectively shape their own role. On the other hand, other buyers may have no interest in prescribing their role activities and accept their role as given to them. Such a buyer is most concerned with merely implementing prescribed company activities and buying policies with sanctioned products. Thus, some buyers will be highly committed to play the role as the firm dictates it (that is, the formal organization's perception of their role) while others might be extremely innovative and uncommitted to the expected role performance.[13] Obviously, roles may be heavily influenced by the organizational climate existing in the particular organization.

Kernan and Sommers have expressed the differences in degree of commitment as innovative, adaptive, and lethargic.[14] In innovative firms, individuals approach their occupational roles with a weak commitment to expected norms of behavior. In an adaptive organization, there is a moderate commitment, while in a lethargic organization, individuals express a strong commitment to traditionally accepted behavior and behave accordingly. Thus, a buyer in a lethargic firm would probably be less innovative in order to maintain acceptance and status within the organization and would keep conflict within the firm to a minimum.

Buyers' perception of their role may differ from the perception of their role held by others in the organization. This can result in variance in perception of the proper and the actual purchase responsibility to be held by the buyer. One study involving purchasing agents revealed that in every firm included in the study, the purchasing agents believed they had more responsibility and control over certain decisions than the other influential purchase decision makers in the firm perceived them as having. The decisions were (1) design of the product, (2) cost of the product, (3) performance life, (4) naming of the specific supplier, (5) assessing the amount of engineering help available from the supplier, and (6) reduction of rejects. This variance in role perception held true regardless of the size of the firm or the significance of the item purchased

---

13 Ibid.
14 Ibid.

to the overall success of the firm.[15] It is important, therefore, that the marketer be aware that such perceptual differences may exist and to determine as accurately as possible the amount of control and responsibility over purchasing decisions held by each purchase decision influencer in the firm.

STAGES IN THE BUYING PROCESS

As with consumer buying, most industrial purchases are made in response to a particular need or problem faced by the firm. Recognition of the need, however, is only the first step in the industrial buying process. The following four stages have been suggested as a model of the industrial buying process:

1. Problem recognition.
2. Organizational assignment of buying responsibility and authority.
3. Search procedures for identifying product offerings and for establishing selection criteria.
4. Choice procedures for evaluating and selecting among alternatives.[16]

Problem Recognition

As mentioned previously, most industrial purchases are made in response to a particular need or problem. The product purchased is hopefully the means to solve the particular problem. Industrial buyers must be concerned with budgets and profits since the firm cannot put forth a great amount of financial resources if it does not have sufficient funds, regardless of the benefits that might be derived from the purchase. However, as was mentioned, there is more "subjective" buying and "persuasion" in the industrial buying process than some earlier writers have indicated.

Assignment of Buying Authority

The influence of individuals on the buying decision will be determined in part by their responsibility as defined by the formal organiza-

---

[15] Robert E. Weigand, "Identifying Industrial Buying Responsibility," *Journal of Marketing Research* 3 (February 1966), pp. 81–84.

[16] Frederick E. Webster, Jr., "Modeling the Industrial Buying Process," *Journal of Marketing Research* 3 (November 1965), pp. 370–76; also see Frederick E. Webster, Jr. and Yoram Wind, "A General Model for Understanding Organizational Buying Behavior," *Journal of Marketing* 36 (April 1972), pp. 12–19; Frederick E. Webster, Jr. and Yoram Wind, *Organizational Buyer Behavior* (Englewood Cliffs, N.J.: Prentice-Hall, Inc., 1972).

HIGHLIGHT 4–5

Realities of Industrial Buying

To view the industrial buying process as completely objective and rational is to ignore the essential fact that industrial buyer-seller relationships involve interaction among people. Likewise, some companies may buy goods and services because of something like pride of possession, just as an individual may buy a new car when he does not really need one. The company-owned computer, the modern glass and steel office building, the services of a consultant, and the "institutional" advertisement in a prestigious business publication all may be purchased for reasons not related to strict economic considerations.

Source: Frederick E. Webster, Jr., "Modeling the Industrial Buying Process," *Journal of Marketing Research* 2 (November 1965), pp. 370–76.

---

tion. An individual's responsibility in a given buying situation will be a function of (1) the technical complexity of the product, (2) the importance of the product to the firm either in dollar terms or in terms of its relationship with the process or system which will use the product, (3) the product-specific technical knowledge which the individual has, (4) the individual's centrality in the process or system which will use the product.[17]

In some organizations the responsibility for the purchasing decision is assigned to a centralized purchasing unit. When centralization of the buying function occurs it is usually based on the assumption that knowledge of the market and not knowledge of the physical product itself is the major consideration in the buying decision. Therefore, the purchasing agent will concentrate on such market variables as price, delivery, and seller performance rather than on the technical aspects of the product.[18]

Search Procedures

This stage involves the search procedures for identifying product offerings and for establishing selection criteria. Basically, industrial buyers perform two key tasks related to the collection and analysis of information. First, the criteria against which to evaluate potential sellers have to be developed. These are usually based on a judgment as to what is needed compared to what is available. Second, alternative product

---

[17] Ibid., p. 372.
[18] Ibid., p. 372.

candidates must be located in the market. The important point here is that buyers seek sellers just as sellers seek buyers.[19]

Choice Procedures

The final stage in the industrial buying process involves establishing choice procedures for evaluating and selecting among alternatives. Once alternative products and alternative suppliers have been identified, the buyer must choose from among the alternatives. The choice process is guided by the use of decision rules and specific criteria for evaluating the product offering. These decision rules evolve from objectives, policies, and procedures established for buying actions by management.[20] Often some type of rating scheme or value index is used.

The above stages in the industrial buying process have particular significance for industrial marketers in their method of approach to potential buyers. This is not to say that these stages are the only activities industrial buyers go through before making a purchase or that they are even aware that they are going through them. The stages are presented here only as a convenient way to examine the industrial buying process and the importance of certain activities during particular stages.

For example, two writers have specifically examined the last stage of the above model (choice procedures) and have divided it into three substages: (1) awareness of the purchase sources, (2) interest in a select group of these sources, and (3) evaluation of these sources. In a study of 90 decision makers in 52 firms, it was found that the use of personal versus impersonal information as a means of maintaining interest in a potential purchase source is dependent on the stage in the buying process. It was also found that the further along potential buyers are in the buying process, the greater is their need for information inputs in terms of quantity and variety.[21]

CONCLUSION

The industrial sector has long been regarded as the stepchild of marketing in terms of the amount of research effort devoted to its problems.[22] However, in this chapter an overview of the industrial buy-

---

[19] Ibid., p. 373.

[20] Ibid., p. 374.

[21] Urban B. Ozanne and Gilbert A. Churchill, "Adoption Research: Information Sources in the Industrial Purchasing Decision," *Proceedings: The American Marketing Association*, Fall 1968, pp. 352–59.

[22] Gary L. Lilien, Alvin J. Silk, Jean-Marie Chaffray, and Murlidhar Rao, "Industrial Advertising Effects and Budgeting Practices," *Journal of Marketing* 40 (January 1976), pp. 16–24.

ing process has been presented. Basically, the model viewed industrial buying as a process of problem recognition, assignment of buying authority, search procedures and choice procedures. Product, organizational, and behavioral influences were recognized as playing important roles in terms of the speed and complexity of this process.

ADDITIONAL READINGS

Leavitt, Theodore. *Industrial Purchasing Behavior: A Study of Communications Effects.* Boston: Harvard University Press, 1965.

Pooler, Victor H. *The Purchasing Man and His Job.* New York: American Management Association, 1964.

Strauss, George. "Tactics of Lateral Relationships: The Purchasing Agent," *Administrative Science Quarterly* 7 (September 1962), pp. 161–86.

Webster, Frederick E., Jr. "New Product Adoption in Industrial Markets: A Framework for Analysis," *Journal of Marketing* 33 (July 1969), pp. 35–39.

Wind, Yoram. "The Determinants of Industrial Buyers' Behaviors," Patrick J. Robinson and Charles W. Faris, eds., *Industrial Buying and Creative Marketing.* Boston: Allyn and Bacon, Inc., 1967.

Wind, Yoram; Green, Paul E.; and Robinson, Patrick J. "The Determinants of Vendor Selection: The Evaluation Function Approach," *Journal of Purchasing* 4 (August 1968), pp. 29–41.

The Marketing Mix

Chapter 5
Product Strategy

Chapter 6
New Product Planning and Development

Chapter 7
Promotion Strategy: Advertising and Sales Promotion

Chapter 8
Promotion Strategy: Personal Selling

Chapter 9
Distribution Strategy

Chapter 10
Pricing Strategy

5

PRODUCT STRATEGY

The primary focus of marketing management in the business organization is on the product. As pointed out previously, marketing has evolved along several different lines. Prior to World War II marketing emphasized "selling." Products were produced and either simply marketed for sale or aggressively promoted to generate sales. During the last three decades the marketing concept philosophy developed; this was a restatement of the ancient idea of consumer sovereignty and it emphasized customer satisfaction as the key to sales and profits. However, the marketing concept philosophy is, for the most part, a product innovation and product development concept. More specifically, this means that a company operating under such a philosophy must be measured not only by the profits it earns, but also by the usefulness of the products and services which it makes available to the larger society. Given today's economy, the firm's survival and long-run growth depends primarily on its ability to create, produce, and market products that satisfy consumer needs and wants.[1]

There are four ways by which a company can grow.[2] It can increase sales from products it is presently marketing. It can acquire other companies by sale or merger. It can obtain rights (licenses) to manufacture

---

[1] For a more detailed discussion of the evolution of marketing management philosophies, see Philip Kotler, *Marketing Management: Analysis, Planning, and Control,* 3d ed. (Englewood Cliffs, N.J.: Prentice-Hall, Inc., 1976), pp. 12–18.

[2] Victor P. Buell, *Marketing Management in Action* (New York: McGraw-Hill, Inc., 1966), pp. 139–45.

products developed by others. It can develop new products internally by its own research departments. Each of these approaches centers on the product variable in the marketing mix. Pricing, promotion, and the other marketing variables play a subsidiary role in the firm's long-run program. This idea is clearly stated by Booz, Allen, and Hamilton: "If the concept is accepted that products are the medium of business conduct, then business strategy is fundamentally product planning."[3]

HIGHLIGHT 5–1

Elements of Product Strategy

1. An audit of the firm's actual and potential resources.
    a. Financial strength.
    b. Access to raw materials.
    c. Plant and equipment.
    d. Operating personnel.
    e. Management.
    f. Engineering and technical skill.
    g. Patents and licenses.
2. Approaches to current markets.
    a. More of the same products.
    b. Variations of present products in terms of grades, sizes and packages.
    c. New products to replace or supplement current lines.
    d. Product deletions.
3. Approaches to new or potential markets.
    a. Geographical expansion of domestic sales.
    b. New socioeconomic or ethnic groups.
    c. Overseas markets.
    d. New uses of present products.
    e. Complementary goods.
4. State of competition.
    a. New entrys into the industry.
    b. Product imitation.
    c. Mergers or acquisitions.

PRODUCT DEFINITION

The way in which the product variable is defined can have important implications for the survival, profitability, and long-run growth of the firm. For example, the same product can be viewed at least three different

---

[3] Booz, Allen, and Hamilton, Inc., *Management of New Products* (Chicago: Booz, Allen, and Hamilton, Inc., 1964), p. 7.

ways. First, it can be viewed in terms of the tangible product—the physical entity or service that is offered to the buyer. Second, it can be viewed in terms of the extended product—the tangible product along with the whole cluster of services that accompany it. Third, it can be viewed in terms of the generic product—the essential benefits the buyer expects to receive from the product.[4]

From the standpoint of the marketing manager, to define the product solely in terms of the tangible product is to fall into the error of "product provincialism."[5] Executives who are guilty of committing this error define their company's product too narrowly since overemphasis is placed upon the physical object itself. The classic example of this mistake can be found in railroad passenger service. Although no amount of product improvement could have staved off its decline, if the industry had defined itself as being in the transportation business rather than the railroad business, it might still be profitable today. On the positive side, toothpaste manufacturers have been willing to exercise flexibility in defining their product. For years toothpaste was an oral hygiene product where emphasis was placed solely on fighting tooth decay and bad breath, e.g., Crest with fluoride. Recently many manufacturers have recognized the need to market toothpaste as a cosmetic item—to clean teeth of stains. As a result, special purpose brands have been designed to serve these particular needs, such as MacLeans, Ultra Brite and Close-Up.

In line with the marketing concept philosophy, a reasonable definition of product is that it is *the sum of the physical, psychological, and sociological satisfactions that the buyer derives from purchase, ownership, and consumption.* From this standpoint, products are consumer-satisfying objects that include such things as accessories, packaging, and service.

PRODUCT CLASSIFICATION

A product classification scheme can be useful to the marketing manager as an analytical device to assist in planning marketing strategy and programs. A basic assumption underlying such classifications is that products with common attributes can be marketed in a similar fashion. In general, products are classed according to two basic criteria: (1) end use or market, and (2) degree of processing or physical transformation.

---

[4] Philip Kotler, *Marketing Management: Analysis, Planning, and Control,* 2d ed. (Englewood Cliffs, N.J.: Prentice-Hall, Inc., 1972), pp. 424–25. Although this classification is useful for the purpose of our text, it is not included in the 3d edition (1976) of the Kotler text.

[5] Theodore Levitt, "Marketing Myopia," *Harvard Business Review* 38 (July-August 1960), pp. 45–56.

1. *Agricultural products and raw materials.* These are goods grown or extracted from the land or sea, such as iron ore, wheat, sand. In general these products are fairly homogenous, sold in large volume, and have low value per unit or bulk weight.

2. *Industrial goods.* These are products purchased by business firms for the purpose of producing other goods or for running their business. This category includes the following:
   a. Raw materials and semifinished goods.
   b. Major and minor equipment such as basic machinery, tools, and other processing facilities.
   c. Parts or components, which become an integral element of some other finished good.
   d. Supplies or items used to operate the business but that do not become part of the final product.

3. *Consumer goods.* Consumer goods can be divided into three classes:
   a. Convenience goods, such as food, which are purchased frequently with minimum effort. Impulse goods would also fall into this category.
   b. Shopping goods, such as appliances, which are purchased after some time and energy is spent comparing the various offerings.
   c. Speciality goods, which are unique in some way so that the consumer will make a special purchase effort to obtain them.

In general, the buying motive, buying habits, and character of the market are different for industrial goods vis-a-vis consumer goods. A primary purchasing motive for industrial goods is, of course, profit. As mentioned in the previous chapter, industrial goods are usually purchased as means to an end, and not as an end in themselves. This is another way of saying that the demand for industrial goods is a derived demand. Industrial goods are often purchased directly from the original source with few middlemen because many of these goods can be bought in large quantities; they have high unit value; technical advice on installation and use is required; and the product is ordered according to the user's specifications. Many industrial goods are subject to multiple-purchase influence and a long period of negotiation is often required.

The market for industrial goods has certain attributes which distinguish it from the consumer goods market. Much of the market is concentrated geographically, as in the case of steel, auto, or shoe manufacturing. For certain products there are a limited number of buyers; this is known as a *vertical market*, which means that (a) it is narrow because customers are restricted to a few industries and (b) it is deep, in that a very large percentage of the producers in the market use the product. Some products, such as office supplies, have a *horizontal market*, which means that the goods are purchased by all types of firms in many different industries. In general, buyers of industrial goods are

HIGHLIGHT 5–2

A. Classes of Industrial Products—Some Characteristics and Marketing Considerations

Characteristics and Marketing Considerations	Type of Product				
	Raw Materials	Fabricating Parts and Materials	Installations	Accessory Equipment	Operating Supplies
Characteristics:					
1. Unit price	Very low	Low	Very high	Medium	Low
2. Length of life	Very short	Depends on final product	Very long	Long	Short
3. Quantities purchased	Large	Large	Very small	Small	Small
4. Frequency of purchase	Frequent delivery; long term purchase contract	Infrequent purchase but frequent delivery	Very infrequently	Medium	Frequent
5. Standardization of competitive products	Very high; grading is important	Very high	Very low; custom-made	Low	High
6. Limits on supply	Limited; cannot be increased quickly or at all	Usually no problem	No problem	Usually no problem	Usually no problem
Marketing considerations:					
1. Nature of channel	Short; no middlemen	Short; middlemen only for small buyers	Short; no middlemen	Middlemen used	Middlemen used
2. Negotiation period	Hard to generalize	Medium	Long	Medium	Short
3. Price competition	Important	Important	Not important	Not main factor	Important
4. Presale/postsale service	Not important	Not important	Very important	Important	Very little
5. Demand stimulation	Very little	Moderate	Salesmen very important	Important	Not too important
6. Brand preference	None	Generally unimportant but some sellers try	High	High	Low
7. Advance buying contract	Important; use of long-term contracts	Important use of long-term contracts	Not usually	Not usually	Not usually

reasonably well informed. As noted previously heavy reliance is often placed on price, quality control, and reliability of supply source.

In terms of consumer products, many marketing scholars have found the convenience, shopping, and specialty classification inadequate and have attempted to either refine it or to derive an entirely new typology.

Highlight 5–2 (continued)

B. Characteristics of Classes of Consumer Goods and Some Marketing Considerations

Characteristics and Marketing Considerations	Type of Product		
	Convenience	Shopping	Specialty
Characteristics:			
1. Time and effort devoted by consumer to shopping	Very little	Considerable	Cannot generalize. May go to nearby store and exert minimum effort or may have to go to distant store and spend much time
2. Time spent planning the purchase	Very little	Considerable	Considerable
3. How soon want is satisfied after it arises	Immediately	Relatively long time	Relatively long time
4. Are price and quality compared?	No	Yes	No
5. Price	Low	High	High
6. Frequency of purchase	Usually frequent	Infrequent	Infrequent
7. Importance	Unimportant	Often very important	Cannot generalize
Marketing considerations:			
1. Length of channel	Long	Short	Short to very short
2. Importance of retailer	Any single store is relatively unimportant	Important	Very important
3. Number of outlets	As many as possible	Few	Few; often only one in a market
4. Stock turnover	High	Lower	Lower
5. Gross margin	Low	High	High
6. Responsibility for advertising	Manufacturer's	Retailer's	Joint responsibility
7. Importance of point-of-purchase display	Very important	Less important	Less important
8. Advertising used	Manufacturer's	Retailer's	Both
9. Brand or store name important	Brand name	Store name	Both
10. Importance of packaging	Very important	Less important	Less important

Source: William J. Stanton, *Fundamentals of Marketing* (New York, McGraw-Hill, Inc., 1978), pp. 139, 148.

None of these attempts appear to have met with complete success.[6] Perhaps there is no "best" way to deal with this problem. From the

---

[6] The interested reader may wish to investigate some of the original work on classification schemes. See Gordon E. Miracle, "Product Characteristics and Marketing Strategy," *Journal of Marketing* 29 (January 1965), pp. 18–24; L. P. Bucklin, "Retail Strategy and the Classification of Consumer Goods," *Journal of Marketing* 27 (January 1963), pp. 50–55; L. Aspinwall, "The Characteristics of Goods and Parallel Systems Theories," in G. T. Kelley and W. Lazer, eds., *Managerial Marketing: Perspectives and Viewpoints* (Homewood, Ill.: Richard D. Irwin, Inc., 1962), pp. 633–43; R. E. Frank and P. E. Green, "Numerical Taxonomy in Marketing Analysis: A Review Article," *Journal of Marketing Research* 5 (February 1968), pp. 83–94.

standpoint of the marketing manager, product classification is useful to the extent that it assists in providing guidelines for developing an appropriate marketing mix. For example, convenience goods generally require broadcast promotion and long channels of distribution as opposed to shopping goods, which generally require more targeted promotion and somewhat shorter channels of distribution.

PRODUCT LIFE CYCLE

A firm's product marketing strategy must take into account the fact that products have a life cycle. Figure 5–1 illustrates this life cycle concept. Products are introduced, grow, mature, and decline. This cycle varies according to industry, product, technology, and market. Marketing executives need to be aware of the life cycle concept because it can be a valuable aid in developing marketing strategies.

During the introduction phase of the cycle, there are usually high production and marketing costs and since sales are only beginning to materialize, profits are low or nonexistent. Profits increase and are positively correlated with sales during the growth stage as the market begins trying and adopting the product. As the product matures, profits for the initiating firm do not keep pace with sales because of competi-

FIGURE 5–1

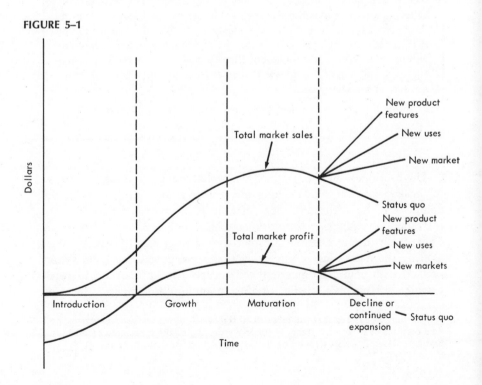

tion. Here the seller may be forced to "remarket" the product, which may involve making price concessions, increasing product quality, or expanding outlays on advertising and sales promotion just to maintain market share. At some point in time sales decline, and the seller must decide whether to (a) drop the product, (b) alter the product, (c) seek new uses for the product, (d) seek new markets, or (e) continue with more of the same.[7]

HIGHLIGHT 5–3

The Used Apple Policy

The fact is, most new products don't have any sort of classical life cycle curve at all. They have instead from the very outset an infinitely descending curve. The product not only doesn't get off the ground; it goes quickly under ground—six feet under.

It is little wonder, therefore, that some disillusioned and badly burned companies have recently adopted a more conservative policy—what I call the "used apple policy." Instead of aspiring to be the first company to see and seize an opportunity, they systematically avoid being first. They let others take the first bite of the supposedly juicy apple that tantalizes them. They let others do the pioneering. If the idea works, they quickly follow suit. They say, in effect, "The trouble with being a pioneer is that the pioneers get killed by the Indians." Hence, they say (thoroughly mixing their metaphors), "We don't have to get the first bite of the apple. The second one is good enough." They are willing to eat off a used apple, but they try to be alert enough to make sure it is only slightly used—that they at least get the second big bite, not the tenth skimpy one.

Source: Theodore Levitt, "Exploit the Product Life Cycle," *Harvard Business Review* 43 (November–December 1965), p. 82.

The usefulness of the product life-cycle concept is primarily that it forces management to take a long-range view of marketing planning. In doing so, it should become clear that shifts in phases of the life cycle correspond to changes in the market situation, competition, and demand. Thus, the astute marketing manager should recognize the necessity of altering the marketing mix to meet these changing conditions. When applied with sound judgment the life cycle concept can aid in forecasting, pricing, advertising, product planning, and other aspects of

---

[7] It should be noted that the labeling of the new product features, new uses, and new markets curves is arbitrary. In other words, any of the three may result in the highest sales and profits depending on the product and situation.

marketing management.[8] However, the marketing manager must also recognize that the length and slope of the product life cycle varies across products. Thus, while the product life cycle is useful for recognizing the stages a product will go through, it is difficult to forecast the exact time periods for these stages.[9]

PRODUCT POLICY CONSIDERATIONS

Economic theory of the firm has evolved on the premise that a company makes and sells only one product. In the actual world of business, the single product firm is the exception rather than the rule. The various kinds of products a company produces and sells are determined by its product policies, which are the outgrowth of top-level management planning. Product planning and development involves the determination of the company's basic product policies, what products to develop and market, their specifications, and their relationships to one another and to those of competition.

Many manufacturers (and middlemen) do not engage in any formal product planning. Some important reasons for this lack of planning are: (1) many executives have failed to recognize and appreciate the need for new products to sustain corporate growth; (2) many are ignorant of the complexities of introducing new products into today's competitive markets; (3) many managers have a production or engineering outlook and feel that marketing people are not qualified to work in the area of product planning and development; and (4) in some organizations managers fear losing control and authority to a product planning committee or department. However, under the marketing concept philosophy, product line planning and development is a vital part of marketing management's responsibility, regardless of the organizational arrangements.

---

[8] For representative literature on managing the product life cycle, consult John E. Smallwood, "The Product Life Cycle: A Key to Strategic Marketing Planning," *MSU Business Topics* (Winter 1973), pp. 29–35; Chester R. Wasson, *Product Management: Product Life Cycles and Competitive Marketing Strategy* (St. Charles, Ill.: Challenge Books, 1971); Thomas A. Staudt and Donald A. Taylor, *A Managerial Introduction to Marketing*, 2d ed. (Englewood Cliffs: Prentice-Hall, Inc., 1970), chap. 10; Eberhard E. Scheving, *New Product Management* (Hinsdale, Ill.: The Dryden Press, 1974), chaps. 12, 13; Bernard Catry and Michel Chevalier, "Market Share Strategy and the Product Life Cycle," *Journal of Marketing* 38 (October 1974), pp. 29–34; Robert Fildes and Stephen Lofthouse, "Marketing Share Strategy and the Product Life Cycle: A Comment," *Journal of Marketing* 39 (October 1975), pp. 57–59; Bernard Catry and Michel Chevalier, "Market Share Strategy: The Concept and the Evidence," *Journal of Marketing* 39 (October 1975), pp. 59–60.

[9] For a further discussion of problems with the product life cycle concept, see Nariman K. Dhalla and Sonia Yuspeh, "Forget the Product Life Cycle Concept!" *Harvard Business Review* 54 (January–February 1976), pp. 102–12.

HIGHLIGHT 5-4

Elements of Marketing Strategy in Product Life Cycle

Stage in Product Life Cycle

Element	Introduction	Growth	Maturation	Decline
Objective	To get trial	Establish strong brand position with distributors and users	Maintain and strengthen customer loyalty	Seek remaining profit
Competition	None	Rapid growth, aggressive competition	Intense. Declining unit profits, competitors drop out	Profit squeeze, fewer competitors
Product	Few models, high quality	Modular, flexible, more models for segments emerging	Tighten lines not serving good markets. Product improvement and differentiation	Reduce line to major profit producers
Price	Good value, trade discounts	Long price line from low to premium	Attention to broadening market. Promotional pricing to extend brand coverage	Maintain profit levels without regard to share of market
Distribution	Exclusive or selective	Intensive and extensive. Quick service to dealers. High dealer inventory	Intensive and extensive. Quick service to dealers. Low dealer inventory	Phase out marginal dealers
Promotion	Create awareness, get early trial. Fairly heavy advertising and free samples	Create strong brand awareness and preference. Maximum use of mass media	Maintain and strengthen consumer-dealer relations. Continue mass media, sales promotion	Rapid phaseout, sustain enough to sell profitable volume only
Marketing research	Discover weaknesses. Identify emerging segments	Market position, market gaps. Product gaps	Attention to product improvement. Search for broader market and new promotion themes	Determine point of product elimination

Source: Adapted from Chester R. Wasson, *Product Management: Product Life Cycles and Competitive Marketing Strategy* (St. Charles, Ill.: Challenge Books, 1971), pp. 168–86.

A reasonable way of viewing product policy is that it consists of forecasting the future nature of the environment and consumer needs in order to predict what products the market may demand. Product policies are the means used to guide decision makers in (a) managing the firm's current products, (b) determining what new products to market, and (c) determining what products to drop from the line. Product policies are the result of planning and must reflect not only the needs of the consumer, but also present and future competition.

Product Mix and Product Line

The *product mix* is the composite of products offered for sale by the firm; *product line* refers to a group of products that are closely related, either because they satisfy a class of need, are used together, are sold to the same customer groups, are marketed through the same types of outlets, or fall within given price ranges.[10] There are three primary dimensions of a firm's product mix: (1) width of the product mix, which refers to the number of product lines the firm handles; (2) depth of the product mix, which refers to the average number of products in each line; (3) consistency of the product mix, which refers to the similarity of product lines. Thus, McDonald's hamburgers represent a product item in their line of sandwiches; whereas their hot cakes or Egg Mac-Muffins represent items in a different line, namely, breakfast foods.

Development of a plan for the existing product line has been called the most critical element of a company's product planning activity.[11] In designing such plans management needs accurate information on the current and anticipated performance of its products, which should encompass:

1. Consumer evaluation of the company's products, particularly their strengths and weaknesses vis-a-vis competition (that is, product positioning by market segment information).
2. Objective information on actual and anticipated product performance on relevant criteria such as sales, profits, and market share.[12]

Market Segmentation

Some years ago, Wendell R. Smith published a now classic article on product differentiation and market segmentation in which he attempted

---

[10] Committee on Definitions of the American Marketing Association, Ralph S. Alexander, Chairman, *Marketing Definitions: A Glossary of Marketing Terms* (Chicago: American Marketing Association, 1960).

[11] Yoram Wind and Henry J. Claycamp, "Planning Product Line Strategy: A Matrix Approach," *Journal of Marketing* 40 (January 1976), p. 2.

[12] Ibid.

to analyze and differentiate these two strategies.[13] Market segmentation involves altering the firm's products to match the specific microsegments of the market.[14] This strategy assumes that the overall market for any (generic) good is heterogeneous, being composed of several homogeneous segments. Each of these microsegments can be considered a target market. To implement this strategy the manufacturer (or seller) modifies or alters the product to accommodate the specific needs of the various segments. In a very general sense, the breadth and depth of a firm's product line can be viewed as an application of a market segmentation strategy. Another application is a "product overlap" strategy where manufacturers compete with themselves, as in the case of Procter and Gamble which markets competing brands of detergents and toothpaste.

Product differentiation is often confused with market segmentation. Smith defines product differentiation as the seller's attempt to "bend

---

HIGHLIGHT 5–5

Some Alternative Bases for Segmentation

1. Geographic—marketing in some areas but not others. Obvious for certain products such as snowmobiles.

2. Demographic—identifying a market in terms of population characteristics such as occupation, race, sex, age, income, stage in family life cycle.

3. Behavioral Characteristics—identifying a market in terms of life style, personality, benefits sought in using the product, social class.

4. Volume—distinguishing heavy, medium, light users and nonusers and determining if they differ demographically and/or behaviorally.

5. Institutional—industrial marketers may identify markets based on size or type of industry.

---

[13] Wendell R. Smith, "Product Differentiation and Market Segmentation as Alternative Marketing Strategies," *Journal of Marketing* 20 (July 1956), pp. 3–8.

[14] Market segmentation has received considerable emphasis in marketing and is the justification for much of the research done in the area of consumer behavior. For in-depth discussions, see James F. Engel, Henry F. Fiorillo, and Murray A. Cayley, eds., *Market Segmentation: Concepts and Applications* (New York: Holt, Rinehart and Winston, Inc., 1972); Ronald E. Frank, William F. Messy, and Yoram Wind, *Market Segmentation* (Englewood Cliffs, N.J.: Prentice-Hall, Inc., 1972); Yoram Wind, "Issues and Advances in Segmentation Research," *Journal of Marketing Research* 15 (August 1978), pp. 317–37.

demand to the will of supply."[15] Thus, the seller attempts to cover a broad market with a single product or limited number of products. Perhaps the difference between the two strategies is in the starting point. In market segmentation the starting point is to determine consumer needs, after which the product is developed or redesigned to meet these needs; in product differentiation the product is developed or modified first, then consumers who have a need for the product are searched for. In any case, these strategies generally complement each other and are used in conjunction with one another.

Private Brands

As a product strategy, many firms produce and market their own products under a so-called private label. For example, A & P uses the Ann Page label, among others, and Sears uses the Kenmore label, among others. Such a strategy is highly important in industries where the middleman has gained control over distribution to the consumer. The advent of large chain stores such as K-Mart has accelerated the growth of private brands. If a manufacturer refuses to supply certain middlemen with private branded merchandise, then the alternative is for these middlemen to go into the manufacturing business, as in the case of Kroger.

As a general rule private brands are lower priced than national brands because there are some cost savings involved, and this has been the strongest appeal of private brand merchandisers. If a manufacturer is selling its national branded products to middlemen under a private label, then the Robinson-Patman Act requires that any price differential reflect (a) genuine differences in grade and quality, or (b) cost savings in manufacturing or distribution. One of the reasons why manufacturers will supply resellers with private branded merchandise is to utilize their production capacity more fully.

Distinctive Packaging

Distinctive or unique packaging is one method of differentiating a relatively homogeneous product. For example, boil-a-pak dinner, pump rather than aerosol deodorant and hair spray containers, and different sizes and designs of tissue packages are attempts to differentiate a product through packaging and satisfy consumer needs at the same time.

In making packaging decisions, the marketing manager must again consider both the consumer and costs. On one hand, the package must be capable of protecting the product through the channel of distribution

---

[15] Ibid., p. 4.

HIGHLIGHT 5–6

Why Branding Is Advantageous to Marketers

There are five basic reasons why it is useful for marketers to brand their merchandise:

1. Encourages repeat buying . . . . A good brand speeds up shopping for the customer and thus reduces the marketer's selling time and effort. When a customer finds it convenient to repeat purchases by brand, promotion costs are reduced and sales volume is increased.

2. Customer franchise . . . . Whether the brander is a manufacturer, wholesaler, or retailer, brand loyalty provides protection from competition because the brander, in effect, is given a customer franchise.

3. Market segmentation . . . . A brander can use various brands to segment markets and meet the needs of various intermediate consumers.

4. Profitability . . . . By offering customers what amounts to a "guarantee" of quality, branders may be able to obtain a price that is higher than the cost of giving this guarantee.

5. Corporate image . . . . Good brands can enhance the company's name, simplifying the introduction of additional products.

Source: Adapted from E. Jerome McCarthy, *Basic Marketing: A Managerial Approach*, 6th ed. (Homewood, Ill.: Richard D. Irwin, Inc., © 1978), pp. 268–69.

---

to the consumer. In addition, it is desirable for packages to be of convenient size and easy to open for the consumer. Hopefully, the package is also attractive and capable of being used as an in-store promotional tool. However, maximizing these objectives may increase the cost of the product to such an extent that consumers are no longer willing to purchase it. Thus, the marketing manager must determine the optimal protection, convenience, and promotional strengths of packages, subject to cost constraints.

PRODUCT MANAGEMENT CONCEPT

Properly executed, the "product management concept" is the complete and profitable administration of a company's products (present and future), through delegated administration, teamwork, and profit responsibility. In a small, one-product company the president is the product manager; however, in a large multiproduct firm other arrangements must be made, because the management problem becomes very complex. The product management concept is the delegation of authority for product marketing to a specialist in the firm. This specialist is entirely responsible for the product with respect to things such as personal selling, distribution, advertising, and so forth. In many respects, the strength of the product management concept lies the need to coordinate the efforts of company specialists in the various functional areas such as production, transportation, forecasting, and advertising. Figure 5–2 is a chart showing how the product manager concept is related to marketing strategy.

There are various product management organizational frameworks, but their basic functions should be the same regardless of the product arrangement. Product policies are usually formulated by top management (the president, the vice president of marketing, or the executive committee). Traditionally, product management is the primary responsibility of the vice president of marketing who is often assisted by a product planning department or committee. There are three basic types of product management orientations.

1. An advertising and sales promotion orientation, which is most common among consumer goods companies such as Procter and Gamble where advertising is such a large and critical part of the marketing program.
2. In the industrial field where customer relations and technical service are paramount requirements, sales get the product manager's major attention. At DuPont, for example, a product manager may report upward through four or five levels of sales executives.
3. The most comprehensive (and rare) kind of product manager is the kind who is more correctly called a general manager. At General Electric, which has more than 100 product departments or "profit centers," each is headed by a general manager responsible for everything about his or her products from manufacturing to marketing.[16]

There are many variations of the product management organizational arrangement. For example, the same job carries different titles (e.g.,

---

[16] "Why Modern Marketing Needs the Product Manager," *Printers' Ink*, October 14, 1960, pp. 25–30. Also see "Product Managers: Just What Do They Do?" *Printers' Ink*, October 28, 1966, pp. 13–21; Victor P. Buell, "The Changing Role of the Product Manager in Consumer Goods Companies," *Journal of Marketing* 39 (July 1975), pp. 3–11.

FIGURE 5–2
How Each Product Manager Develops Marketing Strategy

	Consumer Brand Manager "As Is"	Industrial Product Manager "As Is"	Product Manager "Ideal"
Sales forecast	Tends to neglect technological trends.	Tends to neglect sociological trends.	Consider both sociological and technological trends.
Pricing	At-value to customer.	At times "cost plus."	At-value to customer; pricing should be flexible.
Advertising and promotion	Spends a great deal of time on it.	Spends little time on it.	Time spent on it should be proportionate to expected pay-off. Both should try to look at role of advertising without preconceived notions.
Distribution	Wide distributive chain.	Often relies mostly on own sales force.	Should not rely on habitual distribution.
Product and market development	Well aware of short product life cycle.	Often does not keep track of product life cycle.	Keeps close watch on product life cycle, not only on sales volume but also on net unit profit.
Research and development	Usually specifies what is needed from R&D.	Often specifies not only what, but also how.	Specify only what; leave how up to R&D.
Planning	Concentrates on few items, but not necessarily in order of importance.	Often responsible for many items—some of them not profitable.	Rank opportunities and concentrate on major ones.
	Sometimes lacks proper environment.	Often lacks proper environment.	Top management should ensure proper environment.
	Thoroughness may not be rewarded properly.	Thoroughness may not be rewarded properly.	Top management should set up yardstick to measure planning effectiveness; reward good planning.
Coordination	Usually well done. Thinks of himself as a product manager.	Often could be smoother. Thinks of himself as product manager.	Should be product managers. Know product, know thyself and be familiar with motivational theories.

Source: *Marketing Insights*, March 10, 1969, pp. 14–16.

product manager, brand manager), duties, responsibilities, authority, and status in different companies. However, there are some common dominators.[17]

1. Product management seems to work as well for industrial companies as for consumer companies.

2. Most product managers seem to have sales or marketing experience and are graduates of business schools.

3. The most common characteristic of firms working with product managers is change.

4. Most product managers have heavy responsibility without commensurate authority. Some 60 percent of consumer companies designate their product managers as line executives.

5. All firms require product managers to prepare sales forecasts and price-cost-profit budgets.

6. Generally, the product manager reports to a higher marketing executive (marketing director, merchandise manager, division manager).

Organizing for Product Management

Product management can be instituted in terms of a *program* or a *project* organizational arrangement. The idea of program or project management comes from the defense industry and is a relatively new management technique.[18] This approach is particularly useful in situations where organizational lines must be crossed. Projects (as in the case of product planning, development, and marketing) require a mix of parallel and serial work tasks, a mix of diverse skills and numerous resources such as materials and facilities.

The program concept is different from the product manager concept in that the program manager has authority commensurate with responsibility and almost complete control over the project. Program managers are fairly autonomous with regard to operations and have the prime responsibility for funding, scheduling, and performance standards for the project. They also act as a focal point for customer contact and resolve all conflicts that threaten to disrupt the project. Thus, program management can be defined as actively encompassing planning, control, and supervising the engineering and manufacturing involved in producing an end item. IBM is an example of a company that employs the

---

[17] See, "The Brand Manager: Who Is He? What Is He Doing? What Is His Ad Role?" *Advertising Age,* January 6, 1969, p. 45; "The Brand Manager: No Longer King," *Business Week,* June 9, 1973, pp. 58–66.

[18] David B. Ulman, *New Product Programs: Their Planning and Control* (New York: American Management Association, 1969), chap. 2.

HIGHLIGHT 5-7

**Comparison of the Roles of the
Product Manager in Two Different Firms**

Activity	Consumer Goods Company	Industrial Goods Company
1. Planning	Key duty	Key duty
2. Advertising	Creates plan	Limited role
3. Sales promotion	Originates, may manage	Suggests technical schedule
4. Merchandising	Recommends policies and plans	Limited role
5. Packaging, branding, labelling	Makes recommendations	Limited role
6. Pricing	Studies and makes recommendations	Bid pricing, estimating, volume pricing
7. Product development, new products	Studies and makes recommendations	Works with laboratories and may approve modifications
8. Product line planning	Recommends changes	Recommends and may have authority over mix
9. Market research	Makes request for studies	May do his own research
10. Production planning	Forecasts sales volume	Establishes mix and schedule
11. Inventories and warehousing	Estimates inventory needs	Estimates inventory needs
12. Field sales and distribution	Recommends channels of distribution	May be primary technical advisor to field

Source: G. H. Evans, "The Product Manager's Job," *American Management Association Research Study*, No. 69 (New York: American Management Association).

---

program manager concept. Figure 5–3 illustrates the difference between a program or project approach versus a functional approach.

THE PRODUCT AUDIT

The product audit is a marketing management technique whereby the company's current product offerings are reviewed to ascertain whether

FIGURE 5–3
Matrix Organization Showing the Relationship between Program Management and Functional Management

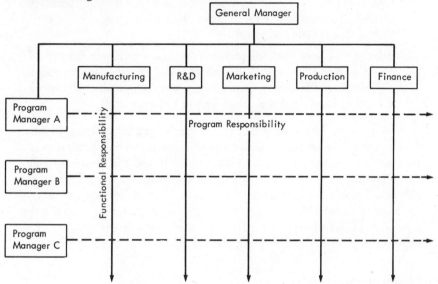

Source: Ulman, *New Product Programs,* p. 101.

each product should be continued as is, improved or modified, or deleted. The audit is a task that should be carried out at regular intervals as a matter of policy. Product audits are the responsibility of the product manager unless specifically delegated to someone else.

Deletions

It can be argued that the major purpose of the product audit is to detect "sick" products and then bury them.[19] Criteria must be developed for deciding whether or not a product is a candidate for deletion. Some of the more obvious factors to be considered are:

Sales Trends. How have sales moved over time? What has happened to market share? Why have sales declined? What changes in sales have occurred in competitive products both in our line and those of other manufacturers?

_____

[19] See R. S. Alexander, "The Death and Burial of Sick Products," *Journal of Marketing* 28 (April 1964), pp. 1–7; Philip Kotler, "Phasing Out Weak Products," *Harvard Business Review* 43 (March–April 1965), pp. 107–18; P. W. Hamelman and Edward M. Mazze, "Improving Product Abandonment Decisions," *Journal of Marketing* 36 (April 1972), pp. 20–26.

Profit Contribution. What has been the profit contribution of this product to the company? If profits have declined, how are these tied to price? Have selling, promotion, and distribution costs risen out of proportion to sales? Does the product require excessive management time and effort.

Product Life Cycle. Has the product reached a level of maturity and saturation in the market? Are there more effective substitutes on the market? Has the product outgrown its usefulness? Can the resources used on this product be put to better use?

The above factors should be used as guidelines for making the final decision to delete a product. Deletion decisions are very difficult to make because of their potential impact on customers and the firm. For example, eliminating a product may force a company to lay off some employees. There are other factors to consider such as keeping consumers supplied with replacement parts and repair service and maintaining the good will of distributors who have an inventory of the product. The deletion plan should provide for the clearing out of stock in question.

Product Improvement

One of the other important objectives of the audit is to ascertain whether or not to alter the product in some way or to leave things as they are. Altering the product means changing one or more of the product's attributes or marketing dimensions. Attributes refer mainly to product features, design, package, and so forth. Marketing dimensions refer to such things as price, promotion strategy, channels of distribution.

It is possible to look at the product audit as a management device for controlling the product strategy. Here, control means feedback on product performance and corrective action in the form of product improvement. Product improvement is a top-level management decision, but the information needed to make the improvement decision may come from the consumer or the middlemen. Suggestions are often made by advertising agencies or consultants. Reports by the sales force should be structured in such a way as to provide management with certain types of product information; in fact, these reports can be the firm's most valuable product improvement tool. Implementing a product improvement decision will often require the coordinated efforts of several specialists plus some research. For example, product design improvement decisions involve engineering, manufacturing, accounting, and marketing. When a firm becomes aware that a product's design can be improved, it is not always clear as to how consumers will react to the various alterations. Consequently, it may be very advisable to conduct some market tests.

CONCLUSION

This chapter has been concerned with a central element of marketing management, product strategy. Emphasis was initially placed on definition and classification of various types of products. Emphasis was also placed on the product life cycle concept and the decision areas in product management. Although product considerations are extremely important, it must be remembered that the product is only one element in the marketing mix. Focusing on product decisions alone without consideration of the other marketing mix variables would be an ineffective marketing strategy.

ADDITIONAL READINGS

Goslin, Lewis N. *The Product-Planning System*. Homewood, Ill.: Richard D. Irwin, Inc., 1967.

Luck, David J. *Product Policy and Strategy*. Englewood Cliffs, N.J.: Prentice-Hall, Inc., 1972.

Melville, Donald R. "Product Management—A Portfolio of Businesses," Edward M. Mazze, ed., *1975 Combined Proceedings*. Chicago: American Marketing Association, 1975, pp. 359–62.

Phelps, Maynard D., ed., *Product Management: Selected Readings (1960–1969)*. Homewood, Ill.: Richard D. Irwin, Inc., 1970.

Spitz, A. Edward, ed., *Product Planning*. Princeton, N.J.: Averbach Publishers, Inc., 1972.

Staudt, Thomas A. "Higher Management Risks in Product Strategy." *Journal of Marketing* 37 (January 1973), 4–9.

Trombetta, William L.; and Wilson, Timothy L. "Foreseeability of Misuse and Abnormal Use of Products by the Consumer." *Journal of Marketing* 39 (July 1975), pp. 48–55.

Twedt, Dik Warren. "How to Plan New Products, Improve Old Ones, and Create Better Advertising." *Journal of Marketing* 32 (January 1969), pp. 53–57.

Wind, Yoram; and Claycamp, Henry J. "Planning Product Line Strategy: A Matrix Approach." *Journal of Marketing* 40 (January 1976), pp. 2–9.

6

NEW PRODUCT PLANNING AND DEVELOPMENT

New products are a vital part of a firm's competitive growth strategy. Booz, Allen, and Hamilton, a leading management consultant firm whose experience with over 4,000 firms dates back to 1914, made an early study of the problem of new product management and development. Some of the important conclusions of their research can be briefly summarized:

1. Most manufacturers cannot live without new products. It is commonplace for major companies to have 50 percent or more of current sales in products new in the past 10 years.
2. Most new products are failures. Estimates of new product failure range from 33 percent to 90 percent.
3. Companies vary widely in the effectiveness of their new product programs.
4. Common elements tend to appear in the management practices which generally distinguish the relative degree of efficiency and success between companies.
5. About four out of five hours devoted by scientists and engineers to technical development of new products are spent on projects which do not reach commercial success.[1]

In one recent year, almost 10,000 supermarket items were introduced

---

[1] Booz, Allen, and Hamilton, Inc., *Management of New Products* (Chicago: Booz, Allen, and Hamilton, Inc., 1964), pp. 2–3. Also see David S. Hopkins and Earl L. Bailey, "New Product Pressures," *Conference Board Record*, June 1971, pp. 16–24.

HIGHLIGHT 6–1

Some Important New Product Decisions

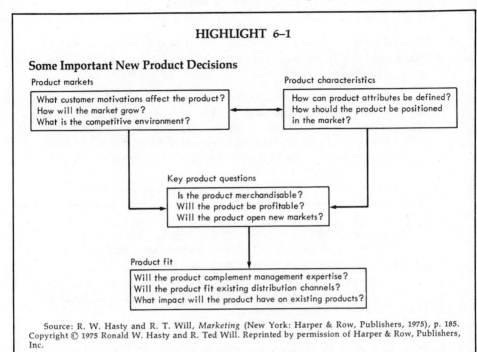

Product markets

> What customer motivations affect the product?
> How will the market grow?
> What is the competitive environment?

Product characteristics

> How can product attributes be defined?
> How should the product be positioned in the market?

Key product questions

> Is the product merchandisable?
> Will the product be profitable?
> Will the product open new markets?

Product fit

> Will the product complement management expertise?
> Will the product fit existing distribution channels?
> What impact will the product have on existing products?

Source: R. W. Hasty and R. T. Will, *Marketing* (New York: Harper & Row, Publishers, 1975), p. 185. Copyright © 1975 Ronald W. Hasty and R. Ted Will. Reprinted by permission of Harper & Row, Publishers, Inc.

into the market. Less than 20 percent met sales goals. A single product failure can cost from $75,000 in a test market to $20 million for a national introduction. In addition to the outlay cost of new product failures, there are also opportunity costs. These opportunity costs refer not only to the alternative uses of funds spent on product failures, but also the time spent in unprofitable product development. For example, the Campbell Soup Company began developing its Red Kettle Soups (dry soup mixes) before 1943 and introduced them on a national scale almost 20 years later. Hills Brothers spent 22 years in developing its instant coffee, while it took General Foods 10 years to develop Maxim, its concentrated instant coffee.[2]

Good management with heavy emphasis on planning (and organization) seems to be a key factor contributing to a firm's success in launching new products. However, if the causes of new product failure are analyzed, faulty marketing management does not show up as a primary cause. Instead, the secondary causes are revealed, which can be traced back to poor decision making and inadequate marketing planning.

---

[2] Lee Adler, "Time Lag in New Product Development," *Journal of Marketing* 30 (January 1966), pp. 17–21. In this study the range was from six months for Sinclair Power X Gasoline to 55 years for television.

NEW PRODUCT POLICY

In developing new product policies, the first question a marketing manager must ask is: "In how many ways can a product be new?" For purpose of analysis there are four basic "new" product situations.

> *Situation I.*   A new model or feature. This involves changes in such things as construction material, method of construction ("unitized" automobile chassis), kind of performance (T.V. combined with stereo, tape cassette recorder, and so forth); method of performance (gas dryer versus electric); new elements (power steering) arrangement of parts (freezer at bottom of refrigerator) and style.
>
> *Situation II.*   A new product (not just an improvement or minor alteration) in a familiar market. The introduction of microwave ovens is a good example of this.
>
> *Situation III.*   A product new to the company but not new to the market. The entry of Smith & Wesson into the holster business to complement its line of handguns is an example.
>
> *Situation IV.*   New products being introduced into new (unfamiliar) markets. An example here can be found in the ethical drug industry (for example, the birth control pill).[3]

Another approach to the "new" product question has been developed by H. Igor Ansoff in the form of "growth vectors."[4] This is a simple matrix which indicates the direction in which the organization is moving with respect to its current products and markets. This is shown in Figure 6–1.

FIGURE 6–1
Growth Vector Components

Markets	Products	
	Present	*New*
Present	Market penetration	Product development
New	Market development	Diversification

Market penetration denotes a growth direction through the increase in market share for present product-markets. *Market development* refers to finding new customers for present products. *Product develop-*

---

[3] For a more detailed list of possibilities see Chester Wasson, "What Is 'New' about a New Product," *Journal of Marketing* 24 (July 1960), pp. 52–56 and James H. Donnelly, Jr. and Michael J. Etzel, "Degrees of Product Newness and Early Trial," *Journal of Marketing Research* 10 (August 1973), pp. 295–300.

[4] H. Igor Ansoff, *Corporate Strategy* (New York: McGraw-Hill, Inc., 1965), pp. 109–10.

ment refers to creating new products to replace existing ones. *Diversification* refers to developing new products and cultivating new markets.

In Figure 6–1 market penetration and market development are product line strategies where the focus is upon altering the breadth and depth of the firm's existing product offerings. Product development and diversification can be characterized as product mix strategies. New products, as defined in the growth vector matrix, usually require the firm to make significant investments in research and development and may require major changes in its organizational structure.

HIGHLIGHT 6–2

Ten Steps in the Development of a New Product Policy

1. Prepare a long-range industry forecast for existing product lines.
2. Prepare a long-range profit plan for the company, using existing product lines.
3. Review the long-range profit plan.
4. Determine what role new products will play in the company's future.
5. Prepare an inventory of company capabilities.
6. Determine market areas for new products.
7. Prepare a statement of new company objectives.
8. Prepare a long-range profit plan, incorporating new products.
9. Assign new product responsibility.
10. Provide for evaluation of new product performance.

It has already been stated that new products are the lifeblood of today's successful business firm. Thus, the critical product policy question is not whether to develop new products but in what direction to move. One way of dealing with this problem is to formulate standards or norms which new products must meet if they are to be considered candidates for launching. In other words, as part of its new product policy, management must ask itself the basic question: "What is the potential contribution of each anticipated new product to the company?"

Each company must answer this question in accordance with its long-run goals, corporate mission, resources, and so forth. Unfortunately, some of the reasons commonly given to justify the launching of new products are so general that they become meaningless. Phrases such as "additional profits" or "increased growth" or "cyclical stability" must be translated into more specific objectives. For example, one objective may be to reduce manufacturing overhead costs by utilizing plant capacity better. This may be accomplished by using the new product as an off-season filler. Naturally, the new product proposal would also have to include production and accounting data to back up this cost argument.

In every new product proposal some attention must be given to the ultimate economic contribution of each new product candidate. If the argument is that a certain type of product is needed to "keep up with competition" or "to establish leadership in a market," then it is fair to ask, "Why?" To put the question another way, top management can ask: "What will be the effect on the firm's long-run profit picture if we do not develop and launch this or that new product?" Policy making criteria on new products should specify (a) a working definition of the profit concept acceptable to top management, (b) a minimum level or floor of profits, and (c) the availability and cost of capital to develop a new product.

NEW PRODUCT PLANNING AND DEVELOPMENT PROCESS

Ideally, products that generate a maximum dollar profit with a minimum amount of risk should be developed and marketed. However, it is very difficult for planners to implement this idea because of the number and nature of the variables involved. What is needed is a systematic, formalized process for new product planning. Although such a process does not provide management with any magic answers, it can increase the probability of new product success. Initially, the firm must establish some new product policy guidelines that include: the product fields of primary interest, organizational responsibilities for managing the various stages in new product development, criteria for making go-ahead decisions. After these guidelines are established, a process such as the following should be useful in new product planning. This process includes six stages: (1) idea generation, (2) idea screening, (3) project planning, (4) product development, (5) test marketing, and (6) commercialization.

Idea Generation

Every product starts as an idea. It goes without saying that all new product ideas do not have equal merit with regard to their potential for economic or commercial success. Some estimates indicate that as many as 60 or 70 ideas are necessary to yield one successful product. This is an average figure but it serves to illustrate the fact that new product ideas have a high mortality rate. In terms of money, of all the dollars of new product expense, almost three fourths go to unsuccessful products.

The problem at this stage is to insure that all new product ideas available to the company at least have a chance to be heard and evaluated. This includes recognizing available sources of new product ideas and funneling these ideas to appropriate decision makers for screening.[5]

HIGHLIGHT 6–3

Some Sources of New Product Ideas

1. Sales force
   a. Knowledge of customers' needs
   b. Inquiries from customers or prospects
   c. Knowledge of the industry and competition
2. Research and engineering
   a. Application of basic research
   b. Original or creative thinking
   c. Testing existing products and performance records
   d. Accidental discoveries
3. Other company sources
   a. Suggestions from employees
   b. Utilization of by-products or scrap
   c. Specific market surveys
4. Outside sources
   a. Inventors
   b. Stockholders
   c. Suppliers or vendors
   d. Middlemen
   e. Ad agencies
   f. Customer suggestions

Idea Screening

The primary function of the screening stage is twofold: first, to eliminate ideas for new products that could not be profitably marketed by the firm and second, to expand viable ideas into a full product concept. New product ideas may be eliminated either because they are outside the fields of the firm's interest or because the firm does not have the necessary resources or technology to produce the product at a profit. However, other ideas are accepted for further study because they appear

---

[5] For additional discussion, see Edward M. Tauber, "HIT: Heuristic Ideation Technique—A Systematic Procedure for New Product Search," *Journal of Marketing* 36 (January 1972), pp. 58–61.

to have adequate profit potential and offer the firm a competitive advantage in the market.

Project Planning

This stage of the process involves several steps. It is here that the product proposal is evaluated further and responsibility for the project is assigned to a project team. The proposal is analyzed in terms of production, marketing, financial, and competitive factors. A development budget is established and some preliminary marketing and technical research is undertaken. The product is actually designed in a rough form. Alternative product features and component specifications are outlined. Finally, a project plan is written up which includes estimates of future development, production, and marketing costs along with capital requirements and manpower needs. A schedule or timetable is also included. Finally, the project proposal is given to top management for a go or no-go decision.

Product Development

At this juncture the product idea has been evaluated from the standpoint of engineering, manufacturing, finance, and marketing. If it has met all expectations, it is considered a candidate for further research and testing. In the laboratory the product is converted into a finished good and tested. A development report to management is prepared which spells out in fine detail: (*a*) the results of the studies by the engineering department, (*b*) required plant design, (*c*) production facilities design, (*d*) tooling requirements, (*e*) marketing test plan, (*r*) financial program survey, and (*g*) an estimated release date.

Test Marketing

Up until now the product has been a company secret. Now management goes outside the company and submits the product candidate for customer approval. Test marketing programs are conducted in line with plans for launching the product. At this stage primary attention is given to the general marketing strategy to be used and the appropriate marketing mix. Test findings are analyzed, the product design is frozen into production, and a marketing plan is finalized.

Commercialization

This is the launching step. It requires top management to commit itself to investing in plant facilities, equipment, manpower, raw materials, and a substantial marketing effort. During this stage heavy emphasis is on the organization structure and management talent needed to implement the product proposal. Secondary emphasis is given to following up such things as bugs in the design, production costs, quality control, and inventory requirements. Procedures and responsibility for evaluating the success of the new product by comparison with projections are also finalized.

PROFIT PLANNING FOR NEW PRODUCTS

Profit planning for new products is essentially trying to forecast the dollar worth of the new product investment. In other words, a new product ought to be viewed as an investment and treated as such in making the decision to launch it. This, of course, is easier said than done because the problem is very complicated. Initially, management must determine the appropriate formula for estimating the profitability of the new product investment. Once this is done, then the variables in the formula must be measured or estimated. Below are some examples of methods of profitability estimation.

Estimating Investment Worth

The profit-oriented marketing manager must understand that the capital invested in new products has a cost. It is a basic principle in business that whoever wishes to use capital must pay for its use. Dollars invested in new products could be diverted to other uses—to pay off debts, pay out to stockholders, place in U.S. treasury bonds—which would yield economic benefits to the corporation. If, on the other hand, all of the dollars used to develop a new product have to be borrowed from lenders outside the corporation, then interest has to be paid on the loan.

There are many ways of measuring the profitability of a new product investment and one of the best is *net present value analysis*. This method employs a "discounted cash flow," which takes into account the time value of money and its price to the borrower. The following example will illustrate this method.

In order to compute the net present value of an investment proposal, the cost of capital must be estimated. The cost of capital can be defined as the required rate of return on an investment that would leave the owners of the firm as well off as if the project was not undertaken. Thus, it is the minimum percentage return on investment that a project must make to be worth undertaking. There are many methods of estimating the cost of capital. However, since these methods are not the concern of this text, we will simply assume that the cost of capital for the Ajax

Corporation has been determined to be 10 percent.[6] Again, it should be noted that once the cost of capital is determined, it becomes the minimum rate of return required for an investment—a type of cutoff point. However, some firms in selecting their new product investments, select a minimum rate of return that is above the cost of capital figure to allow for errors in judgement or measurement.

The Ajax Corporation is considering a proposal to market instant developing movie film. After conducting considerable marketing research, sales were projected to be $1,000,000 per year. In addition, the finance department compiled the following information concerning the project:

New equipment needed $700,000
Useful life of equipment ....   10 years
Depreciation ....   10% per year
Salvage value $100,000
Cost of goods and expenses .... $700,000 per year
Cost of capital 10%
Tax rate 50%

In order to compute the net present value of this project, the net cash flow for each year of the project must first be determined. This can be done in four steps:

1. Sales — Cost of goods and expenses = Gross income

or

$$\$1,000,000 - 700,000 = \$300,000.$$

2. Gross income — Depreciation = Taxable income

or

$$\$300,000 - (10\% \times 600,000) = \$240,000.$$

3. Taxable income — Tax = Net income

or

$$\$240,000 - (50\% \times 240,000) = \$120,000.$$

4. Net income + Depreciation = Net cash flow

or

$$\$120,000 + 60,000 = \$180,000 \text{ per year.}$$

---

[6] For methods of estimating the cost of capital, see James C. Van Horne, *Financial Management and Policy*, 4th ed. (Englewood Cliffs, N.J.: Prentice-Hall, Inc., 1977), chap. 8.

Since the cost of capital is 10 percent, this figure is used to discount the net cash flows for each year. For example, the $180,000 received at the end of the first year would be discounted by the factor $1/(1 + 0.10)$ which would be $180,000 \times 0.9091 = \$171,288$; the $180,000 received at the end of the second year would be discounted by the factor $1/(1 + 0.10)^2$, which would be $180,000 \times 0.8264 = \$154,998$, and so on. (Most finance textbooks have present value tables that can be used to simplify the computations). Below are the present value computations for the ten-year project. It should be noted that the net cash flow for year 10 is $280,000 since there is an additional $100,000 inflow from salvage value.

Year	Net Cash Flow	0.10 Discount Factor	Present Value
1	$180,000	0.9091	$171,288
2	180,000	0.8264	154,998
3	180,000	0.7513	140,238
4	180,000	0.6830	126.900
5	180,000	0.6209	114,822
6	180,000	0.5645	103,896
7	180,000	0.5132	44,014
8	180,000	0.4665	85,068
9.	180,000	0.4241	76,968
10	280,000	0.3855	108,332
Total ...	$1,900,000		$1,176,524

Thus, at a discount rate of 10 percent, the present value of the net cash flow from new product investment is greater than the $700,000 outlay required, and so the decision can be considered profitable by this standard. Here the *net present value* is $476,524 which is the difference between the $700,000 investment outlay and the $1,176,524 discounted cash flow. The present value ratio is nothing more than the present value of the net cash flow divided by the cash investment. If this ratio is one or larger than one, then the project gets the go-ahead signal from top management.

There are many other measures of investment worth, but only one additional method will be discussed. It is the very popular and easily understood "payback method." Payback refers to the amount of time required to pay back the original outlay from the cash flows. Staying with the example, the project is expected to produce a stream of cash proceeds that is constant from year to year, so the payback period can be arrived at by dividing the investment outlay by this annual cash flow. Dividing $700,000 by $180,000, the payback period is approximately 3.9 years. Firms often set a minimum payback period before a project will be accepted. For example, many firms refuse to take on a project if the payback period exceeds five years.

This example should illustrate the difficulty in evaluating new products from a profitability or economic worth standpoint. The most challenging problem is that of developing accurate cash flows, because during this step there are many possible alternatives such as price of the product, and channels of distribution, and the consequences of each alternative must be forecast in terms of sales volumes, selling costs, and other expenses. In spite of all the problems, management must evaluate the economic worth of new product decisions not only to reduce some of the guesswork and ambiguity surrounding new product planning, but also to reinforce the objective of trying to make profitable decisions.

CAUSES OF NEW PRODUCT FAILURE

Many new products with satisfactory potential have failed to make the grade. Many of the reasons for new product failure relate to execution and control problems. Below is a brief list of some of the more important causes of new product failures after they have been carefully screened, developed and marketed.

1. Faulty estimates of market potential.
2. Unexpected reactions from competitors.
3. Poor timing in the introduction of the product.
4. Rapid change in the market (economy) after the product was approved.
5. Inadequate quality control.
6. Faulty estimates in production costs.
7. Inadequate expenditures on initial promotion.
8. Faulty marketing testing.
9. Improper channel of distribution.

Some of the above problems are beyond the control of management, but it is very clear that successful new product planning requires large amounts of reliable information in diverse areas. Each department assigned functional responsibility for product development automatically becomes an input to the information system needed by the new product decision maker. For example, when a firm is considering developing a new product, it is wise for the engineers and the marketers to decide first on the kind of market they expect to enter (for example, consumer, industrial, defense, or export) and secondarily on the specific target segments. These decisions will be of paramount influence on the design and cost of the finished good which will, of course, directly influence price, sales, and profits.

Need for Research

In many respects it can be argued that the keystone activity of any new product planning system is research—not just marketing research but technical research as well. Regardless of the way in which the new product planning function is organized in the company, whether by committee, project team, or department, development decisions by top management require data that will provide a base for making more intelligent choices. New product project reports ought to be more than a collection of "expert" opinions. Top management has a responsibility to ask certain questions and the new product planning team has an obligation to generate answers to these questions based on research that provides marketing, economic, engineering, and production information. This need will be more clearly understood if some of the specific questions commonly raised in evaluating product ideas are examined:

1. What is the anticipated market demand over time? Are the potential applications for the product restricted?
2. Can the item be patented? Are there any antitrust problems?
3. Can the product be sold through present channels and sales force? What will be the number of new salespersons needed? What additional sales training will be required?
4. At different volume levels, what will be the unit manufacturing costs?
5. What is the most appropriate package to use in terms of color, material, design, and so forth?
6. What is the estimated return on investment?
7. What is the appropriate pricing strategy?

While this list is not intended to be exhaustive, it serves to illustrate the serious need for reliable information. In addition, it should be noted that some of the essential facts required to answer these questions can only be obtained through time consuming and expensive marketing research studies. Other data can be generated in the engineering laboratories or pulled from accounting records. Certain types of information must be based on assumptions, which may or may not hold true, and on expectations about what will happen in the future, as in the case of "anticipated competitive reaction" or the projected level of sales.

Another complication is that many different types of information must be gathered and formulated into a meaningful program for decision making. For example, in trying to answer questions about return on investment of a particular project, the analyst must know something about (1) the pricing strategy to be used and (2) the investment outlay. Regardless of the formula used to measure the investment worth of a new product, different types of information are required. Using one of the simplest approaches—the payback method (the ratio of investment outlay to annual cash flow)—one needs to estimate the magnitude of the product investment outlay and the annual cash flow. The investment outlay requires estimates of such things as production equipment, R&D costs, and nonrecurring introductory marketing expenditures; the annual cash flow requires a forecast of unit demand and price. These data must be collected or generated from many different departments and processed into a form that will be meaningful to the decision maker.

ORGANIZING FOR NEW PRODUCT DEVELOPMENT

There are three basic organizational arrangements for dealing with new product effort; (1) new product department (2) team approach and (3) new product committee. The most popular is the new product department, headed by a single executive. New product departments usually report to a top executive—the president, top marketing officer, top R&D officer. The department's responsibilities range from idea generation to test marketing and final evaluation of a product's performance, and usually include recommendations to top management of how the product should be marketed.

A team approach to new product management usually amounts to a working committee that is created to carry out particular assignments associated with a specific product. Such teams usually report in a staff or advisory relationship to the new products director or new products committee. These teams are seldom involved in generating or screening new product ideas and are generally disbanded after the product is launched.

New product committees differ from teams in that they are usually a permanent arrangement. Such committees are composed of high-level executives, such as vice president of marketing, vice president of manufacturing, director of R&D, who not only formulate policy but also attempt to coordinate and supervise the entire new product development program. The formation of a new product committee is frequently a step that precedes the establishment of a new product department. Many firms have both arrangements; the committee recommends policy and makes line decisions based on competent staff work and then the new product department completes the job.

There is no best way to organize for managing the new product development function. In fact, the organizational arrangement may not be the most important factor in new product development. The key factor is probably management's philosophy and attitude toward innovation. Regardless of the organizational arrangement a firm employs, sound management requires that the responsibility and authority for new product planning and development be clearly delegated to some person or unit. This also implies that the new product function should be well defined and compatible with the company's overall goals and objectives.[7]

CONCLUSION

. This chapter has focused on the nature of new product planning and development. Attention has been given to the management process required to have an effective program for new product development. It should be obvious to the reader that this is one of the most important and difficult aspects of marketing management. The problem is so complex that unless management develops a plan for dealing with the problem, it is likely to operate at a severe competitive disadvantage in the marketplace.

ADDITIONAL READINGS

Cardozo, Richard N.; Ross, Ivan; and Rudelius, William. "New Product Decisions by Marketing Executives: A Computer-Controlled Experiment." *Journal of Marketing* 36 (January 1972), pp. 10–16.

Drucker, Peter. "The Care and Feeding of Profitable Products." *Fortune*, March 1964, pp. 133–35.

Dussenbury, Warren. "CPM for New Product Introductions." *Harvard Business Review* 45 (July–August 1967), pp. 124–39.

Green, Paul G. "Bayesian Statistics and Product Decisions." *Business Horizons*, Fall 1962, pp. 101–9.

Harper, Paul C., Jr. "New Product Management: The Cutting Edge of Corporate Policy." *Journal of Marketing* 40 (April 1976), pp. 76–79.

Kotler, Phillip. "Marketing Mix Decisions for New Products," *Journal of Marketing Research* 1 (February 1964), pp. 43–49.

Levitt, Theodore. "Exploit the Product Life Cycle." *Harvard Business Review* 43 (November–December 1965), pp. 81–94.

Marting, Elizabeth, ed. *New Products, New Profits: Company Experience in New Product Planning.* New York: American Marketing Association, 1964.

Pessemier, Edgar A. *New Product Decisions: An Analytical Approach.* New York: McGraw-Hill, Inc., 1966.

Pessemier, Edward A., and Root, H. Paul. "The Dimensions of New Product Planning." *Journal of Marketing* 37 (January 1973), pp. 10–18.

Tauber, Edward M. "Reduce New Product Failures: Measure Needs as Well as Purchase Interest." *Journal of Marketing* 37 (July 1973), pp. 61–64.

Weber, John A. *Growth Opportunity Analysis.* Reston, Va.: Reston Publishing Co., 1976.

---

[7] The interested reader should also see Gert Assmus, "NEWPROD: The Design and Implementation of a New Product Model," *Journal of Marketing* 39 (January 1975), pp. 16–23.

7

PROMOTION STRATEGY: ADVERTISING AND SALES PROMOTION

In order to simplify the discussion of the general subject of promotion the topic has been divided into two basic categories, personal selling and nonpersonal selling. Personal selling will be discussed in detail in the next chapter and this chapter will be devoted to nonpersonal selling.

Nonpersonal selling includes all demand creation and demand maintenance activities of the firm other than personal selling. It is mass selling. In more specific terms, nonpersonal selling includes (a) advertising, (b) sales promotion, and (c) publicity. For the purposes of this text, primary emphasis will be placed on advertising and sales promotion. Publicity is a special form of promotion which amounts to "free advertising," such as a writeup about the firm's products in a newspaper article. It will not be dealt with in this text.

THE PROMOTION MIX

The promotion mix concept refers to *the combination of the types of promotional effort the firm puts forth during a specified time period.* Most business concerns make use of more than one form of promotion, but some firms rely on a single selling technique. An example of a company using only one promotional device would be a manufacturer of novelties who markets its products exclusively by means of mail order. Small business concerns tend to use a simple promotion mix, as in the case of most retailers.

In devising its promotion mix the firm should take into account three basic factors: (1) the role of promotion in the overall marketing mix, (2) the nature of the product, and (3) the nature of the market. Also, it must be recognized that a firm's promotion mix is likely to change over time to reflect changes in the market, competition, the product's life cycle, and the adoption of new strategies. The following example illustrates how one firm developed its promotion mix along these lines.

During the 1960s IBM began to market its magnetic character sensing equipment for banks. The company defined the 500 largest banks as its likeliest market and a research firm was commissioned to study the marketing problems.[1] They selected a representative sample of 185 banks and interviewed the officer designated by each bank as the person who would be most influential in deciding whether or not to purchase the equipment. Researchers sought to establish which of the following stages each banker had reached in the sales process (1) *awareness* of the new product; (2) *comprehension* of what it offered; (3) *conviction* that it would be a good investment; or (4) the *ordering* stage. They also tried to isolate the promotional factors that had brought the bankers to each stage. IBM's promotional mix consisted of personal selling, advertising, education (IBM schools and in-bank seminars), and publicity (through news releases). Figure 7–1 illustrates the process.

The findings were a revelation to IBM. In the marketing of such equipment IBM had consistently taken the position that advertising had a very minor role to play; that nothing could replace the sales call. IBM found it could cut back on personal selling in the early stages of the selling process, thereby freeing salespeople to concentrate on the vital phase of the process—the actual closing of the sale. While these results may not hold true for all products, they are an excellent example of the concept of the promotion mix and the effectiveness of different combinations of promotion tools for achieving various objectives.

ADVERTISING: PLANNING AND STRATEGY

Advertising seeks to promote the seller's product by means of printed and electronic media. This is justified on the grounds that messages can reach large numbers of people and inform, persuade, and remind them about the firm's offerings. The traditional way of defining advertising is as follows: It is any paid form of nonpersonal presentation of ideas, goods, or services by an identified sponsor.[2]

From a management viewpoint, advertising is a strategic device for

---

[1] "Advertising Saves Sales Calls," *Business Week*, December 5, 1969, pp. 69–70.

[2] Committee on Definitions of the American Marketing Association, *Marketing Definitions: A Glossary of Marketing Terms* (Chicago: American Marketing Association, 1960).

FIGURE 7–1

An Example of the Role of Various Promotion Tools in the Selling Process

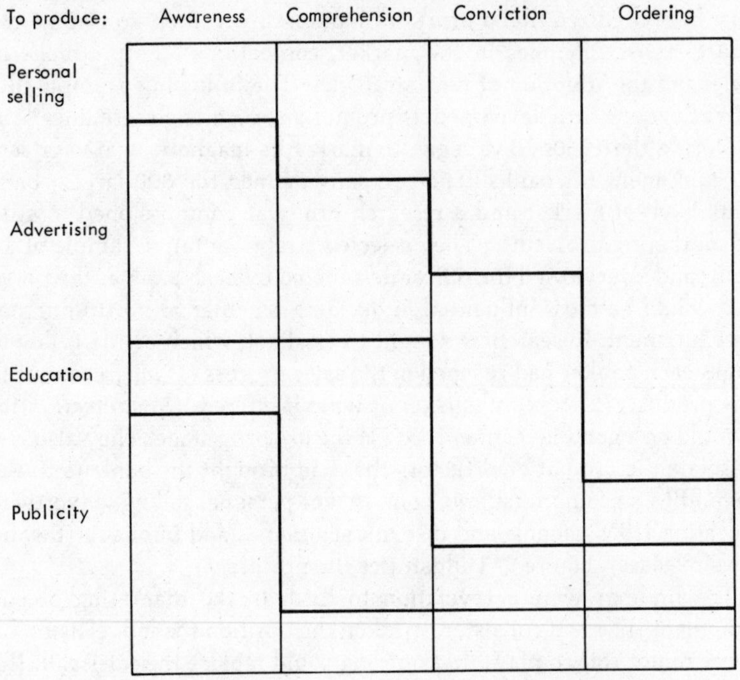

To produce:	Awareness	Comprehension	Conviction	Ordering
Personal selling				
Advertising				
Education				
Publicity				

gaining or maintaining a competitive advantage in the marketplace. For manufacturers and resellers alike, advertising budgets represent a large and growing element in the cost of marketing goods and services. For example, in 1974 the top 100 advertisers spent $6 billion on advertising[3] and in 1977 this figure had grown to nearly $9 billion.[4] As part of the seller's promotion mix, advertising dollars must be appropriated and budgeted according to a marketing plan that takes into account such factors as:

1. Nature of the product, including life cycle.
2. Competition.
3. Government regulations.
4. Nature and scope of the market.
5. Channels of distribution.

---

[3] Merle Kingman, "Top 100 Advertisers Spend Record $6 Billion," *Advertising Age*, August 18, 1975, p. 1.

[4] Kathryn Sederberg, "Top 100 Near $9 Billion in Ads," *Advertising Age*, August 28, 1978, p. 1.

6. Availability of media.
7. Availability of funds.
8. Outlays for other forms of promotion.

HIGHLIGHT 7–1

Steps in Appraising the Primary Advertising Opportunity

To appraise properly the primary advertising opportunity, attention should be directed toward:

1. The number of present users and nonusers, unless, of course, the product is a new concept and no present users exist.
2. The wants satisfied by the product.
3. Competing wants.
4. Nature and strength of available product appeals.
5. Alternate ways for satisfying the wants with other types of products.
6. The nature and strength of appeals available for those alternative products.
7. Social and environmental trends affecting product demand.

Source: Albert F. Frey and Jean C. Halterman, *Advertising*, 4th ed. (New York: The Ronald Press, 1970), p. 201.

Objectives of Advertising

In the long run, and often in the short run, advertising is justified on the basis of the revenues it produces. Revenues in this case may refer either to sales or profits. Economic theory assumes that firms are profit maximizers and that advertising outlays should be increased in every market and medium up to the point where the additional cost of getting more business just equals the incremental profits. Since most business firms do not have the data required to use the marginal analysis of economic theory, they usually employ a less sophisticated decision-making model. There is also evidence to show that many executives advertise to maximize sales on the assumption that higher sales mean more profits (which may or may not be true).

The point to be made here is that the ultimate goal of the business advertiser is sales and profits. To achieve this goal an approach to advertising is needed that provides guidelines for intelligent decision making. This approach must recognize the need for measuring the results of advertising, and these measurements must be as valid and reliable as possible. Marketing managers must also be aware of the fact that advertising not only complements other forms of selling but also is subject to the law of diminishing returns. This means that for any advertised product it can be assumed that a point is eventually reached at which additional advertising produces little or no additional sales.

HIGHLIGHT 7–2

Preparing the Advertising Campaign: The Eight-M Formula

Effective advertising should follow a plan. There is no one best way to go about planning an advertising campaign, but, in general, marketers should have good answers to the following eight questions:

1. *The management question:* Who will manage the advertising program?
2. *The money question:* How much should be spent on advertising as opposed to other forms of selling?
3. *The market question:* To whom should the advertising be directed?
4. *The message question:* What should the ads say about the product?
5. *The media question:* What types and combinations of media should be used?
6. *The macro-scheduling question:* How long should the advertising campaign be in effect before changing ads or themes?
7. *The micro-scheduling question:* At what times and dates would it be best for ads to appear during the course of the campaign?
8. *The measurement question:* How will the effectiveness of the advertising campaign be measured and how will the campaign be evaluated and controlled?

Specific Tasks of Advertising

In attempting to evaluate the contribution of advertising to the economic health of the firm, there are at least three different viewpoints on the subject. The generalist viewpoint is primarily concerned with sales, profits, return on investment, and so forth. At the other extreme the specialist viewpoint is represented by advertising experts who are primarily concerned with measuring the effects of specific ads or campaigns; here primary attention is given to such matters as the Neilsen Index, Starch Reports, copy appeal, and so forth. A middle view, one that might be classified as more of a marketing management approach, understands and appreciates the other two viewpoints but in addition, views advertising as a competitive weapon. Emphasis in this approach is given to the strategic aspects of the advertising problem. Following are some of the marketing tasks generally assigned to the advertising function as part of the overall marketing mix:

1. Maintaining dealer cooperation.
2. Familiarizing the consumer with the use of the product.
3. Emphasizing a trademark or brand.
4. Obtaining a list of prospects.
5. Creating goodwill for the product, brand, or company.
6. Stressing unique features of the product.
7. Introducing new products.
8. Generating store traffic.
9. Informing customers of sales prices.
10. Building customer or brand loyalty.
11. Establishing a relationship between the producer and distributor.

The above list is representative but not exhaustive, and it should be noted that some of the points pertain more to middlemen than to producers. For example, the first point is a "channel task" where advertising and other forms of sales promotion are employed to facilitate the flow of the producer's goods through distributors to the ultimate consumer; "cooperative advertising" programs are specifically designed to meet this objective. This is where a channel member such as a retailer will receive a certain percentage of gross sales as an advertising allowance. Some manufacturers also provide advertising copy, illustrations, and so forth.

HIGHLIGHT 7–3

An Advertising Process Model

Consumer Psycho-social State	*Marketing Situation*
1. Ignorance	Consumer has no knowledge of the product.
2. Indifference	Consumer is conscious of product's existence by means of advertising.
3. Awareness	Advertising messages generate an awareness of a need for the product or reinforce a need once generated.
4. Interest	Consumer begins seeking more product-brand information by paying closer attention to various ads.

Highlight 7–3 (continued)

5. Comprehension ...... Consumer knows main features of product and various brands after intense ad exposure.
6. Conviction .... Consumer is receptive to purchase and ready to act.
7. Action .... Consumer shops for the product often as a result of the "act now" advertisements or special sales.

ADVERTISING DECISIONS

In line with what has just been said, there are two key decisions the marketing manager must make. The first decision deals with determining the size of the advertising budget, and the second deals with how the advertising budget should be allocated. Although these decisions are highly interrelated, we will deal with them separately in order to achieve a better understanding of the problems involved.

The Expenditure Question

Most firms determine how much to spend on advertising by one of the following methods:

Percent of Sales. This is one of the most popular rule-of-thumb methods and its appeal is found in its simplicity. The firm simply takes a percentage figure and applies it to either past or future sales. For example, if next year's sales are estimated to be one million dollars, then using a two percent of sales criterion, the ad budget would be $20,000. This approach is usually justified by its advocates in terms of the following argument: (*a*) advertising is needed to generate sales; (*b*) a number of cents, that is, the percentage used, out of each dollar of sales should be devoted to advertising in order to generate needed sales; and (*c*) the percentage is easily adjusted and can be readily understood by other executives. The percent of sales approach is very popular in the field of retailing.

Per Unit Expenditure. Closely related to the above technique is one in which a fixed monetary amount is spent on advertising for each unit of the product expected to be sold. This method is popular with higher priced merchandise such as automobiles or appliances. For example, if a company is marketing color televisions priced at $500, then it may decide that it should spend $30 per set on advertising. Since this $30 is a fixed amount for each unit, this method amounts to the same thing as the percent of sales method. The big difference is in the rationale used to justify each of the methods. The per unit expenditure method attempts to determine the retail price by using production costs as a base. Here the seller realizes that a reasonably competitive price must be established for the product in question and attempts to cost out the gross margin. All this means is that if the suggested retail price is to be $500 and manufacturing costs are $250, then there is a gross margin of $250 available to cover certain expenses such as transportation, personal selling, advertising, dealer profit, and so forth. Some of these expense items are flexible, such as advertising, while others are nearly fixed, as in the case of transportation. The basic problem with this method and the percentage of sales method is that they view advertising as a function of sales rather than sales as a function of advertising.

All You Can Afford.   Here the advertising budget is established as a predetermined share of profits or financial resources. The availability of current revenues sets the upper limit of the ad budget. The only advantage to this approach is that it sets reasonable limits on the expenditures for advertising. However, from the standpoint of sound marketing practice, this method is undesirable because there is no necessary connection between liquidity and advertising opportunity. In addition, any firm that limits its advertising outlays to the amount of available funds will probably miss out on opportunities for both sales and increased profits.

Competitive Parity.   This approach is often used in conjunction with other approaches such as the percent of sales method. The basic philosophy underlying this approach is that advertising is defensive. Advertising budgets are based on those of competitors or other members of the industry. From a strategy standpoint, this is a "followership" technique and assumes that the other firms in the industry know what they are doing and have similar goals. Competitive parity is not a preferred method although some executives feel it is a "safe" approach. This may or may not be true depending in part on the relative market share of competing firms and their growth objectives.

The Research Approach.   Here the advertising budget is argued for and presented on the basis of research findings. Advertising media are studied in terms of their productivity by the use of (a) media reports, such as the Starch Reports, (b) experiments, and (c) surveys. Costs are also estimated and compared with study results. A typical experiment is one in which three or more test markets are selected.[5] The first test market is used as a control either with no advertising or with normal levels

    [5] For example, see Bill R. Miller and Charles E. Strain, "Determining Promotional Effects by Experimental Design," *Journal of Marketing Research* 7 (November 1970), pp. 513–16.

of advertising. Advertising with various levels of intensity are used in different markets and comparisons are made between markets to see what effect different levels of intensity have. The advertising manager then evaluates the costs and benefits of the different approaches and intensity levels to determine the overall budget. Although the research approach is generally more expensive than some other models, it is a more rational approach to the expenditure decision.

The Task Approach.   Well-planned advertising programs usually make use of the task approach, which initially formulates the advertising goals and defines the tasks to accomplish these goals. Once this is done management determines how much it will cost to accomplish each task and adds up the total. This approach is often used in conjunction with the research approach. A variation of the task approach is referred to as the *marketing-program approach.* Here all promotional or selling programs are budgeted in relation to each other, and, given a set of objectives, the goal is to find the optimum promotional-mix. It should be clear that in the task or marketing-program approach, the expenditure and allocation decisions are inseparable.

The Allocation Question

This question deals with the problem of deciding upon the most effective way of spending advertising dollars. A general answer to the question is that management's choice of strategies and objectives determines the media and appeals to be used. In other words, the firm's or product division's overall marketing plan will function as a general guideline for answering the allocation question.

From a practical standpoint, however, the allocation question can be framed in terms of message and media decisions. A successful ad campaign has two related tasks: (1) say the right things in the ads themselves, and (2) use the appropriate media in the right amounts at the right time to reach the target market.

Message Strategy.   The advertising process involves creating messages with words, ideas, sounds, and other forms of audio-visual stimuli that are designed to affect consumer (or distributor) behavior. It follows that much of advertising is a communication process. To be effective, the advertising message must meet two general criteria: (1) it must take into account the basic principles of communication; and (2) it must be predicated upon a valid theory of consumer motivation.[6]

The basic communication process involves three elements: (1) the sender or source of the communication; (2) the communication or

---

[6] For a full discussion of message strategy, see S. W. Dunn and A. M. Barban, *Advertising: Its Role in Modern Marketing,* 4th ed. (Hinsdale, Ill.: The Dryden Press, 1978), chaps. 16–24.

message; and (3) the receiver or audience. Advertising agencies are considered experts in the communications field and are employed by most large firms to create meaningful messages and assist in their dissemination. Translating the product idea or marketing message into an effective ad is termed "encoding." In advertising, the goal of encoding is to generate ads that are understood by the audience. For this to occur, the audience must be able to decode the message in the ad so that the perceived content of the message is the same as the intended content of the message. From a practical standpoint, all this means is that advertising messages must be sent to consumers in an understandable and meaningful way.

Advertising messages must, of course, be transmitted and carried by particular communication channels commonly known as advertising media. These media or channels vary as to efficiency, selectivity, and cost. Some channels are preferred to others because they have less "noise" and thus messages are more easily received and understood. For example, a particular newspaper ad must compete with other ads, pictures, or stories on the same page. In the case of radio or TV while only one firm's message is usually broadcast at a time, there are other distractions (noise) that can hamper clear communications, such as driving while listening to the radio.

The relationship between advertising and consumer behavior is quite obvious. For many products and services advertising is an "influence" that may affect the consumer's decision to purchase a particular product or brand. It is clear that consumers are subjected to many selling influences, and the question arises as to how important advertising is or can be. Here is where the advertising expert must operate on some theory of consumer behavior. The reader will recall from the discussion of the buying process that the buyer was viewed as progressing through various stages from an unsatisfied need through and beyond a purchase decision. The relevance of this discussion is illustrated in Figure 7–2, which compares the role of advertising in various stages of the buying process.

The planning of an advertising campaign and the creation of persuasive messages requires a curious mixture of marketing skill and creative know-how. Relative to the dimension of marketing skills, there are some important pieces of marketing information needed before launching an ad campaign. Most of this information must be generated by the firm and kept up to date. Listed below are some of the critical types of information an advertiser should have:

1. *Who* the firm's customers and potential customers are; their demographic, economic, and psychological characteristics; and any other factors affecting their likelihood of buying.

FIGURE 7–2
Advertising and the Buying Process

Stage in the Buying Process	Possible Advertising Objective	Examples
1. Unsatisfied need	Awareness	"The reciprocating engine is inefficient."
		"Dishwashing roughens hands."
2. Prepurchase behavior	Comprehension	"The Wankel engine is efficient."
		"Palmolive is mild."
3. Purchase decision . . .	Conviction-ordering	"Come in and see for yourself."
		"Buy some today."
4. Postpurchase feelings	Reassurance	"Thousands of satisfied owners."
		"Compare with any other brand."

Source: Adapted for the purposes of this text from Ben M. Enis, *Marketing Principles: The Management Process* (Pacific Palisades, Calif.: Goodyear Publishing Co., 1974), p. 424.

2. *How many* such customers there are.
3. *How much* of the firm's type and brand of product they are currently buying and can reasonably be expected to buy in the short-term and long-term future.
4. *What* individuals other than customers and potential customers *influence* purchasing decisions.
5. *Where* customers, potential customers, and influencers live.
6. *Where* they *buy* the firm's brand of product.
7. *When* they buy, or frequency of purchase.
8. *What* competitive brands they buy and the extent to which they buy them.
9. *How* they buy.
10. *How* they *use* the product.
11. *Why* they buy particular *types* and *brands* of products.

Media Mix. Media selection is no easy task. To start with, there are numerous types and combinations of media to choose from. Below is a general outline of some of the more common advertising media.

A. Printed Media
1. National
     a. Magazines
     b. Newspapers
     c. Direct mail

    2. Local
       a. Newspapers
       b. Magazines
       c. Direct mail
       d. Handbills or flyers
       e. Yellow Pages

B. Electronic Media
    1. National (network)
       a. Radio
       b. Television
    2. Local
       a. Radio (AM–FM)
       b. Television

C. Other
    1. Outdoor (example: billboards)
    2. Transit
    3. Specialty (give aways)
    4. Point-of-purchase
    5. Telephone selling

Of course, each of the above media categories can be further refined. For example, magazines can be broken down into more detailed classes, such as mass monthlies (*Reader's Digest*), news weeklies (*Time*), men's magazines (*Playboy*), women's fashion magazines (*Vogue*), sports magazines (*Sports Illustrated*), business magazines (*Forbes*), and so forth. Clearly, one dimension of this advertising management problem involves having an overabundance of media to select from. With only four media to choose from there are 16 possible go or no-go decisions. With ten media, there would be approximately 1,000 combinations.

Although the number of media and media combinations available for advertising is overwhelming at first glance, there are four interrelated factors that limit the number of practical alternatives. First, *the nature of the product* limits the number of practical and efficient alternatives. For example, a radically new and highly complex product could not be properly promoted using billboard advertisements. Second, *the nature and size of the target market* also limits appropriate advertising media. For example, it is generally inefficient to advertise industrial goods in mass media publications. Third, *the advertising budget* may restrict the use of expensive media such as television and fourth, *the availability* of some media may be limited in particular geographic areas. Although these factors reduce media alternatives to a more manageable number, specific media must still be selected. A primary consideration at this point is media effectiveness or efficiency.

HIGHLIGHT 7–4

Some Relative Merits of Major Advertising Media

Newspapers

Advantages
1. Flexible and timely
2. Intense coverage of local markets
3. Broad acceptance and use
4. High believability of printed word

Disadvantages
1. Short life
2. Read hastily
3. Small "Pass-Along" audience

Radio

Advantages
1. Mass use (over 25 million radios sold annually)
2. Audience selectivity via station format
3. Low cost (per unit of time)
4. Geographic flexibility

Disadvantages
1. Audio presentation only
2. Less attention than T.V.
3. Chaotic buying (nonstandardized rate structures)
4. Short life

Outdoor

Advantages
1. Flexible
2. Relative absence of competing advertisements
3. Repeat exposure
4. Relatively inexpensive

Disadvantages
1. Creative limitations
2. Many distractions for viewer
3. Public attack (ecological implications)
4. No selectivity of audience

Television

Advantages
1. Combination of sight, sound, and motion
2. Appeals to senses
3. Mass audience coverage
4. Psychology of attention

Disadvantages
1. Non-selectivity of audience
2. Fleeting impressions
3. Short life
4. Expensive

Magazines

Advantages
1. High geographic and demographic selectivity
2. Psychology of attention
3. Quality of reproduction
4. Pass-along readership

Disadvantages
1. Long closing periods (6 to 8 weeks prior to publication)
2. Some waste circulation
3. No guarantee of position (unless premium is paid)

Direct Mail

Advantages
1. Audience selectivity
2. Flexible
3. No competition from competing advertisements
4. Personalized

Disadvantages
1. Relatively high cost
2. Consumers often pay little attention since they receive a great deal

Source: Leonard L. Berry and James H. Donnelly, Jr., *Marketing for Bankers* (Washington, D.C.: American Bankers Association, 1975), p. 145.

For a given task or sales objective not all advertising media will be equally efficient. At the conceptual level, efficiency refers to the marginal productivity of sales dollars.[7] Figure 7–3 is a simple graphic illustration of the efficiency principle using three different media.

Each of the curves in Figure 7–3 can be considered a productivity measure for the various practical media available for promoting a particular product. Each curve shows the relationship between dollars spent and sales generated and has two characteristics that should be noted. First is the *ceiling effect,* where the curve flattens out and additional dollars spent on advertising in this media yield zero (sometimes negative) sales. Second is the *threshold effect,* which is illustrated on the horizontal axis by points A, B, and C. Each curve starts at some distance to the right of the point of origin representing the fact that for a given ad medium, some fixed amount of money might have to be spent before advertising has any effect at all. It also illustrates the point that the

FIGURE 7–3
Efficiency of Three Different Media

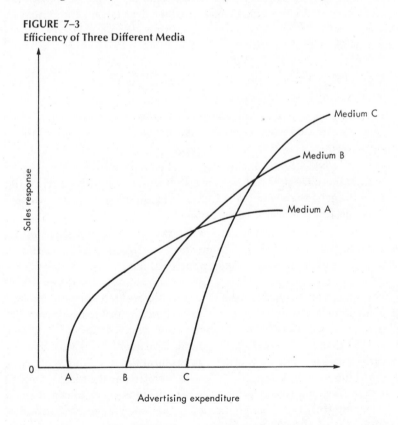

Advertising expenditure

---

[7] Marginal productivity refers to the advertising "effects" such as readership, inquiries, and sales generated by the expenditure of additional dollars in each particular medium.

desired amount of a particular advertising medium may not always be available. Such is the case when particular types of advertising media are sold in different size blocks. For example, NBC may not sell 15-second commercials or a 15-second commercial may be of no sales value and the money would be wasted.

In the advertising industry a common measure of efficiency or productivity of media is "cost per thousand." This figure generally refers to the dollar cost for reaching one thousand prospects and its chief advantage is in making media comparisons. Generally, measures such as circulation, audience size, and sets in use per commercial minute are used in the calculation. Of course, different relative rankings of media can occur depending on the measure used. Another problem deals with what is meant by "reaching" the prospect and at least five levels of reaching are possible:

1. *Distribution.* This level refers to circulation or physical distribution of the vehicle into households or other decision-making units. In only some of these households or decision-making units are there genuine prospects for the product.

2. *Exposure.* This level refers to actual exposure of prospects to the message. If the TV set is on distribution is taking place, but only if the program is being watched can exposure occur.

3. *Awareness.* This level refers to the prospect becoming alert to the message in the sense of being conscious of the ad. Actual information processing starts at this point.

4. *Communication.* This level goes one step beyond awareness, to the point where the prospect becomes affected by the message. Here the effect is to generate some sort of change in the prospect's knowledge, attitude, or desire concerning the product.

5. *Response.* This level represents the overt action that results because of the ad. Response can mean many things, such as a simple telephone or mail inquiry, a shopping trip, or a purchase.

The advertiser has to decide at what level to evaluate the performance of a medium and this is a particularly difficult problem. Ideally, the advertiser would like to know exactly how many dollars of sales are generated by ads in a particular medium. However, this is very difficult to measure since so many other factors are simultaneously at work which could be producing sales. On the other hand, the distribution of a medium is much easier to measure but distribution figures are much less meaningful. For example, a newspaper may have a distribution (circulation) of 100,000 people, yet none of these people may be prospects for the particular product being advertised. Thus, if this media were evaluated in terms of distribution, it might be viewed as quite effective even though it may be totally ineffective in terms of producing

---

HIGHLIGHT 7–5

Factors Affecting Media Selection

Selection of the most effective television shows, radio programs, magazines, newspapers, and other media vehicles to convey a message to a target population has always been more involved than simply selecting the set of media vehicles with the lowest cost-per-thousand. Other factors to be considered include the editorial climate of the vehicle, its prestige, the visual and/or audio qualities in relation to the requirements of the product message, interactions among vehicles, and the social environment in which the audience reads or views the vehicles.

Source: Dennis H. Gensch, "Media Factors: A Review Article," *Journal of Marketing Research* 8 (May 1970), p. 216.

---

sales. This problem further illustrates the importance of insuring that the media selected are those used by the target market.

From what has been said so far, it should be clear that advertising decisions involve a great deal of complexity and a myriad of variables. It is not surprising, therefore, that application of quantitative techniques have become quite popular in the area. Linear programming, dynamic programming, heuristic programming, and simulation have been applied to the problem of selecting media schedules[8] and more comprehensive models of advertising decisions have also been developed. For example, a recently developed model simultaneously addresses the budget decision, the copy decision and the media-allocation decision.[9] Although these models can be extremely useful as an aid in advertising decision making, they must be viewed as tools and not as replacement for sound managerial decisions and judgement.

SALES PROMOTION

In marketing, the word *promotion* is used in many ways. For example, it is sometimes used to refer to a specific activity such as advertising or publicity. In the general sense, promotion has been defined as "any identifiable effort on the part of the seller to persuade buyers to accept

---

[8] For a review, see Dennis H. Gensch, "Computer Models in Advertising Media Selection," *Journal of Marketing Research* 5 (November 1968), pp. 414–24. Also see Peter Doyle and Ian Fenwick, "Planning and Estimation in Advertising," *Journal of Marketing Research* 12 (February 1975), pp. 1–6.

[9] David A. Aaker, "ADMOD: An Advertising Decision Model," *Journal of Marketing Research* 12 (February 1975), pp. 37–45.

the seller's information and store it in retrievable form.[10] However, the term *sales promotion* has a more restricted and technical meaning and has been defined by the American Marketing Association as follows:

> . . . those marketing activities, other than personal selling, advertising and publicity, that stimulate consumer purchasing and dealer effectiveness, such as display, shows, and exhibitions, demonstrations, and various nonrecurrent selling efforts not in the ordinary routine.[11]

This definition illustrates that the term *sales promotion* is used for categorizing selling activities that cannot be conveniently classified as one of the other types of promotion. Listed below are some of the more common forms of sales promotion activities.[12]

Catalogs	Fixtures
Contests	Games
Conventions	Missionary salespeople
Coupons	Point-of-purchase displays
Deals—merchandise, price	Premiums
Films	Salesperson's aids
Free Samples	Trading stamps
Rebates	Trade exhibits

In examining this list, it should be noted that in some cases it is not always possible to distinguish between certain types of sales promotion activities and advertising. For example, point-of-purchase displays are sometimes classified as advertising. Likewise, coupon offers and contests are frequently considered part of an advertising campaign. However, regardless of this ambiguity, sales promotion activities are generally thought of as complementary activities which facilitate advertising and personal selling.

Because sales promotion involves so many diverse activities, it is difficult to make meaningful generalizations. For example, some sales promotion tools such as special price deals or coupon offers may be easy to justify on the basis of measured responses; however, other activities such as missionary salespersons or catalogues are more difficult to evaluate in terms of sales response or goodwill. Two common justifications for sales promotion in the latter case are (1) it is customary in the trade (as in the case of giving free drug samples to doctors) or (2) it is necessary because competition does it (as in the case of trading stamps).

---

[10] Jerome B. Kernan, William P. Dommermuth, and Montrose S. Sommers, *Promotion: An Introductory Analysis* (New York: McGraw-Hill, Inc., 1970), p. 9.

[11] Ralph S. Alexander et al., *Marketing Definitions: A Glossary of Marketing Terms* (Chicago: American Marketing Association, 1960), p. 20.

[12] For a discussion of recent trends in methods of sales promotion, see William A. Robinson, "How Marketers Responded to the Big Money Crunch in '75," *Advertising Age*, January 5, 1976, p. 32.

Finally, it should be noted that some sales promotion activities can be classified as semiprice competition rather than as nonprice competition. For example, trading stamps and special deals or merchandise offers have the effect of giving the buyer a lower price and giving the seller a way of engaging in price competition in a subtle or indirect manner. Another dimension to the problem is that with these types of promotion competitors can easily retaliate and in some cases cancel out the benefits to all sellers. For example, one reason for the decline in the use of trading stamps in grocery stores is that once all major competitors offered them this form of sales promotion no longer gave the individual stores or chains a differential advantage.

CONCLUSION

This chapter has been concerned with nonpersonal selling. It should be remembered that advertising and sales promotion are only two of the ways by which sellers can affect the demand for their products. Advertising and sales promotion are only part of the firm's promotion mix and in turn, the promotion mix is only part of the overall marketing mix. Thus, it should be noted that advertising begins with the marketing plan and not with the advertising plan. Ignoring this point can produce ineffective promotional programs because of a lack of coordination with other elements of the marketing mix.

ADDITIONAL READINGS

Aaker, David A., and Myers, John G.   *Advertising Management.* Englewood Cliffs, N.J.: Prentice-Hall, Inc., 1975.

Banks, Seymour.   "Trends Affecting the Implementation of Advertising and Promotion," *Journal of Marketing* 37 (January 1973), pp. 19–28.

Cohen, Dorothy.   *Advertising.* New York: John Wiley and Sons, Inc., 1972.

Kernan, Jerome B., and McNeal, James V.   "The Closest Thing to Measuring Advertising Effectiveness." *Business Horizons,* Winter 1964, pp. 73–80.

Kotler, Philip.   "Toward an Explicit Model for Media Selection." *Journal of Advertising Research,* March 1974, pp. 34–41.

Nylen, David W.   *Advertising: Planning, Implementation, and Control.* Cincinnati: South-Western Publishing Co., 1975.

Sandage, C. H.; Fryburger, Vernon; and Rotzoll, Kim.   *Advertising Theory and Practice.* 10th ed. Homewood, Ill.: Richard D. Irwin, Inc., 1979.

Woodside, Arch G., and Reid, David M.   "Is CPM Related to the Advertising Effectiveness of Magazines?" *Journal of Business Research* 3 (October 1975), pp. 323–34.

8

PROMOTION STRATEGY: PERSONAL SELLING

Personal selling, unlike advertising or sales promotion, involves direct face-to-face relationships between the seller and the prospect or customer. The behavioral scientist would probably characterize personal selling as a type of personal influence. Operationally, it is a complex communication process; one not completely understood by marketing scholars.

IMPORTANCE OF PERSONAL SELLING

Most business firms find it impossible to market their products without some form of personal selling. For example, some years ago vending machines became quite popular. The question may be raised as to whether or not these machines replaced the salesperson. The answer is both yes and no. In a narrow sense of the word, the vending machine has replaced some retail sales clerks who, for most convenience goods, merely dispensed the product and collected money. On the other hand, vending machines and their contents must be "sold" to the vending machine operators, and personal selling effort must be exerted to secure profitable locations for the machines.

The policies of self-service and self-selection have done much to eleminate the need for personal selling in some types of retail stores. However, the successful deployment of these policies have required manufacturers to do two things: (a) presell the consumer by means of larger advertising and sales promotion outlays; and (b) design packages for their products that would "sell" themselves, so to speak.

The importance of the personal selling function depends partially on the nature of the product. As a general rule, goods that are new, technically complex, and/or expensive require more personal selling effort. The salesperson plays a a key role in providing the consumer with information about such products in order to reduce the risks involved in purchase and use. Insurance, for example is a complex and technical product which needs significant amounts of personal selling. In addition, many industrial goods cannot be presold and the salesperson (or sales team) has a key role to play in finalizing the sale. On the other hand, most national branded convenience goods are purchased by the consumer without any significant assistance from store clerks.

The importance of personal selling also is determined to a large extent by the needs of the consumer. In the case of pure competition (a large number of small buyers with complete market knowledge of a homogeneous product), there is little need for personal selling. A close approximation to this situation is found at auctions for agricultural products such as tobacco or wheat. At the other extreme when a product is highly differentiated, such as housing, and marketed to consumers with imperfect knowledge of product offerings, then personal selling becomes a key factor in the promotion mix. In fact in some cases the consumer may not even be seeking the product; for example, life insurance is often categorized as an unsought good. Finally, sellers who differentiate their products at the point of sale will usually make heavy use of personal selling in their promotion mix. For example, in the case of automobile purchase the buyer is given the opportunity to purchase various extras or options at the time of purchase.

THE SALES PROCESS

Personal selling is as much an art as it is a science. The word *art* is used to describe that portion of the selling process that is highly creative in nature and difficult to explain. This does not mean that there is little control over the personal selling element in the promotion mix. It does imply that, all other things equal, the trained salesperson can outsell the untrained one.

Before management selects and trains salespeople, it should have an understanding of the sales process. Obviously, the sales process will differ according to the size of the company, the nature of the product, the market, and so forth, but there are some elements common to almost all selling situations that should be understood. For the purposes of this text, the term *sales process* refers to two basic factors: (1) the sequence of stages or steps the salesperson should follow in trying to sell goods and services and (2) a set of basic principles which, if adhered to, will increase the likelihood of a sale being made.

The traditional approach to personal selling involves a formula or step-by-step procedure. It is known as the AIDAS formula and has five steps: (1) get the prospect's *attention;* (2) arouse the prospect's *interest;* (3) stimulate the prospect's *desire* for the product; (3) get buying *action;* and (5) build *satisfaction* into the transaction. This approach to selling implies two things. First, the prospect or potential buyer goes through these five steps. Second, the salesperson can, to a large extent, control the behavior of the prospect if this process is managed skillfully. Although this model represents a logical approach to explaining the sales process, it emphasizes a how-to approach to selling rather than attempting to explain why sales are made or conversely, why purchases are made.

An explanation of the selling process in terms of why individuals purchase would require a full understanding of consumer behavior. Obviously, as we saw in Chapter 3, this is a difficult task, since there are so many variables involved that are difficult to measure or control. However, a useful framework for a better understanding of the selling process is illustrated in Figure 8–1.

FIGURE 8–1
A Model of the Selling Process

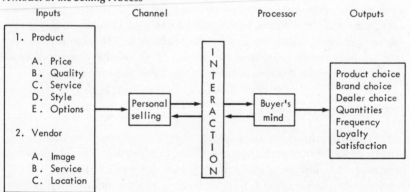

This approach views the selling process as an input-output system: the inputs are marketing stimuli such as price, quality, service, style, and so forth. Personal selling is viewed as one of the channels by which knowledge about these marketing stimuli are transmitted to the buyer. In this model the buyer's mind is a processor of the various stimuli, and since the workings of the mind are only partially understood, it can be considered a "black box." The explanation of what goes on in this black box depends on which approach or theory of behavior is employed.[1] The outputs for the model represent purchasing responses such as brand choice, dealer choice, and so forth. Here the sales process is viewed as a social situation involving two persons. The interaction of the two persons depends upon the economic, social, physical, and personality characteristics of both the seller and the buyer. A successful sale is situationally determined by these factors and can be considered social behavior as well as individual behavior. The prospect's perception of the salesperson is a key factor in determining the salesperson's effectiveness and role expectations.[2] The salesperson's confidence and ability to "play the role" of a salesperson is crucial in determining behavior and is influenced by personality, knowledge, training, and previous experience.[3]

Selling Fundamentals

From what has been said so far, the only reasonable conclusion that can be drawn is that there is no one clear-cut theory of personal selling nor one single technique that can be applied universally. Most sales training programs attempt to provide the trainee with the fundamentals of selling, placing emphasis on the "how" and "what" and leaving the "why" questions to the theorists.

A primary objective of any sales training program is to impart knowledge and techniques to the participants. An analysis of numerous training manuals reveals subjects or topics common to many programs. Following is a brief description of some fundamentals well-trained salespeople should know.

---

[1] Philip Kotler, "Behavioral Models for Analyzing Buyers," *Journal of Marketing* 29 (October 1965), pp. 37–45. Also see Thomas S. Robertson and Richard B. Chase, "The Sales Process: An Open Systems Approach," *MSU Business Topics* 16 (Autumn 1968), pp. 45–52; Robert F. Gwinner, "Base Theory in the Formulation of Sales Strategy," *MSU Business Topics* 16 (Autumn 1968), pp. 37–44; and Robert F. Gwinner, "Coordinating Strategy Tactics in Sales Administration," *MSU Business Topics* 18 (Summer 1970), pp. 56–62.

[2] For an example see Edward A. Riordan, Richard L. Oliver, and James H. Donnelly, Jr., "The Unsold Prospect: Dyadic and Attitudinal Determinants," *Journal of Marketing Research* 14 (November 1977), pp. 530–37.

[3] Frederick E. Webster, Jr. "Interpersonal Communication and Salesman Effectiveness," *Journal of Marketing* 32 (July 1968), pp. 7–12. Also see Gary M. Grikscheit and William J. E. Crissy, "Improving Interpersonal Communications Skill," *MSU Business Topics* 21 (August 1973), pp. 63–68. For discussions of the salesperson's role, see Orville C. Walker, Jr., Gilbert A. Churchill, Jr., and Neil M. Ford, "Organizational Determinants of the Industrial Salesman's Role Conflict and Ambiguity," *Journal of Marketing* 39 (January 1975), pp. 32–39; James H. Donnelly, Jr. and John M. Ivancevich, "Role Clarity and the Salesman," *Journal of Marketing* 39 (January 1975), pp. 71–74. John H. Scheibelhut and Gerald Albaum, "Self-Other Orientations among Salesmen and Nonsalesmen," *Journal of Marketing Research* 10 (February 1973), pp. 97–99; Arch G. Woodside and J. William Davenport, Jr., "The Effects of Salesman Similarity and Expertise on Consumer Purchasing Behavior," *Journal of Marketing Research* 11 (May 1974), pp. 198–202.

1. They should have thorough knowledge of the company they represent including its past histroy. This includes the philosophy of management as well as the firm's basic operating policies.

2. They should have thorough technical and commercial knowledge of their products or product lines. This is particularly true when selling industrial goods. When selling very technical products, many firms require their salespeople to have training as engineers.

3. They should have good working knowledge of competitor's products. This is a vital requirement because the successful salesperson will have to know the strengths and weaknesses of those products that are in competition for market share.

4. They should have in-depth knowledge of the market for their merchandise. The market here refers not only to a particular sales territory but also to the general market, including the economic factors that affect the demand for their goods.

5. They should have accurate knowledge of the buyer or the prospect (the decision-making unit) to whom they are selling. Under the marketing concept, knowledge of the customer is a vital requirement; also, effective selling requires salespeople to understand the unique characteristics of each account.

6. They should have some basic knowledge of sales tactics, which will permit them to overcome obstacles encountered in the field. Tactics here refer to such matters as how to handle objections or how to close a sale.

There are no magic secrets of successful selling. The difference between good salespeople and mediocre ones is often the result of training plus experience. Training is no substitute for experience; the two complement each other. The difficulty with trying to discuss the selling job in terms of basic principles is that experienced, successful salespeople will always be able to find exceptions to these principles. Often successful selling seems to defy logic and sometimes, common sense. Trying to program salespeople to follow definite rules or principles in every situation can stifle their originality and creativity.[4]

MANAGING THE SALES PROCESS

Management can significantly affect the productivity of its field sales force. Whenever salespeople make calls on accounts or prospective buyers they are operating as a member of a marketing team, because

---

[4] This is not meant to imply that structured sales approaches have no value. See Marvin A. Jolson, "The Underestimated Potential of the Canned Sales Presentation," *Journal of Marketing* 39 (January 1975), pp. 75–78.

excellent antecedent promotional effort can go for naught if salespeople are not effective. Thus, the primary mission of the sales management function is to ensure that personal selling effort is as effective as possible.

Every personal sale can be divided into two parts: the part done by the salespeople and the part done for the salespeople by the company. For example, from the standoint of the product the company should provide the salesperson with a product skillfully designed, thoroughly tested, attractively packaged, adequately advertised, and priced to compare favorably with competitive products. Salespeople have the responsibility of being thoroughly acquainted with the product, its selling features, points of superiority and a sincere belief in the value of the product. From a sales management standpoint, the company's part of the sale involves the following:

1. Efficient and effective sales tools, including continuous sales training, promotional literature, samples, trade shows, product information, and adequate advertising.
2. An efficient delivery and reorder system to insure that customers will receive the merchandise as promised.
3. An equitable compensation plan that rewards performance, motivates the salesperson, and promotes company loyalty. It should also reimburse the salesperson for all reasonable expenses incurred while doing the job.
4. Adequate supervision and evaluation of performance as a means of helping salespeople do a better job, not only for the company but for themselves as well.

The Sales Management Task

Since the advent of the marketing concept in the 1950s, a clear-cut distinction has been made between marketing management and sales management. As was seen in Chapter 1, marketing management refers to all activities in the firm that have to do with satisfying demand. Sales management is a narrower concept dealing with those functions directly related to personal selling. Generally speaking, sales managers are in middle management and report directly to the vice president of marketing. Their basic responsibilities can be broken down into at least seven major areas: (1) developing an effective sales organization for the company; (1) formulating short-range and long-range sales programs; (3) recruiting, training and supervising the sales force; (4) formulating sales budgets and controlling selling expenses; (5) coordinating the personal selling effort with other forms of promotional activities; (6) maintaining lines of communication between the sales force, customers and other relevant parts of the business such as advertising, production, and logistics; and in some firms, (7) developing sales forecasts and other types of relevant marketing studies to be used in sales planning and control.

Sales managers are line officers whose primary responsibility is establishing and maintaining an active sales organization. In terms of authority, they usually have equivalent rank to that of other marketing executives who manage aspects of the marketing program such as advertising, product planning, or physical distribution. The sales organization may have separate departments and department heads to perform specialized tasks such as training, personnel, promotion, and forecasting. Figure 8–2 is an example of such a sales organization.

FIGURE 8–2
An Example of a Sales Organization

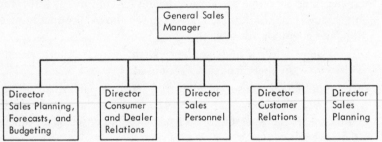

In other cases, general sales managers may have product managers, or directors, reporting to them. This is common in cases where the firm sells numerous products and each product or product line is handled by a separate manager. Another common arrangement is to have sales managers assigned to specific geographic regions or customer groups. This type of specialization enables the sales force to operate more efficiently by avoiding overlaps. Regardless of the method used, the sales force should be structured to meet the unique needs of the consumer, the company, and its management.

Controlling the Sales Force

There are two obvious reasons why it is critical that the sales force be properly controlled. First, personal selling is very often the largest marketing expense component in the final price of the product. Second, unless the sales force is somehow directed, motivated, and audited on a continual basis, it is likely to be less efficient than it is capable of being. Controlling the sales force involves four key functions: (1) forecasting

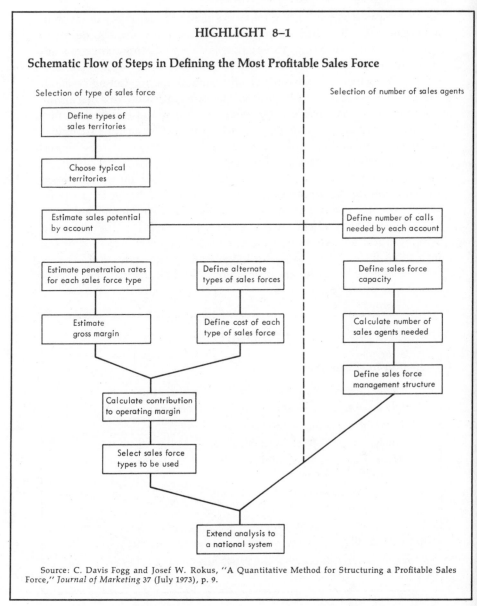

HIGHLIGHT 8–1

Schematic Flow of Steps in Defining the Most Profitable Sales Force

Selection of type of sales force   Selection of number of sales agents

Define types of
sales territories

Choose typical
territories

Estimate sales potential
by account

Define number of calls
needed by each account

Estimate penetration rates
for each sales force type

Define alternate
types of sales forces

Define sales force
capacity

Estimate
gross margin

Define cost of each
type of sales force

Calculate number of
sales agents needed

Define sales force
management structure

Calculate contribution
to operating margin

Select sales force
types to be used

Extend analysis to
a national system

Source: C. Davis Fogg and Josef W. Rokus, "A Quantitative Method for Structuring a Profitable Sales Force," *Journal of Marketing* 37 (July 1973), p. 9.

sales; (2) establishing sales territories and quotas; (3) analyzing expenses and (4) motivating and compensating performance.

Forecasting Sales. Sales planning begins with a forecast of sales for some future period or periods. From a practical standpoint, these forecasts are made on a short-term basis of a year or less, although long-range forecasts of one to five years are made for purposes other than managing the sales force, such as financing, production, and development. Generally speaking, forecasting is the marketing manager's responsibility. In large firms, because of the complexity of the task, it is usually delegated to a specialized unit such as the marketing research department. Forecast data should be integrated into the firm's marketing information system for use by sales managers and other corporate executives. For many companies the sales forecast is the key instrument in the planning and control of operations.[5]

The sales forecast is a scientific estimate of how much of the company's output, either in dollars or in units, can be sold during a specified future period under a proposed marketing plan and under an assumed set of economic conditions. A sales forecast has several important uses: (1) it is used to establish sales quotas; (2) it is used to plan personal selling efforts as well as other types of promotional activities in the marketing mix; (3) it is used to budget selling expenses; and (4) it is used to plan and coordinate production, physical distribution, inventories, manpower, and so forth.

HIGHLIGHT 8–2

Steps in Forecasting Sales

1. Determine purpose for which forecasts are to be used.
2. Divide company's products into homogeneous groups.
3. Choose forecasting method best suited to the job.
4. Analyze and check all available data.
5. Make assumptions regarding the effect of the factors that cannot be measured or forecasted.
6. Convert deductions and assumptions into specific product and territorial forecasts.
7. Apply to company operations.
8. Periodically review performance and revise forecasts.

Source: National Industrial Conference Board, "Forecasting Sales," *Studies in Business Policy*, No. 106.

Sales forecasting has become very sophisticated in recent years, especially with the increased availability of computer hardware and software. It should be mentioned, however, that a forecast is never a

---

[5] For a review of computerized systems in sales management, see James B. Comer, "The Computer, Personal Selling, and Sales Management," *Journal of Marketing* 39 (July 1975), pp. 27–33.

substitute for sound business judgement. At the present time there is no single method of sales forecasting known that gives uniformly accurate results with infallible precision. Outlined below are some commonly used sales forecasting methods.[6]

1. *Jury of executive opinion method*—This combines and averages the views of top management representing marketing, production, finance, purchasing, and administration.

2. *Sales force composite method*—This is similar to the first method in that it obtains the combined views of the sales force as to the future outlook for sales. In some companies all salespeople, or district managers, submit estimates of the future sales in their territory or district.

3. *Customer expectations method*—This approach involves asking customers or product users about the quantity they expect to purchase.

4. *Time series analyses*—This approach involves analyzing past movements and the interaction of the basic factors that largely determine the pattern of a company's sales (long-term growth trends, cyclical fluctuations, seasonal variations).

5. *Correlation analysis*—This involves measuring the relationship between the dependent variable, sales, and one or more independent variables that can explain increases or decreases in sales volumes.

6. *Other Quantitative techniques*—There are numerous statistical and mathematical techniques that can be used to predict or estimate future sales. Two of the more important techniques are (*a*) growth functions, which are mathematical expressions specifying the relationship between demand and time; (*b*) simulation models, where a statistical model of the industry is developed and programmed on the computer to develop values for the key parameters of the model.

Establishing Sales Territories and Quotas. The sales forecast is the starting point for all future planning of marketing effort throughout the company. It forces management to take a critical look at past performance and compare it with established sales goals or volume targets. These norms represent market potential based on estimates derived from forecasts by product and territory. The establishment of sales territories and sales quotas represents management's need to match personal selling effort with sales potential (or opportunity).

Sales territories are usually specified geographic areas assigned to individual salespeople. These areas represent an attempt to make the

---

[6] Based on a survey by the National Industrial Conference Board. "Forecasting Sales," *Studies in Business Policy*, No. 106.

selling task more efficient.[7] The underlying rationale is that the control of sales operations will be facilitated by breaking the total market down into smaller and more manageable units. Implied here is the notion that there are some distinct economic advantages to dividing the total market into smaller segments. These segments should represent clusters of customers, or prospects within some degree of physical proximity. Of course, there are criteria for establishing territories other than geography. One important criterion is that of product specialization. In this case, salespeople are specialists relative to particular product or customer situations.

From a marketing management point of view there are many advantages to establishing sales territories. First, it facilitates the process of sales planning by making it easier to coordinate personal selling, transportation, storage, and other forms of promotion. Second, it promotes better customer relations because the salespeople will be more familiar with the accounts they service. Third, it is an effective way of making sure that each market is well covered. Fourth, it aids management in the evaluation and control of selling costs. And fifth, it helps in the evaluation of performance.[8]

The question of managing sales territories cannot be discussed meaningfully without saying something about quotas. Sales quotas represent specific sales goals assigned to each territory or sales unit over a designated time period. Quotas are primarily a planning and control device because they provide management with measurable, quantitative standards of performance. The most common method of establishing quotas for territories is to relate sales to forecasted sales potential. For example, if the Ajax Drug Company's territory M has an estimated industry sales potential for a particular product of $400,000 for the year, then the quota might be set at 25 percent of that potential, or $100,000. The 25 percent figure represents the market share Ajax assumes as a reasonable target. This $100,000 quota may represent an increase of $20,000 in sales over last year (assuming constant prices) which is expected from new business.

In establishing sales quotas for its individual territories or sales personnel, management needs to take into account three key factors.[9]

---

[7] For a quantitative approach to this problem, see Leonard M. Lodish, "Sales Territory Alignment to Maximize Profit," *Journal of Marketing Research* 12 (February 1975), pp. 30–36.

[8] For additional discussion, see David W. Cravens, Robert B. Woodruff, and Joe C. Stamper, "An Analytical Approach for Evaluating Sales Territory Performance," *Journal of Marketing* 36 (January 1972), pp. 31–37.

[9] It should be noted that the term *sales budget* in accounting is what we are talking about here. When a sales forecast is translated into a sales budget it means the total figure is broken down by product line, region, customers, and salespeople. See Carl L. Moore and Robert K. Jadicke, *Managerial Accounting* (Cincinnati: South-Western Publishing Co., 1976), pp. 560–67.

First, all territories will not have equal potential and therefore, compensation must be adjusted accordingly. Second, all salespeople will not have equal ability and assignments may have to be made accordingly. Third, the sales task in each territory may differ from time period to time period. For example, the nature of some territories may require that salespeople spend more time seeking new accounts rather than servicing established accounts, especially in the case of so-called new territories. The point to be made here is that quotas can vary, not only by territory, but also by assigned tasks. The effective sales manager should assign quotas not only for dollar sales but also for each major selling function. Figure 8–3 is an example of how this is done for the Ajax Drug Company, where each activity is assigned a quota and a weight reflecting its relative importance so that performance can be measured quantitatively.

FIGURE 8–3
Ajax Drug Company Sales Activity Evaluation

Territory: M
Salesperson: Smith

Functions	(1) Quota	(2) Actual	(3) Percent (2÷1)	(4) Weight	(5) Score (3×4)
Sales volume					
A. Old business	380,000	300,000	79	0.7	55.7
B. New business	20,000	20,000	100	0.5	50.0
Calls on prospects					
A. Doctors	20	15	75	0.2	15.0
B. Druggists	80	60	75	0.2	15.0
C. Wholesalers . . .	15	15	100	0.2	20.0
D. Hospitals	10	10	100	0.2	20.0
				2.0	175.7

Performance Index = 175.7

Analyzing Expenses.   Most of what sales managers do in the performance of their job can be classified as control in one form or another. One of the most important control activities involves what is known as expense control. Expense control is important because of its direct relationship to profits. Sales planning should include the sales expense budget. The starting point is the (forecasted) sales potential figure.

More often than not sales expense budgets are developed from the bottom up. Each territorial or district manager submits estimates of expenses and forecasted sales quotas. These estimates are usually prepared for a period of a year and then broken down into quarters and months. The chief sales executive then reviews the budget requests from the field offices and from staff departments. Usually expenses are classified as fixed, semivariable or variable and direct or indirect. Certain items such as rent or administrative salaries are fixed. In the field offices, manpower is the principal expense and it may be fixed or semivariable, depending upon the compensation plan. Other items such as travel, samples, or other promotional material are variable in nature. Some expenses are directly traceable to the sale of specific products such as samples, or displays, while other expenses are indirect, as in the case of administrative salaries and rent. Sales commissions and shipping expenses tend to vary in direct proportion to sales, while travel expense and entertainment may not be tied to sales volume in any direct proportion.

It should be understood that selling costs are budgeted much in the same way as manufacturing costs. Selling costs are usually broken down by product lines, sales region, customers, salespersons, or some other unit. Proper budgeting requires a reasonable cost accounting system. From a budgeting standpoint, the firm should use its accounting system to analyze marketing costs as a means of control.[10]

Motivating and Compensating Performance.   The sales manager's personnel function includes more than motivating and compensating the sales force, but from the vantage point of sales force productivity, these two tasks are of paramount importance. Operationally, it means that the sales manager has the responsibility of keeping the morale of the sales force at a high level through supervision and motivation.

These closely related tasks are accomplished through interaction with the sales force (1) by contacts with supervisors, managers or sales executives individually or in group meetings, such as conventions, (2) through communication by letters or telephone, and (3) through incentive schemes by which greater opportunity for earnings (as in sales contests) or promotion may be achieved.

Compensation is a principal method by which firms motivate and retain their sales forces. Devising a compensation plan for a company is a technical matter but there are some general guidelines in formulating such a plan. First of all, a firm should be mindful of any modifications necessary to meet its particular needs when adopting another company's compensation plan. Second, the plan should make sense (that is, should have a logical rationale) to both management and the sales force. Third, the plan should not be overly complex so that it cannot be understood by the average salesperson. Fourth, as suggested in the section on quotas, the plan should be fair and equitable to avoid penalizing the sales force because of factors beyond their control; conversely, the plan should insure reward for performance in proportion to results.

---

[10] For a discussion of some useful accounting procedures for marketing analysis, see Frank H. Mossman, Paul M. Fischer, and W. J. E. Crissy, "New Approaches to Analyzing Marketing Profitability," *Journal of Marketing* 38 (April 1974), pp. 43–48.

Fifth, the plan should allow the sales force to earn salaries that permit them to maintain an acceptable standard of living. Finally, the plan should attempt to minimize attrition by giving the sales force some incentive, such as a vested retirement plan, for staying with the company.

There are two basic types of compensation: salary and commission. Salary usually refers to a specific amount of monetary compensation at an agreed rate for definite time periods. Commission is usually monetary compensation provided for each unit of sales and expressed as a percentage of sales, profit, or unit of product sales. The base on which commissions are computed may be: volume of sales in units of product, gross sales in dollars, net sales after returns, sales volume in excess of a quota, and net profits. Very often, several compensation approaches are combined. For example, a salesperson might be paid a base salary, a commission on sales exceeding a volume figure, and a percentage share of the company's profits for that year.

Some other important elements of sales compensation plans are:

1. *Drawing account*—Periodic money advances at an agreed rate. Repayment is deducted from total earnings computed on a commission or other basis, or is repaid from other assets of the salesperson if earnings are insufficient to cover the advance (except in the case of a guaranteed drawing account).

2. *Special payments for sales operations*—Payments in the nature of piece rates on operations rather than commissions on results. Flat payments per call or payments per new customer secured can be included in this category. To the extent that these payments are estimated by size of customers' purchases, they resemble commissions and are sometimes so labeled. Other bases for special payments are demonstrations, putting up counter or window displays, and special promotional work.

3. *Bonus payments*—usually lump-sump payments, over and above contractual earnings, for extra effort or merit or for results beyond normal expectation. Bonuses that vary directly with sales or profit results, however, are really commissions.

4. *Special prizes*—monetary amounts or valuable merchandise to reward the winners of sales contests and other competitions. Practices vary from firms that never use this device to firms where there is continuous use and almost every member of the sales force expects to get some compensation from this source during the year, in which case prizes amount to a form of incentive payment.

5. *Profit sharing*—a share of the profits of the business as a whole, figured on the basis of earnings, retail sales, profits in an area, or other factors. Sometimes profit sharing is intended to build up a retirement fund.

6. *Expense allowances*—provision for travel and other business expenses, which becomes an important part of any compensation plan. No agreement for outside sales work is complete without an understanding as to whether the company or the salesperson is to pay the travel and other business expenses incurred in connection with work; and, if the company is responsible, just what the arrangements should be. Automobile, hotel, entertainment, and many other items of expense may be included in the agreement.

7. *Maximum earnings or cutoff point*—a limitation on earnings. This figure may be employed for limiting maximum earnings when it is impossible to predict the range of earnings under commission or other types of incentive plans.

8. *Fringe benefits.* Pensions, group insurance, health insurance, and so forth. More and more frequently these are given to sales forces as a matter of policy and become a definite part of the compensation plan.[11]

CONCLUSION

This chapter has attempted to outline and explain the personal selling aspect of the promotion mix. Before ending the discussion a brief comment might be made concerning the overall value of personal selling. Personal selling in a growing economy must always play an important part in the marketing of goods and services. As long as production continues to expand through the development of new and highly technical products, personal selling will occupy a key role in our marketing system.

ADDITIONAL READINGS

Baer, Earl A. *Salesmanship.* New York: McGraw-Hill, Inc., 1972.

Bird, Monroe M.; Clayton, Edward R.; and Moore, Laurence J. "Sales Negotiation Cost Planning for Corporate Level Sales." *Journal of Marketing* 37 (April 1973), pp. 7–13.

Dunn, Albert H.; Johnson, Eugene M.; and Kurtz, David L. *Sales Management: Concepts, Practices, and Cases.* Morristown, N.J.: General Learning Press, 1975.

Greif, Edwin C. *Personal Salesmanship: New Concepts and Directions.* Reston, Va.: Reston Publishing Co., Inc., 1974.

Haas, Kenneth B., and Ernest, John W. *Creative Salesmanship: Understanding Essentials*, 2d ed. Beverly Hills, Calif.: Glencoe Press, 1974.

---

[11] See Rene Y. Darmon, "Salesmen's Response to Financial Incentives: An Empirical Study," *Journal of Marketing Research* 11 (November 1974), pp. 418–26; Henry O. Pruden, William H. Cunningham, and Wilke D. English, "Nonfinancial Incentives for Salesmen," *Journal of Marketing* 36 (October 1972), pp. 55–59.

Jolson, Marvin A.   "The Salesman's Career Cycle." *Journal of Marketing* 38 (July 1974), pp. 39–46.

Kurtz, David L.; Dodge, H. Robert; and Klompmaker, Jay E.   *Professional Selling*, Rev. ed. Dallas: Business Publications, Inc., 1979.

Oliver, Richard L.   "Expectancy Theory Predictions of Salesmen's Performance," *Journal of Marketing Research* 11 (August 1974), pp. 243–53.

Robertson, Dan H.   "Sales Force Feedback on Competitor's Activities." *Journal of Marketing* 38 (April 1974), pp. 69–71.

Russell, Frederic A.; Beach, Frank H.; and Buskirk, Richard H.   *Textbook of Salesmanship*, 9th ed. New York: McGraw-Hill, Inc., 1974.

Stanton, William J., and Buskirk, Richard H.   *Management of the Sales Force*, 5th ed. Homewood, Ill.: Richard D. Irwin, Inc., 1978.

Thompson, Joseph W.   *Selling: A Managerial and Behavioral Analysis.* New York: McGraw-Hill, Inc., 1973.

Winer, Leon.   "The Effects of Product Quotas on Sales Force Productivity," *Journal of Marketing Research* 10 (May 1973), pp. 180–83.

9

DISTRIBUTION STRATEGY

Channel of distribution decisions involve numerous interrelated variables that must be integrated into the total marketing mix. Because of the time and money required to set up an efficient channel, and since channels are often hard to change once they are set up, these decisions are critical to the success of the firm.

This chapter is concerned with the development and management of channels of distribution and the process of goods distribution in an extremely complex, highly productive, and specialized economy. It should be noted at the outset that channels of distribution provide the ultimate consumer or industrial user with time, place, and possession utility. Thus, an efficient channel is one that delivers the product when and where it is wanted at a minimum total cost.

THE NEED FOR MARKETING INTERMEDIARIES

A channel of distribution is the combination of institutions through which a seller markets products to the user or ultimate consumer. The need for other institutions or intermediaries in the delivery of goods is sometimes questioned, particularly since the profits they make are viewed as adding to the cost of the product. However, this reasoning is generally falacious, since producers use marketing intermediaries because the intermediary can perform functions *more cheaply and more efficiently* than the producer can. This notion of efficiency is critical when the characteristics of our economy are considered.

142

For example, our economy is characterized by heterogeneity in terms of both supply and demand. In terms of numbers alone, there are over five million establishments comprising the supply segment of our economy and there are over sixty million households making up the demand side. Clearly, if each of these units had to deal on a one-to-one basis to obtain needed goods and services and there were no intermediaries to collect and disperse assortments of goods, the system would be totally inefficient. Thus, the primary role of intermediaries is to bring supply and demand together in an efficient and orderly fashion.

CLASSIFICATION OF MARKETING INTERMEDIARIES AND FUNCTIONS

There are a great many types of marketing intermediaries, many of which are so specialized by function and industry that they need not be discussed here. Figure 9–1 presents the major types of marketing intermediaries common to many industries. Although there is some overlap in this classification, these categories are based on the marketing functions performed. That is, various intermediaries perform different mar-

FIGURE 9–1
Major Types of Marketing Intermediaries

Middleman—any intermediary between manufacturer and end-user markets; synonymous with *reseller*.

Agent—any middleman with legal authority to act on behalf of the manufacturer.

Manufacturer's representative—a middleman who sells the product but usually does not take legal title to or physical possession of the merchandise.

Wholesaler—a middleman who sells to other middlemen, usually to retailers. This term usually applies to consumer markets.

Retailer—a middleman who sells to consumers.

Broker—a middleman who performs limited selling functions, usually only writing orders to be turned over to the manufacturer for delivery, and usually specializing in sales to a particular kind of customer such as grocery stores.

Sales agent—a middleman who agrees to sell all of the output of a manufacturer, at a stated commission rate or for a stated fee, but who usually does not take physical possession of or legal title to the merchandise.

Distributor—an imprecise term, usually used to describe a middleman who performs a variety of distribution functions, including selling, maintaining inventories, extending credit, and so on. It is a more common term in industrial markets but may also be used to refer to wholesalers.

Dealer—an even more imprecise term that can mean the same as distributor, retailer, wholesaler, and so forth. It is virtually synonymous with *middleman*.

Jobber—usually used in an industrial marketing context to refer to distributors, or in certain fields such as paper and hardware to refer to wholesalers characterized by broad lines and reasonably complete service offerings.

Source: Frederick E. Webster, Jr., *Marketing for Managers* (New York: Harper & Row, Publishers, 1974), p. 191. Copyright © 1974 by Frederick E. Webster, Jr. Reprinted by permission of Harper & Row, Publishers, Inc.

keting functions and to different degrees. Figure 9–2 is a listing of the more common marketing functions performed in the channel.

FIGURE 9–2
Marketing Function Performed in Channels of Distribution

Selling—promoting the product to potential customers.

Buying—purchasing a variety of products from various sellers, usually for resale.

Assorting—providing an assortment of items (often interrelated) for potential customers.

Financing—offering credit to potential customers to facilitate the transaction; also, providing funds to sellers to help them finance their affairs.

Storage—protecting the product and maintaining inventories to offer better customer service.

Sorting—buying a quantity and breaking bulk items into amounts desired by customers.

Grading—judging products and labelling them as to quality.

Transportation—physically moving the product between manufacturer and end user.

Market information—information needed by manufacturers about market conditions, including expected sales volume, fashion trends, and pricing conditions.

Risk taking—absorbing business risks, especially risks of maintaining inventories, product obsolescence, et cetera.

Source: Frederick E. Webster, Jr., *Marketing for Managers* (New York: Harper & Row, Publishers, 1974), p. 191. Copyright © 1974 by Frederick E. Webster, Jr. Reprinted by permission of Harper & Row, Publishers, Inc.

It should be remembered that whether or not a manufacturer utilizes intermediaries to perform these functions, the functions have to be performed by someone. In other words, the managerial question is not whether to perform the functions but who will perform them and to what degree.

CHANNELS OF DISTRIBUTION

As previously noted, a channel of distribution is the sequence of firms comprised of all the intermediaries involved in moving goods and the title to them from the producer to the consumer. Some of these links assume the risks of ownership, others do not. Some perform marketing functions while others perform nonmarketing or facilitating functions, such as transportation. The typical channel of distribution patterns for consumer goods markets are shown in Figure 9–3.

Some manufacturers use a direct channel, selling directly to the ultimate consumer, for example, Avon cosmetics. In other cases, one or more intermediaries may be used. For example, a manufacturer of paper cartons may sell to retailers, or a manufacturer of small appliances may sell to retailers under a private brand. The most common channel in the consumer market is the one in which the manufacturer sells through

FIGURE 9–3
Typical Channels of Distribution for Consumer Goods

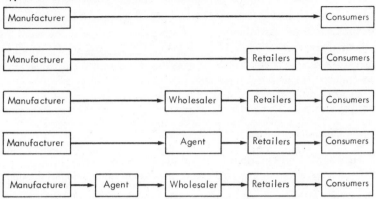

wholesalers to retailers. For example, a cold remedy manufacturer may sell to drug wholesalers who in turn sell a vast array of drug products to various retail outlets. Small manufacturers may also use agents, since they do not have sufficient capital for their own sales forces. Agents are commonly-used intermediaries in the jewelry industry. The final channel in Figure 9–3 is used primarily when small wholesalers and retailers are involved. Channels with one or more intermediaries are referred to as indirect channels.

In contrast to consumer products, the direct channel is often used in the distribution of industrial goods. The reason for this stems from the structure of most industrial markets, which often have relatively few but extremely large customers. Also many industrial products, such as computers need a great deal of presale and postsale service. Distributors are used in industrial markets when the number of buyers is large and the size of the buying firm is small. As in the consumer market, agents

FIGURE 9–4
Typical Channels of Distribution for Industrial Goods

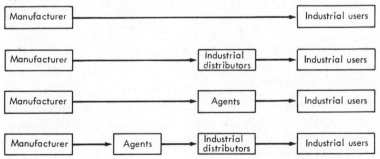

are used in industrial market in cases where manufacturers do not wish to have their own sales forces. Such an arrangement may be used by small manufacturers or when the market is geographically dispersed. The final channel arrangement in Figure 9–4 may also be used by a small manufacturer or when the market consists of many small customers. Under such conditions it may not be economical for sellers to have their own sales organization.

HIGHLIGHT 9–1

"Are Channels of Distribution What the Textbook Say?"

The middleman is not a hired link in a chain forged by a manufacturer, but rather an independent market, the focus of a large group of customers for whom he buys. Subsequent to some market analysis of his own, he selects products and suppliers, thereby setting at least one link in the channel.

After some experimentation, he settles upon a method of operation, performing those functions he deems inescapable in the light of his own objectives, forming policies for himself wherever he has freedom to do so. Perhaps these methods and policies conform closely to those of a Census category of middleman, but perhaps they do not.

It is true that his choices are in many instances tentative proposals. He is subject to much influence from competitors, from aggressive suppliers, from inadequate finances and faulty information, as well as from habit. Nonetheless, many of his choices are independent.

As he grows and builds a following, he may find that his prestige in his market is greater than that of the suppliers whose goods he sells. In some instances his local strength is so great that a manufacturer is virtually unable to tap that market, except through him. In such a case the manufacturer can have no channel policy with respect to that market.

Source: Phillip McVey, "Are Channels of Distribution What the Textbooks Say?" *Journal of Marketing* 24 (January 1960), pp. 61–65. This article can be considered a classic in the field of marketing.

SELECTING CHANNELS OF DISTRIBUTION

General Considerations

Given the numerous types of channel middlemen and functions that must be performed, the task of selecting and designing a channel of distribution may at first appear to be overwhelming. However, in many industries, channels of distribution have developed over many years and have become somewhat traditional. In such cases the producer may be limited to this type of channel in order to operate in the industry. This is not to say that a traditional channel is always the most efficient and that there are no opportunities for innovation, but the fact that such a channel is widely accepted in the industry suggests that it is highly efficient. A primary constraint in these cases and in cases where no traditional channel exists is that of *availability* of the various types of middlemen. All too often in the early stages of channel design, executives map out elaborate channel networks only to find out later that no such independent middlemen exist for the firm's product in selected geographic areas. Even if they do exist, they may not be willing to accept the seller's products. In general, there are six basic considerations in the initial development of channel strategy. These are outlined in Figure 9–5.[1]

It should be noted that for a particular product any one of these characteristics may greatly influence choice of channels. For example,

---

FIGURE 9–5
Considerations in Channel Planning

1. Customer characteristics.
   a. Number.
   b. Geographical dispersion.
   c. Purchasing patterns.
   d. Susceptibilities to different selling methods.
2. Product characteristics.
   a. Perishability.
   b. Bulkiness.
   c. Degree of standardization.
   d. Installation and maintenance services required.
3. Middleman characteristics.
   a. Availability.
   b. Willingness to accept product or product line.
   c. Strengths.
   d. Weaknesses.
4. Competitive characteristics.
   a. Geographic proximity.
   b. Proximity in outlet.
5. Company characteristics.
   a. Financial strength.
   b. Product mix.
   c. Past channel experience.
   d. Present company marketing policies.
6. Environmental characteristics.
   a. Economic conditions.
   b. Legal regulations and restrictions.

---

[1] This figure was formulated from Philip Kotler, *Marketing Management: Analysis, Planning, and Control,* 3d ed. (Englewood Cliffs, N.J.: Prentice-Hall, Inc., 1976), pp. 287–89.

highly perishable products generally require direct channels, or a firm with little financial strength may require middlemen to perform almost all of the marketing functions.

Specific Considerations

The above characteristics play an important part in framing the channel selection decision. Based on them, the choice of channels can be further refined in terms of (1) distribution coverage required, (2) degree of control desired, (3) total distribution cost and (4) channel flexibility.

Distribution Coverage Required. Because of the characteristics of the product, the environment needed to sell the product, and the needs and expectations of the potential buyer, products will vary in the intensity of distribution coverage they require. Distribution coverage can be viewed along a continuum ranging from intensive, to selective, to exclusive distribution.

Intensive Distribution. Here the manufacturer attempts to gain exposure through as many wholesalers and retailers as possible. Most convenience goods require intensive distribution based on the characteristics of the product (low-unit value) and the needs and expectations of the buyer (high frequency of purchase and convenience).

Selective Distribution. Here the manufacturer limits the use of middlemen to the ones believed to be the best available. This may be based on the service organization available, the sales organization, or the reputation of the middleman. Thus, appliances, home furnishings, and better clothing are usually distributed selectively. For appliances the middleman's service organization could be a key factor, while for better clothing and home furnishings the middleman's reputation would be an important consideration.

Exclusive Distribution. Here the manufacturer severely limits distribution and the middleman is provided the fullest protection and has exclusive rights within a particular territory. The characteristics of the product are a determining factor here. Where the product requires certain specialized selling effort and/or investment in unique facilities or large inventories, this arrangement is usually selected.[2] Retail paint stores are an example of such a distribution arrangement.

Degree of Control Desired. In selecting channels of distribution the seller must make decisions concerning the degree of control desired over

---

[2] For a discussion of legality of restrictive distribution arrangements, see James R. Burley, "Territorial Restriction in Distribution Systems: Current Legal Developments," *Journal of Marketing* 39 (October 1975), pp. 52–56.

the marketing of the firm's products. Some manufacturers prefer to keep as much control over the policies surrounding their product as possible. Ordinarily the degree of control achieved by the seller is proportionate to the directness of the channel. One Eastern brewery, for example, owns its own fleet of trucks and operates a wholly owned delivery system direct to grocery and liquor stores. Its market is very concentrated geographically with many small buyers, so such a system is economically feasible. However, all other brewers in the area sell through wholesalers or distributors.

When more indirect channels are used the manufacturer must surrender some control over the marketing of the firm's product. However, attempts are usually made to maintain a degree of control through some other indirect means such as sharing promotional expenditures, providing sales training, or other operational aids such as accounting systems, inventory systems, or marketing research data on the dealer's trading area.[3]

Total Distribution Cost. The total distribution cost concept has developed out of the more general topic of systems theory. The concept suggests that a channel of distribution should be viewed as a total system composed of interdependent subsystems and that the objective of the system (channel) manager should be to optimize total system performance. In terms of distribution costs, it is generally assumed that the total system should be designed to minimize costs, other things being equal. The following is a representative list of the major distribution costs to be minimized.

1. Transportation.
2. Order processing.
3. Cost of lost business (an "opportunity" cost due to inability to meet customer demand).
4. Inventory carrying costs, including.
   a. Storage-space charges.
   b. Cost of capital invested.
   c. Taxes.
   d. Insurance.
   e. Obsolescence and deterioration.
5. Packaging.
6. Materials handling.[4]

---

[3] For further discussion, see Louis P. Bucklin, "A Theory of Channel Control," *Journal of Marketing* 37 (January 1973), pp. 39–47; Adel I. El-Ansary and Robert A. Robicheaux, "A Theory of Channel Control: Revisited," *Journal of Marketing* 38 (January 1974), pp. 2–7.

[4] Webster, *Marketing for Managers*, p. 185.

HIGHLIGHT 9–2

Franchising: An Alternative to Traditional Channels

Basically, the franchise is a means by which a producer (of products or services) achieves a direct channel of distribution without wholly owning or managing the physical facilities in the market. It is "a continuing relationship between the franchisor and the franchisee in which the sum total of the franchisor's knowledge, image, successes, and manufacturing and marketing techniques are supplied to the franchisee for a consideration."

Ingredients of a Franchised Business

Six key ingredients should be included within a well-balanced franchise offered to a franchisee. These are given here in order of importance:

1. *Technical knowledge* in its practical form is supplied through an intensive course of study.

2. *Managerial techniques* based upon proven and time-tested programs are imparted to the franchisee on a continuing basis, even after the business has been started or taken over by the franchisee.

3. *Commercial knowledge* involving prescribed methods of buying and selling is explained and codified. Most products to be obtained, processed, and sold to the franchisee are supplied by the franchisor.

4. *Financial instruction* on managing funds and accounts is given to the franchisee during the indoctrination period.

5. *Accounting controls* are set up by the franchisor for the franchisee.

6. *Protective safeguards* are included in the intensive training of the franchisee for his employees and customers, including the quality of his product, as well as the safeguards for his assets through adequate insurance controls.

Source: Aaron M. Rothenberg, "A Fresh Look at Franchising," *Journal of Marketing* 31 (July 1967), pp. 52–54.

The important qualification to the total cost concept is the statement "other things being equal." The purpose of the total cost concept is to emphasize total system performance to avoid suboptimization. However, other important factors must be considered, not the least of which are level of customer service, sales, profits, and interface with the total marketing mix.

Channel Flexibility. A final consideration relates to the ability of the manufacturer to adapt to changing conditions. For example, in recent years much of the population has moved from inner cities to suburbs and thus make most of their purchases in shopping centers and malls. If a manufacturer had long-term, exclusive dealership with retailers in the inner city, the ability to adapt to this population shift could have been severely limited. In general, the less certain the future seems to be, the less favorable are channel alternatives involving long commitments.[5]

MANAGING A CHANNEL OF DISTRIBUTION

Once the seller has decided on the type of channel structure to use and selected the individual members, the entire coalition should operate as a total system. From a behavioral perspective, the system can be viewed as a social system since each member interacts with the others, each member plays a role vis-a-vis the others and each has certain expectations of the other.[6] Thus, the behavioral perspective views a channel of distribution as more than a series of markets or participants extending from production to consumption.

A Channel Leader

If a channel of distribution is viewed as a social system comprised of interacting firms with a common set of objectives, then integration among them seems desirable. This is because the channel, as a system, can be conceived as a competitive unit in and of itself; in other words, any success that the product has is determined largely by the effectiveness and efficiency with which human material and monetary resources have been mobilized throughout the entire interfirm network.[7]

If the above view is taken, the question arises as to who should exert primary leadership in the channel, that is, becomes the "channel captain" or "channel commander." There is little agreement as to the answer. Some marketers believe the manufacturer or the owner of the brand name should be the channel captain. The argument here is that the manufacturer or brand name owner (1) has the most to lose if the system malfunctions or fails, (2) has the most technical expertise, and (3) in many cases has greater resources than other channel members. Others believe the retailer should be the channel captain since the

---

[5] Philip Kotler, *Marketing Management: Analysis Planning, and Control*, 3d ed. (Englewood Cliffs, N.J.: Prentice-Hall, Inc., 1976), p. 296.

[6] For a complete work devoted to the behavioral dimensions of channels of distribution see Louis W. Stern, ed., *Distribution Channels: Behavioral Dimensions* (Boston: Houghton-Mifflin Co., 1969).

[7] Ibid., p. 1.

retailer is the closest link to the consumer and therefore can judge consumer needs and wants better. Still others argue the wholesaler should seek to gain channel control or that the locus of control should be at the level where competition is greatest.

In some channels of distribution one member may be large and powerful with respect to other members. It may be a manufacturer, wholesaler, or large retailer. Consider the power Sears Roebuck has over a small supplying manufacturing firm, since 90 percent of Sears products are under its own label. In such cases the powerful member may assume leadership.

HIGHLIGHT 9–3

The Battle of the Brands

The competition between manufacturers' and distributors' brands has been labeled the "battle of the brands." In this confrontation, the distributor has many advantages on his side. Retail shelf space is scarce, and many manufacturers, especially newer and smaller ones, cannot introduce products into distribution under their own name. The distributors take special care to maintain the quality of their brands, building consumers' confidence. Many buyers know that the private label is often manufactured by one of the big manufacturers anyway. The distributors' brands are often priced lower than comparable manufacturers' brands, thus appealing to budget-conscious shoppers, especially in times of inflation. The distributors give more prominent display to their own brands and make sure they are better stocked. For these and other reasons, the former dominance of the manufacturers' brands is ending. Indeed, some marketing commentators predict the distributors' brands will eventually knock out most manufacturers' brands.

Source: Philip Kotler, *Marketing Management: Analysis, Planning and Control*, 3d ed. (Englewood Cliffs, N.J.: Prentice-Hall, Inc., 1976), p. 192.

While the issue is certainly not clear, the tendency appears to lean toward channels controlled by the manufacturer, with a few notable exceptions. For example, for their own brands Sears Roebuck and Montgomery Ward undoubtedly play the primary leadership role while the manufacturer plays a subordinate role. In some cases where wholesalers have their own brands, the manufacturer and retailer probably assume a subordinate role. However, in many cases, manufacturers have absorbed functions previously performed by middlemen and thereby obtained even greater channel control.

HIGHLIGHT 9–4

Pushing or Pulling through the Channel System

A producer has a special challenge with respect to channel systems: How to win channel cooperation to ensure that his product reaches the end of the channel. Middlemen, and especially retailers, don't have this problem, since they already control that end of the channel.

The two basic methods of achieving channel cooperation are *pushing* and *pulling*.

Pushing a product through the channels means using normal promotional effort—personal salesmen and advertising—to help sell the whole marketing mix to possible channel members. This method is common, since these sales transactions are usually between rational, presumably profit-oriented businessmen. The approach emphasizes the importance of building a channel and securing the wholehearted cooperation of prospective channel members in a total system of action. The channel captain, in effect, tries to develop a team that will work well together to get the product to the user.

By contrast, a manufacturer pulls a product through the channels when he tries to develop channel support by making consumers want his product. This entails highly aggressive promotion to final consumers or users, perhaps using coupons or samples, and temporary bypassing of middlemen. If the promotion works, the middlemen are forced to carry the product to satisfy their customers.

Source: E. Jerome McCarthy, *Basic Marketing,* 6th ed. (Homewood, Ill.: Richard D. Irwin, 1978), pp. 325–26.

CONCLUSION

The purpose of this chapter has been to introduce the reader to the process of distribution of goods in an extremely complex, highly productive and highly specialized economy. It is important that the reader understand the vital need for marketing intermediaries in such an economy to bring about exchanges between buyers and sellers in a reasonably efficient manner. If the reader appreciates this concept, then the major objective of this chapter has been achieved. The chapter also examined the typical channels of distribution for both consumer goods and industrial goods and the various types of marketing intermediaries available to a seller. Finally, two important aspects of channels of distribution were discussed: the selection and management of channels of distribution.

ADDITIONAL READINGS

Boone, Louis E., and James C. Johnson, eds.   *Marketing Channels.* Morristown, N.J.: General Learning Press, 1973.

Bowersox, Donald J.   "Planning Physical Distribution Operations with Dynamic Simulation." *Journal of Marketing* 36 (January 1972), pp. 17–25.

Bucklin, Louis P.   *Competition and Evolution in the Distributive Trades.* Englewood Cliffs, N.J.: Prentice-Hall, Inc., 1972.

El-Ansary, Adel I., and Louis W. Stern, "Power Measurement in the Distribution Channel." *Journal of Marketing Research* 9 (February 1972), pp. 47–52.

Hollingsworth, A. Thomas.   "Applying Organization Theory to Marketing Channels." *Journal of Retailing* 49 (Summer 1973), pp. 51–64.

Mallen, Bruce.   "Functional Spin-off: A Key to Anticipating Change in Distribution Structure." *Journal of Marketing* 37 (July 1973), pp. 18–25.

Michman, Ronald.   *Marketing Channels.* Columbus, Ohio: Grid, Inc., 1973.

Moller, William G., Jr.; and Wilemon, David L., eds.   *Marketing Channels: A Systems Viewpoint.* Homewood, Ill.: Richard D. Irwin, Inc., 1971.

Rosenbloom, Bert.   "Conflict and Channel Efficiency: Some Conceptual Models for the Decision Maker." *Journal of Marketing* 37 (July 1973), pp. 26–30.

Stern, Louis, ed. *Distribution Channels: Behavioral Dimensions.* Boston: Houghton-Mifflin, 1969.

Walker, Bruce J.; and Haynes, Joel B., eds.   *Marketing Channels and Institutions: Readings on Distribution Concepts and Practices.* Columbus, Ohio: Grid, Inc., 1978.

10

PRICING STRATEGY

One of the most important and complex decisions a firm has to make relates to pricing its products. In America the price system is generally an "administered" one in contrast to a system where prices are determined solely by the interaction of supply and demand.[1] This does not mean that market forces are not important considerations in determining prices. What it does mean is that executive decisions are juxtaposed between demand and supply forces. Thus, it is executive decisions that determine not only the initial price of new products but also changes in price after products have been on the market for some time.

This chapter discusses demand, supply, and environmental influences that affect pricing decisions and emphasizes that consideration of all three are necessary for effective pricing. However, as will be discussed throughout the chapter, many firms price their products without explicitly considering all of these influences.

DEMAND INFLUENCES ON PRICING DECISIONS

Demand influences on pricing decisions concern primarily the nature of the target market and expected reactions of consumers to a given price or change in price. There are three primary considerations here: demographic factors, psychological factors, and price elasticity.

---

[1] Much of economic price theory is based on the latter assumption and thus is not completely useful for this treatment of pricing strategy. For a full discussion of the limitations of economic price theory, see Philip Kotler, *Marketing Management*, 3d ed. (Englewood Cliffs, N.J.: Prentice-Hall, Inc., 1976), pp. 250–54.

Demographic Factors.   In the initial selection of the target market that the firm intends to serve, a number of demographic factors are usually considered. Demographic factors that are particularly important for pricing decisions include the following:

1.   Number of potential buyers.
2.   Location of potential buyers.
3.   Position of potential buyers (resellers or final consumers).
4.   Expected consumption rates of potential buyers.
5.   Economic strength of potential buyers.

These factors help determine market potential and are useful for estimating expected sales.

Psychological Factors.   Psychological factors related to pricing concern primarily how consumers will perceive various prices or price changes. For example, marketing managers should be concerned with such questions as

1.   Will potential buyers use price as an indicator of product quality?
2.   Will potential buyers be favorably attracted by odd pricing?
3.   Will potential buyers perceive the price as too high relative to the service the product gives them?
4.   Are potential buyers prestige-oriented and therefore willing to pay higher prices to fulfill this need?
5.   How much will potential buyers be willing to pay for the product?

While psychological factors can have a significant effect on the success of a pricing policy and ultimately on marketing strategy, answers to the above questions may require considerable marketing research. In fact, a review of buyers' subjective perceptions of price concluded that very little is known about how price affects buyers' perceptions of alternative purchase offers and how these perceptions affect purchase response.[2] However, some tentative generalizations about how buyers perceive price have been formulated. For example, one study found that persons who chose high-priced items perceived large quality variations within product categories and saw the consequences of a poor choice as being undesirable.[3] They were confident that quality was related to price and saw themselves as good judges of product quality. Their

---

[2] Kent B. Monroe, "Buyers' Subjective Perceptions of Price," *Journal of Marketing Research* 10 (February 1973), pp. 70–80.

[3] Zarrel V. Lambert, "Price and Choice Behavior," *Journal of Marketing Research* 9 (February 1972), p. 40. See also James R. Bettman, "Perceived Price, and Product Perceptual Variables," *Journal of Marketing Research*, February 1973, pp. 100–102.

perceived experience in purchasing was often high, and they thought brand choice was likely to affect other people's social judgments of them. In general, the reverse held true for persons who selected low-priced items in the same product categories. Thus, although information on psychological factors involved in purchasing may be difficult to obtain, marketing managers must at least consider the affects of such factors on their desired target market and marketing strategy.

Price Elasticity. Both demographic and psychological factors affect price elasticity. Price elasticity is a measure of consumers' price sensitivity, which is estimated by dividing relative changes in the quantity sold by the relative changes in price:

$$e = \frac{\Delta Q/Q}{\Delta P/P}$$

Although difficult to measure, there are two basic methods commonly used to estimate price elasticity. First, price elasticity can be estimated from historical data or from price-quantity data across different sales districts. Second, price elasticity can be estimated by sampling a group of subjects from the target market and polling them concerning various price-quantity relationships. While both of these approaches provide estimates of price elasticity, the former approach is limited to the consideration of price changes while the latter approach is often expensive and there is some question as to the validity of subjects' responses.[4] However, even a crude estimate of price elasticity is a useful input to pricing decisions.

A practical example of how the price elasticity works can be seen using automobiles. Assume that the price elasticity of Ajax Electric Automobiles is estimated to be 1.5. The key question is whether or not a price reduction of $100 would be profitable for Ajax. Let us assume that the average price of Ajax's line is $2,500 with a forecasted sales volume of 1 million units at this price. A price cut of $100 from $2,500 to $2,400 is a 4 percent reduction. A price elasticity of 1.5 would result in an increase in sales of 6 percent ($1.5 \times 4\% = 6\%$) and so the anticipated new sales volume would be increased from 1 million units to 1.06 million autos. At the price of $2,500, sales revenue would be $2.5 billion (1 million cars $\times$ $2,500). At the new price of $2,400 the anticipated sales revenue would be $2.544 billion ($2,400 $\times$ 1.6 million cars). Thus Ajax would have increased revenue of $44 million.

---

[4] For additional discussion of price elasticity, see Kotler, *Marketing Management*, pp. 261–64; Douglas J. Dalrymple and Leonard J. Parsons, *Marketing Management: Text and Cases* (New York: John Wiley and Sons, Inc., 1976), pp. 353–57.

SUPPLY INFLUENCES ON PRICING DECISIONS

For the purpose of this text, supply influences on pricing decisions can be discussed in terms of three basic factors. These factors relate to objectives, costs, and nature of the product.

Pricing Objectives

Pricing objectives should be derived from overall marketing objectives, which in turn should be derived from corporate objectives. Since it is traditionally assumed that business firms operate to maximize profits in the long run, it is often thought that the basic pricing objective is solely concerned with long-run profits. However, the profit maximization norm does not provide the operating marketing manager with a

---

HIGHLIGHT 10–1

Some Potential Pricing Objectives

1. Target return on investment.
2. Target market share.
3. Maximum long-run profits.
4. Maximum short-run profits.
5. Growth.
6. Stabilize market.
7. Desensitize customers to price.
8. Maintain price-leadership arrangement.
9. Discourage entrants.
10. Speed exit of marginal firms.
11. Avoid government investigation and control.
12. Maintain loyalty of middlemen and get their sales support.
13. Avoid demands for "more" from suppliers—labor in particular.
14. Enhance image of firm and its offerings.
15. Be regarded as "fair" by customers (ultimate).
16. Create interest and excitement about the item.
17. Be considered trustworthy and reliable by rivals.
18. Help in the sale of weak items in the line.
19. Discourage others from cutting prices.
20. Make a product "visible."
21. "Spoil market" to obtain high price for sale of business.
22. Build traffic.
23. Maximum profits on product line.
24. Recover investment quickly.

Source: Adapted from Alfred R. Oxenfeldt, "A Decision-Making Structure for Price Decisions," *Journal of Marketing* 37 (January 1973), p. 50.

---

single, unequivocal guideline for selecting prices. In addition, the marketing manager does not have perfect cost, revenue, and market information so as to be able to evaluate whether or not this objective is being reached. In practice, then, many other objectives are employed as guidelines for pricing decisions. In some cases, these objectives may be considered as operational approaches to achieve long-run profit maximization.

Research has found that the most common pricing objectives are (1) pricing to achieve a target return on investment, (2) stabilization of price and margin; (3) pricing to achieve a target market share; and (4) pricing to meet or prevent competition.

Cost Considerations in Pricing

The price of a product usually must cover costs of production, promotion, and distribution, plus a profit in order for the offering to be of value to the firm. In addition, when products are priced on the basis of costs plus a "fair" profit, there is an implicit assumption that this sum represents the economic value of the product in the marketplace.

Cost-oriented pricing is the most common approach in practice and there are at least three basic variations: *markup pricing, cost-plus pricing* and *rate-of-return pricing.* Mark-up pricing is commonly used in retailing, where a percentage is added to the retailer's invoice price to determine the final selling price. Closely related to mark-up pricing is cost-plus pricing, where the costs of producing a product or completing a project are totalled and a profit amount or percentage is added on. Cost-plus pricing is most often used to describe the pricing of jobs that are nonroutine and difficult to "cost" in advance, such as construction and military weapon development.[5]

Rate-of-return, or *target pricing* is commonly used by manufacturers. In this method, price is determined by adding a desired rate of return on investment to total costs. Generally, a break-even analysis is performed for expected production and sales levels and a rate of return is added on. For example, suppose a firm estimated production and sales to be 75,000 units at a total cost of $300,000. If the firm desired a before-tax return of 20 percent, then the selling price would be (300,000 + 0.20(300,000) ÷ 75,000 = $4.80.

Cost-oriented approaches to pricing have the advantage of simplicity, and at least one writer suggests that they generally yield a good price decision.[6] However, such approaches have been criticized for two basic

[5] Kotler, *Marketing Management,* p. 254.

[6] Douglas G. Brooks, "Cost-Oriented Pricing: A Realistic Solution to a Complicated Problem," *Journal of Marketing* 39 (April 1975), pp. 72–74.

HIGHLIGHT 10–2

Basic Break-Even Formulas

The following formulas are used to calculate break-even points in units and in dollars:

$$BEP_{(in\,units)} = \frac{FC}{(SP-VC)}$$

$$BEP_{(in\,dollars)} = \frac{FC}{1-(VC/SP)}$$

where FC = fixed cost
VC = variable cost
SP = selling price

If, as is generally the case, a firm wants to know how many units or sales dollars are necessary to generate a given amount of profit, profit (P) is simply added to fixed costs in the above formulas. In addition, if the firm has estimates of expected sales and fixed and variable costs, the selling price can be solved for.

---

reasons. First, cost approaches give little or no consideration to demand factors. For example, the price determined by markup or cost-plus methods has no necessary relationship to what people will be willing to pay for the product. In the case of rate-of-return pricing, little emphasis is placed on estimating sales volume. Even if it were, rate-of-return pricing involves circular reasoning since unit cost depends on sales volume but sales volume depends on selling price. Second, cost approaches fail to reflect competition adequately. Only in industries where all firms use this approach and have similar costs and markups can this approach yield similar prices and minimize price competition. Thus, in many industries, cost-oriented pricing could lead to severe price competition, which could eliminate smaller firms. Thus, although costs are a highly important consideration in price decisions, numerous other factors need to be examined.[7]

Product Consideration in Pricing

Although numerous product characteristics can affect pricing, three of the most important are (1) perishability; (2) distinctiveness; and (3) stage in the product life cycle.

---

[7] For an excellent discussion of problems and alternatives to cost-oriented pricing, see Joseph P. Guiltinan, "Risk Aversive Pricing Policies: Problems and Alternatives," *Journal of Marketing* 40 (January 1976), pp. 10–15.

Perishability.   Goods that are very perishable in a physical sense must be priced so as to promote sales without costly delays. Foodstuffs and certain types of raw materials tend to be in this category. Products can also be considered perishable in two other senses. High fashion, fad, and seasonal products are perishable not in the sense that the product deteriorates, but in the sense that demand for the product is confined to a specific time period. Perishability also relates to consumption rate, which means that some products are consumed very slowly, as in the case of consumer durables. Two important pricing considerations here are that (1) such goods tend to be expensive because large amounts of service are purchased at one time, and (2) the consumer has a certain amount of discretionary time available in making replacement purchase decisions.

Distinctiveness.   Products can be classified in terms of how distinctive they are. Homogeneous goods are perfect substitutes for each other, as in the case of bulk wheat or whole milk, while most manufactured goods can be differentiated on the basis of certain features such as package, trademark, engineering design, chemical features, and so forth. Thus, few consumer goods are perfectly homogeneous, and one of the primary marketing objectives of any firm is to make its product distinctive in the minds of buyers. Large sums of money are often invested to accomplish this task and one of the pay-offs for such investments is the seller's ability to charge higher prices for distinctive products. In the language of economics, the more distinctive a product is in the consumer's mind, the more inelastic is the price for the good. All this means is that all other things being equal, sellers can charge higher prices for more distinctive goods.

Life Cycle.   The stage of the life cycle that a product is in can have important pricing implications. With regard to the life cycle, two approaches to pricing are skimming and penetration price policies. A *skimming* policy is one in which the seller charges a relatively high price on a new product. Generally, this policy is used when the firm has a temporary monopoly and in cases where demand for the product is price inelastic. In later stages of the life cycle, as competition moves in and other market factors change, the price may then be lowered. Digital watches and calculators are recent examples of this. A *penetration* policy is one in which the seller charges a relatively low price on a new product. Generally, this policy is used when the firm expects competition to move in rapidly and where demand for the product is, at least in the short run, price elastic. This policy is also used to obtain large economies of scale and as a major instrument for rapid creation of a mass market. A low price and profit margin may also discourage competition. In later stages of the life cycle the price may have to be altered to meet changes in the market.

ENVIRONMENTAL INFLUENCES ON PRICING DECISIONS

Environmental influences on pricing decisions include variables which are uncontrollable by the marketing manager. Two of the most important of these are competition and government regulation.

Competition

In setting or changing prices, the firm must consider its competition and how competition will react to the price of the product. Initially, consideration must be given to such factors as:

1. Number of competitors.
2. Size of competitors.
3. Location of competitors.
4. Conditions of entry into the industry.
5. Degree of vertical integration of competitors.
6. Number of products sold by competitors.
7. Cost structure of competitors.
8. Historical reaction of competitors to price changes.

These factors help determine whether the firm's selling price should be at, below, or above competition. Pricing a product at competition, that is, the average price charged by the industry, is called "going rate pricing" and is popular for homogeneous products since this approach represents the collective wisdom of the industry and is not disruptive of industry harmony.[8] An example of pricing below competition can be found in sealed-bid pricing, where the firm is bidding directly against competition for project contracts. Although cost and profits are initially calculated, the firm attempts to bid below competitors in order to obtain the job contract. A firm may price above competition because it has a superior product or because the firm is the price leader in the industry. For example, U.S. Steel led in 11 of the 12 price increases in the steel industry between World War II and the 1960s, and thus could be considered the price leader.[9]

Government Regulations

Prices of certain goods and services are regulated by state and federal governments. Public utilities and transportation are examples of state regulation of prices. However, for most marketing managers, federal laws that make certain pricing practices illegal are of primary considera-

---

[8] Kotler, *Marketing Management*, p. 258.

[9] Kotler, *Marketing Management*, p. 259.

tion in pricing decisions. The list below is a summary of some of the more important legal constraints on pricing. Of course, since most marketing managers are not trained as lawyers, they usually seek legal counsel when developing pricing strategies to ensure conformity to state and federal legislation.

1. Price-fixing is illegal per se. Sellers must not make any agreements with (a) competitors or (b) distributors concerning the final price of the goods. The Sherman Antitrust Act is the primary device used to outlaw horizontal price fixing. Section 5 of the Federal Trade Commission has been used to outlaw price fixing as an "unfair" business practice.

2. Deceptive pricing practices are outlawed under Section 5 of the Federal Trade Commission Act. An example of deceptive pricing would be to mark merchandise with an exceptionally high price and then claim that the lower selling price actually used represents a legitimate price reduction.

3. Price discrimination that lessens competition or is deemed injurious to it is outlawed by the Robinson-Patman Act (which amends Section 2 of the Clayton Act). Price discrimination is not illegal per se, but sellers cannot charge competing buyers different prices for essentially the same products if the effect of such sales is injurious to competition. Price differentials can be legally justified on certain grounds, especially if the price differences reflect cost differences. This is particularly true of quantity discounts.

4. Basing-point pricing by members of an industry is generally illegal because such "delivered price" systems cannot be maintained without collusion. Such delivered price systems are not illegal per se, but if a firm uses a basing-point plan it must not conspire nor can it charge "phantom freight."[10]

5. Promotional pricing, such as cooperative advertising, and price deals are not illegal per se, but if a seller grants advertising allowances, merchandising service, free goods, or special promotional discounts to customers, it must do so on proportionately equal terms. Sections 2(d) and 2(e) of the Robinson-Patman Act are designed to regulate such practices so that price reductions cannot be granted to some customers under the guise of promotional allowances.

---

[10] Basing-point pricing refers to a situation where the buyer is charged a price f.o.b. the seller's plant. In the steel industry under the "Pittsburgh-plus" plan, buyers paid the mill price plus rail charges to the buyer's plant regardless of the actual point of shipment or actual freight cost. Thus, a Chicago manufacturer who purchased steel in Gary, Indiana, would pay freight from Pittsburgh even though the goods were shipped from Gary. This plan is now illegal.

A GENERAL PRICING DECISION MODEL

From what has been discussed thus far, it should be clear that effective pricing decisions involve the consideration of many factors and, depending on the situation, any of these factors can be the primary consideration in setting price. In addition, it is difficult to formulate an exact sequencing of when each factor should be considered. However, several general pricing decision models have been advanced with the clearly stated warning that all pricing decisions will not fit the framework. Below is one such model, which views pricing decisions as a nine-step sequence.

1. *Define market targets.* All marketing decision making should begin with a definition of segmentation strategy and the identification of potential customers.

2. *Estimate market potential.* The maximum size of the available market determines what is possible and helps define competitive opportunities.

3. *Develop product positioning.* The brand image and the desired niche in the competitive marketplace provide important constraints on the pricing decision as the firm attempts to obtain a unique competitive advantage by differentiating its product offering from that of competitors.

4. *Design the marketing mix.* Design of the marketing mix defines the role to be played by pricing in relation to and in support of other marketing variables, especially distribution and promotional policies.

5. *Estimate price elasticity of demand.* The sensitivity of the level of demand to differences in price can be estimated either from past experience or through market tests.

6. *Estimate all relevant costs.* While straight cost-plus pricing is to be avoided because it is insensitive to demand, pricing decisions must take into account necessary plant investment, investment in R&D, and investment in market development, as well as variable costs of production and marketing.

7. *Analyze environmental factors.* Pricing decisions are further constrained by industry practices, likely competitive response to alternative pricing strategies, and legal requirements.

8. *Set pricing objectives.* Pricing decisions must be guided by a clear statement of objectives that recognizes environmental constraints and defines the role of pricing in the marketing strategy while at the same time relating pricing to the firm's financial objectives.

9. *Develop the price structure.* The price structure for a given product can now be determined and will define selling prices for the product (perhaps in a variety of styles and sizes) and the discounts from list

price to be offered to various kinds of middlemen and various types of buyers.[11]

While all pricing decisions cannot be made strictly on the basis of this model, such an approach has three advantages for the marketing manager. First, it breaks the pricing decision into nine manageable steps. Second, it recognizes that pricing decisions must be fully integrated into overall marketing strategy. Third, it aids the decision maker by recognizing the importance of both qualitative and quantitative factors in pricing decisions.

CONCLUSION

Pricing decisions that integrate the firm's costs with marketing strategy, business conditions, competition, consumer demand, product variables, channels of distribution, and general resources can determine the success or failure of a business. This places a very heavy burden on the price maker. Modern day marketing managers cannot ignore the complexity or the importance of price management. Pricing policies must be continually reviewed and must take into account the fact that the firm is a dynamic entity operating in a very competitive environment. There are many ways for money to flow out of a firm in the form of costs, but there is often only one way to bring revenues in and that is by the price-product mechanism.

ADDITIONAL READINGS

Darden, Bill R. "An Operational Approach to Product Pricing." *Journal of Marketing* 32 (April 1968), pp. 29–33.

Dean, Joel. "The Role of Price in the American Business System." *Pricing: The Critical Decision.* A.M.A. Management Report No. 66. Chicago: American Management Association, pp. 5–11.

Fitzpatrick, Albert A. *Pricing Methods of Industry.* Boulder, Colo.: Pruett Press, Inc., 1969.

Green, Paul. "Bayesian Decision Theory in Pricing Strategy." *Journal of Marketing* 27 (January 1963), pp. 5–14.

Harper, Donald V. *Price Policy and Procedure.* New York: Harcourt, Brace and World, 1966.

Lynn, Robert A. *Price Policies and Marketing Management.* Homewood, Ill.: Richard D. Irwin, Inc., 1967.

Oxenfeldt, Alfred R. "Multi-Stage Approach to Pricing." *Harvard Business Review* 38 (July–August 1960), pp. 125–33.

---

[11] Frederick E. Webster, *Marketing for Managers* (New York: Harper and Row, Inc., 1974), pp. 178–79.

Oxenfeldt, Alfred R.   "A Decision-Making Structure for Price Decisions." *Journal of Marketing* 37 (January 1973), pp. 48–53.

Oxenfeldt, Alfred; Miller, David; Shuckman, Abraham; and Winick, Charles. *Insights into Pricing: From Operations Research and Behavioral Science.* Belmont, Calif.: Wadsworth Publishing Company, 1961.

Mulrichell, Donald F.; and Paranda, Stephen, eds.   *Price Policies and Practices: A Source Book in Readings.* New York: John Wiley and Sons, Inc., 1967.

Palda, Kristian S.   *Pricing Decisions and Marketing Policies.* Englewood Cliffs, N.J.: Prentice-Hall, Inc., 1971.

Reinmuth, James E., and Barnes, Jim D.   "A Strategic Competitive Bidding Approach to Pricing Decisions for Petroleum Industry Drilling Contractors." *Journal of Marketing Research* 12 (August 1975), pp. 362–65.

Stobough, Robert B., and Townsend, Phillip L.   "Price Forecasting and Strategic Planning: The Case of Petrochemicals." *Journal of Marketing Research* 12 (February 1975), pp. 19–29.

Tucker, Spencer A.   *Pricing for Higher Profit.* New York: McGraw-Hill, Inc., 1966.

Marketing in Special Fields

Chapter 11
The Marketing of Services

Chapter 12
International Marketing

11

THE MARKETING OF SERVICES

Since World War II the fastest growing segment of the American economy has not been the production of tangibles, but the performance of services. Spending on services has increased to such an extent that today it captures about 50 cents of the consumer's dollar. However, for the most part, the entire area of service marketing remains undefined or ill defined.

Unfortunately, many marketing textbooks also devote little, if any, attention to program development for the marketing of services.[1] This omission is usually based on the assumption that the marketing of goods and the marketing of services are the same, and therefore the techniques discussed under goods apply as well to the marketing of services. Basically, this assumption is true. Whether selling products or services, the marketer must be concerned with developing a marketing strategy centered around the four controllable decision variables that comprise the marketing mix: the product (or service), the price, the distribution

---

[1] Notable exceptions are Eugene M. Johnson, *An Introduction to the Problems of Service Marketing Management* (Newark, Del.: University of Delaware, Bureau of Economic and Business Research, 1964); Donald D. Parker, *The Marketing of Consumer Services* (Seattle, Wash.: University of Washington, Business Study Series, 1960); John Rathmell, *Marketing and the Service Sector* (Cambridge, Mass.: Winthrop Publishers, 1974); Philip Kotler, *Marketing for Nonprofit Organizations* (Englewood Cliffs, N.J.: Prentice-Hall, Inc., 1975); William J. Stanton, *Fundamentals of Marketing*, 5th ed. (New York: McGraw-Hill Book Co., 1978), chap. 24; Seymour Baranoff and James H. Donnelly, Jr., "Selecting Channels of Distribution for Services," in Victor P. Buell, ed., *Handbook of Modern Marketing* (New York: McGraw-Hill, Inc., 1970).

system, and promotion. In addition, the use of marketing research is as valuable to the marketer of services as it is to the marketer of goods.

However, because services possess certain distinguishing character-istics, the task of determining the marketing mix ingredients for a service marketing strategy may present different and more difficult problems than might appear at first glance. The purpose of this chapter is to acquaint the reader with the special problems of service marketing so that the material in the other chapters of the book can be integrated into a better understanding of the marketing of services.

Before proceeding, some attention must be given to what the authors refer to when using the term *services*. Probably the most frustrating aspect of the available literature on services is that the definition of what constitutes a service remains unclear. The fact is that no common definition and boundaries have been developed to delimit the field of services. The American Marketing Association has defined services as "activities, benefits, or satisfaction which are offered for sale, or are provided in connection with the sale of goods."[2] This definition lacks the precision needed for the purposes of this chapter, since it does not separate those services that are separate and identifiable activities from those services that exist only in connection with the sale of a product or another service. Such a delineation is needed for this chapter.

HIGHLIGHT 11–1

Kinds of Service Establishments

Barber shops	Photo studios
Equipment rental agencies	Nursery schools
Car washes	Truck and car rental agencies
Banks	Savings and loan associations
Health spas and gyms	Beauty salons
Radio, TV, and appliance repair shops	Automotive maintenance and re-pair shops (as well as the more specialized muffler shops and
Laundry (dry cleaning outlets—full service or self-service)	transmission centers)
Movie theaters	Country clubs
Amusement parks	Tax preparation services
Hotels and motels	Shoe-repair shops
Massage parlors	Dance studios
Campgrounds	Film-processing outlets

Source: Don L. James, Bruce J. Walker, and Michael J. Etzel, *Retailing Today* (New York: Harcourt Brace Jovanovich, Inc., 1975), p. 563.

---

[2] Committee on Definitions, *Marketing Definitions: A Glossary of Marketing Terms* (Chicago: American Marketing Association, 1960), p. 21.

Therefore, "services" will be defined here as "separately identifiable, intangible activities which provide want satisfaction, and which are not necessarily tied to the sale of a product or another service."[3] This definition includes such services as insurance, entertainment, airlines, and banking, but does not include such services as wrapping and delivery, because these services exist only in connection with the sale of a product or another service. This is not to suggest, however, that marketers of goods are not also marketers of services.

IMPORTANT CHARACTERISTICS OF SERVICES

Services possess several unique characteristics which often have a significant impact on marketing program development. These special features of services may cause unique problems and often result in marketing mix decisions that are substantially different from those found in connection with the marketing of goods. Some of the more important of these characteristics are intangibility, inseparability, perishability and fluctuating demand, highly differentiated marketing systems, and a client relationship.[4]

Intangibility

The obvious basic difference between goods and services is the intangibility of services, and many of the problems encountered in the marketing of services are due to this intangible nature. These problems are unique to service marketing.

The fact that many services cannot appeal to a buyer's sense of touch, taste, smell, sight, or hearing before purchase places a burden on the marketing organization. Obviously, it is most heavily felt in a firm's promotional program, but as will be discussed later, it may affect other areas as well. Depending on the type of service, the intangibility factor may dictate direct channels of distribution because of the need for personal contact between the buyer and seller. Since a service firm is actually selling an idea, not a product, it must tell the buyer what the service will do, since it is often unable to illustrate, demonstrate, or display the service in use. Such a situation obviously makes promotion difficult.

Inseparability

In many cases a service cannot be separated from the person of the seller. In other words, the service must often be created and marketed

---

[3] Stanton, *Fundamentals of Marketing*, p. 482.

[4] See Stanton, *Fundamentals of Marketing*, pp. 484–85; John R. Rathmell, "What Is Meant by Services?" *Journal of Marketing* 30 (October 1966), pp. 30–36.

simultaneously. Because of the simultaneous production and marketing of most services, the main concern of the marketer is usually the creation of time and place utility. For example, the barber produces the service of a haircut and markets it at the same time. Many services, therefore, are "tailored" and nonmass-produced.

The implications of inseparability for the selection of channels of distribution are important. Inseparable services cannot be inventoried and thus direct sale is the only feasibly channel of distribution. In fact, until recently, most service firms did not differentiate between the production and marketing of services and in many cases, viewed the two as equivalent.[5]

Some industries have been able to modify the inseparability characteristics. In such industries there may be a tangible representation of the service, such as a contract, by someone other than the producer. In other words, if tangible representations of the service are transferable, various middlemen such as agents can be utilized. The reader is probably most familiar with this in the marketing of insurance. The service itself remains inseparable from the seller, but the buyer has a tangible representation of the service in the form of a policy. This enables the use of middlemen in the marketing of insurance. Another example would be service contracts on equipment such as computers, or typewriters. However, often these are product-related in that they are sometimes tied to the actual sale of the tangible product. More will be said about the distribution of services later in the chapter.

Perishability and Fluctuating Demand

Services are perishable, and the markets for most services fluctuate by seasons and for many, even by day or week. Unused telephone capacity, electrical power, vacant seats on trains, buses, planes and in stadiums represent business that is lost forever. (Standby plans in air travel are an attempt at solving this type of problem).

The combination of perishability and fluctuating demand has created many problems for marketers of services. Specifically in the area of distribution, channels must be found in order to have the service available for peak periods and new channels must be developed to make use of the service during slack periods. Many firms are currently attempting to cope with the latter problem, and several innovations in the distribution of services have occurred in recent years. These will be discussed later in the chapter.

---

[5] Rathmell, *Marketing and the Service Sector,* p. 35.

Highly Differentiated Marketing Systems

Although the marketer of a tangible product is not compelled to use an established marketing system, such systems are often available and may be the most efficient. If an established system is not available, the marketer can at least obtain guidelines from the systems used for similar products. In the case of services, however, there may be little similarity between the marketing system needed and those used for other services. For example, the marketing of banking and other financial services bears little resemblance to the marketing of computer services or labor services. The entire area of service marketing, therefore, demands greater creativity and ingenuity on the part of marketing management.

Client Relationship

In the marketing of a great many services a client relationship exists between the buyer and seller as opposed to a customer relationship. Examples of this type of relationship would be the physician-patient and financial institution-investor relationship. The buyer abides by the suggestions or advice provided by the seller and these relationships may be of an ongoing nature. In addition, since many service firms are client-serving organizations, they may approach the marketing function in a more professional manner, as seen in health care, financial, legal, governmental, and educational services.

ROADBLOCKS TO INNOVATION IN SERVICE MARKETING

The factors of intangibility and inseparability make total comprehension of service marketing extremely difficult. However, in view of the size and importance of services in our economy, considerable innovation and ingenuity are needed to make these services available at convenient locations for consumers as well as business people. In fact, the area of services probably offers more opportunities for imagination and creative innovation with respect to distribution than do goods.

Unfortunately, in the past most service firms have lagged in the area of creative marketing.[6] Even those service firms that have done a relatively good marketing job have been extremely slow in recognizing opportunities for innovation in all aspects of their marketing programs. Four reasons have been given for this lack of innovative marketing on the part of service industries: (1) a limited view of marketing; (2) a lack

---

[6] See "Services Grow while the Quality Shrinks," *Business Week*, October 30, 1971, pp. 50–57.

of competition; (3) a lack of creative management; and (4) no obsolescence.[7]

Limited View of Marketing

Because of the nature of their service, many service firms depend to a great extent on population growth to expand sales. A popular example here is the telephone company, which did not establish a marketing department until 1955.[8] It was at that time that the company realized it had to be concerned not only with population growth but also with meeting the needs of a growing population. Increases in educational levels and rises in the standards of living also bring about the need for new and diversified services.

Service firms must meet these changing needs by developing new services, developing new channels and altering existing channels to meet the changing needs of the population. For many service industries, growth potential is limited unless more and new channels of distribution are found.

In terms of specific differences between manufacturing and service firms in handling marketing functions, a recent study found that service firms appear to be (1) generally less likely to have marketing mix activities carried out in the marketing department, (2) less likely to perform industry analysis, (3) more likely to handle their advertising internally rather than go to outside agencies, (4) less likely to have an overall sales plan, (5) less likely to develop sales training programs, (6) less likely to use marketing research firms and marketing consultants, and (7) less likely to spend as much on marketing when expressed as a percentage of gross sales.[9] These results clearly suggest that marketing activities are more limited and less well understood in the service sector.

Limited Competition

A second major cause of the lack of innovative marketing in many service industries is the lack of competition that exists in many of these industries. Many service industries, such as banking, railroads, and public utilities have, throughout their histories, faced very little competition; some have even been regulated monopolies. Obviously, in an environment characterized by little competition, there is not likely to be a great deal of innovative marketing. However, some service industries have

---

[7] Johnson, An Introduction to Problems, pp. 29–45.

[8] See Theodore Levitt, "Marketing Myopia," Harvard Business Review 38 (July–August 1960), pp. 45–56.

[9] William R. George and Hiram C. Barksdale, "Marketing Activities in the Service Industry," Journal of Marketing 38 (October 1974), pp. 65–70.

developed innovative marketing programs. Primary among those industries have been insurance companies and some financial institutions. Each of these industries has been actively seeking new and better ways to market their services. Many of these innovations will be discussed later in the chapter.

Noncreative Management

For many years the managements of service industries have been criticized for not being progressive and creative. Railroad managements were a prime example of an industry in dire need of creative management talent. More recently, however, railroads have been leading innovators in the field of freight transportation, introducing such innovations as piggyback service and containerization. Some other service industries, however, have been slow to develop new services or innovate in the marketing of their existing services as in the field of health care.

No Obsolescence

A great advantage for many service industries is the fact that many services, because of their intangibility, are less subject to obsolescence than goods. While this is an obvious advantage, it has also led some service firms to be sluggish in their approach to marketing. Manufacturers of goods may continually change their marketing plans and seek new and more efficient ways to distribute their product. Since service firms are often not faced with obsolescence, they have often failed to recognize the necessity for formal marketing planning. However, one area in which there is considerable evidence of innovation in service marketing is distribution.

INNOVATIONS IN THE DISTRIBUTION OF SERVICES

As was discussed in Chapter 9, the channel of distribution is viewed as the sequence of firms involved in moving a product from the producer to the user. The channel may be direct, as in the case where the manufacturer sells directly to the ultimate consumer, or it may contain one or more institutional middlemen. Some of the middlemen assume risks of ownership, some perform various marketing functions such as advertising, while others may perform nonmarketing or facilitating functions such as transporting and warehousing.[10]

Apparently using this concept as a frame of reference, most market-

---

[10] This section of the chapter is from James H. Donnelly, Jr., "Marketing Intermediaries in Channels of Distribution for Services," *Journal of Marketing* 40 (January 1976), pp. 55–57.

ing writers generalize that because of the intangible and inseparable nature of services, direct sale is the only possible channel for distributing most services. The only traditional indirect channel used involves one-agent middlemen. This channel is used in the distribution of such services as securities, housing, entertainment, insurance and labor. In some cases, individuals are trained in the production of the service and franchised to sell it as in the case of dance studios and employment agencies. They note that because they are intangible, services cannot be stored, transported, or inventoried; and since they cannot be separated from the person of the seller, they must be created and distributed simultaneously. Finally, because there is no physical product, traditional wholesalers and other intermediaries can rarely operate in such markets and retailing cannot be an independent activity. For these reasons, it is generally concluded that the geographic area in which most service marketers can operate is, therefore, restricted.

All of these generalizations are certainly true, using the concept of "channels of distribution" developed for goods. However, the practice of viewing the distribution of services using the framework developed for goods has severely limited thinking concerning their distribution. It has focused attention away from understanding the problem and identifying means to overcome the handicaps of intangibility and inseparability. Most importantly, however, it has led to a failure to distinguish conceptually between the production and distribution of services; hence, it supports the idea that services must be created and distributed simultaneously. This had resulted in a lack of attention to channel decisions for producers of services.

Marketing Intermediaries in the Distribution of Services

Despite traditional thinking concerning the distribution of services, channels of distribution have evolved in many service industries that use separate organizational entities as intermediaries between the producer and user of the service. These intermediaries play a variety of roles in making the services available to prospective users. Some examples from various service industries illustrate this point.

Financial. The retailer who extends a bank's credit to its customers is an intermediary in the distribution of credit. In the marketing of credit card plans, banks rely heavily on the retail merchant to assist in encouraging customers to apply for and use the cards. In fact, many banks have actually compensated merchants for various kinds of incentive credit card promotions. Thus, when retailers become part of a credit card plan they are, in effect, becoming intermediaries in the channel of distribution for credit.

In recent years the banking industry has been very active in developing new retail banking services, particularly those that use the technology of more sophisticated hardware and data processing systems. One of these, "direct pay deposit," permits employees to have their pay deposited directly into their checking account. By authorizing employers to deposit their pay, employees save a trip to the bank and avoid forgetting to make a deposit. They get a receipt from the employer and deposits are shown on their monthly bank statement. Bankers benefit by the reduced paperwork involved in the processing of checks. In the marketing of such plans banks obviously must rely heavily on employers to encourage employees to apply for the service. Thus, when an organization agrees to become part of such a plan, it becomes an intermediary in the distribution of a bank's service.

Health Care. The distribution of health care services is of vital concern today as the nation faces what has been widely described as a "delivery gap" in health care. In health care delivery the inseparability characteristic presents more of a handicap than in other service industries because users (patients) literally place themselves in the hands of the seller. However, although direct personal contact between producer and user is necessary, new and more efficient channels of distribution appear to be evolving.

While medical care is traditionally associated with the present solo-practice, fee-for-service system, several alternative delivery systems are being developed. One method that has received some attention is the health maintenance organization (HMO) concept.[11] This type of delivery system stresses the creation of group health care clinics using teams of salaried health practitioners (physicians, pharmacists, technicians, and so forth) that serve a specific enrolled membership on a prepaid basis.

The HMO is not a new method of producing health care. It does, however, perform an intermediary role between practitioner and patient. It increases availability and convenience by providing a central location and "one-stop shopping." For example, a member can visit a general practitioner for a particular ailment and undergo treatment by the appropriate specialist in the same visit. The HMO also assumes responsibility for arranging for or providing hospital care, emergency care, and preventive services. In addition, the prepaid nature of the program encourages more frequent preventive visits, while the traditional philosophy of medical care is primarily remedial. HMO programs have

----

[11] M. R. Greelick, "The Impact of Prepaid Group Insurance on American Medical Care: A Critical Evaluation," *Annals of the American Academy of Political and Social Science* 399 (January 1972), pp. 100–113.

inspired similar innovations in other phases of health care, such as dentistry.[12]

Insurance. The vending machines found in airports for aircraft accident insurance have been finding their way into other areas such as travel accident insurance, which is now available in many motel chains. Group insurance written through employers and labor unions has also been extremely successful. In each instance, the insurance industry has used intermediaries to distribute its services.

Communication. With growth potential basically limited to population growth since the mid-1950s, firms in the communication industry have sought ways to increase the availability and convenience of their services. One means has been the walk-up telephone. Companies or organizations that provide space for a walk-up phone serve as intermediaries for the telephone communication.

In each of the examples cited here, means of distribution were used that consisted of separate organizational entities between the producer of the service and the user for the purpose of making the service available. These intermediaries were not the traditional institutional middlemen that comprise the channel of distribution for goods. While the present goods-based concept of channel of distribution does not provide for this, the concept itself is not inadequate. Rather, the concept of "marketing intermediary" must be defined in the context of services. We propose that any extra-corporate entity between the producer of a service and prospective users that is utilized to make the service available and/or more convenient is a marketing intermediary for that service.

Implications for Service Marketers

Services must be made available to prospective users, and this implies distribution in the marketing sense of the word. The revised concept of the distribution of services appears to have at least two important implications for service marketers.

First, service marketers can and must distinguish conceptually between the production and distribution of services. The problem of making services more efficiently and widely available must not be ignored in favor of other elements of the marketing mix that are easier to deal with. For example, many service industries have been criticized for an "overdependence on advertising."[13] The problem of overdependence on

---

[12] See Richard C. Becherer," An Investigation of the Adoption Process Associated with an Innovative Dental Program" (DBA dissertation, University of Kentucky, 1974).

[13] For example, see Robert W. Haas, "The Missing Link in Bank Marketing," *Atlanta Economic Review* 24 (January–February 1974), pp. 35–39.

one or two elements of the marketing mix is one that service marketers cannot afford. The sum total of the marketing mix elements represents the total impact of the firm's marketing strategy. The slack created by severely restricting one element cannot be compensated for by heavier emphasis on another, since each element in the marketing mix is designed to address specific problems and achieve specific objectives.

Second, this discussion points out the critical role of product development in the distribution of services. It indicates that making services available is often a product development as well as a distribution problem. In several of the examples described, indirect distribution of the service was made possible because "products" were developed that included a tangible representation of the service. This facilitates the use of intermediaries, because the service can now be separated from the producer. Of course, the process might be reversed: intermediaries could be located and appropriate "products" developed.

For example, the bank credit card is a tangible representation of the service of credit, though it is not the service itself. As such, it has enabled banks to overcome the inseparability problem and use the retail merchant as an intermediary in the distribution of credit. The credit card has also made it possible for banks to expand their geographic markets by maintaining credit customers far outside their immediate trading areas, since it enables subscribers to maintain an "inventory" of the bank's credit for use at their convenience. The same is true for the HMO membership card. Members can be treated or hospitalized while away from home and still be covered by their HMO membership.

CONCLUSION

This chapter has dealt with the complex topic of service marketing. While the marketing of services has a good deal in common with the marketing of products, there are unique problems in the area that require highly creative marketing management skills. Many of the problems in the service area can be traced to the intangible and inseparable nature of services. However, considerable progress has been made in understanding and reacting to these difficult problems, particularly in the area of distribution. In view of the major role services play in our economy, it is important for marketing practitioners to better understand and appreciate the unique problems of service marketing.

ADDITIONAL READINGS

Berry, Leonard L., and Capaldini, L. A. *Marketing for the Bank Executive.* New York: Petrocelli Books, 1974.

Berry, Leonard L., and Donnelly, James H.   *Marketing for Bankers.* Washington, D.C.: American Bankers Association, 1975.

Durand, Richard M., Eckrich, Donald W., and Sprecher, C. Ronald.   "A New Approach to Bank Image Research." *Bank Marketing* 9 (December 1977), pp. 26–28.

Gitlow, Howard S.   "Abortion Services: Time for a Discussion of Marketing Policies." *Journal of Marketing* 42 (April 1978), pp. 71–82.

Hise, Richard T.   *Basic Product/Service Strategy.* New York: Petrocelli Books, 1977.

Judd, Robert C.   "The Case for Redefining Services." *Journal of Marketing* 28 (January 1964), pp. 58–59.

Kotler, Philip and Connor, Richard A., Jr.   "Marketing Professional Services." *Journal of Marketing* 41 (January 1977), pp. 71–76.

Levitt, Theodore   "Production-Line Approach to Service." *Harvard Business Review* 50 (September–October 1972), pp. 41–52.

Regan, William J.   "The Service Revolution." *Journal of Marketing* 27 (July 1963), pp. 57–62.

Zaltman, Gerald, and Vertinsky, Ilan.   "Health Service Marketing: A Suggested Model." *Journal of Marketing* 35 (July 1971), pp. 19–27.

12

INTERNATIONAL MARKETING

Since the end of World War II a growing number of U.S. corporations have transversed geographical boundaries and become truly multinational in character. These firms are increasing their investments of private capital in overseas divisions, branches, and subsidiaries at a rate of about 10 percent per year,[1] and it has been estimated that at least 5,000 American corporations operate in foreign nations.

These multinational firms have invested in foreign countries for the same basic reasons they invested capital in the domestic United States. These reasons vary from firm to firm, but most fall under the inter-related goals of (1) increasing long-term growth and profit prospects, (2) maximizing total sales revenue, and (3) improving overall market position. As domestic markets approach saturation, American firms look to foreign markets as outlets for surplus productive capacity and as potential sources of wider profit margins and returns on investments.

Basically, marketing abroad is the same as marketing at home. Regardless of which part of the world the firm sells in, the marketing program must still be built around a sound product or service that is properly priced, promoted, and distributed to a target market that has been carefully analyzed. In other words, the marketing manager has the same controllable decision variables in both domestic and nondomestic markets.

Although the development of a marketing program may be the same

---

[1] David S. R. Leighton, "The Internationalization of American Business—The Third Industrial Revolution," *Journal of Marketing* 34 (July 1970), pp. 3–6.

in either domestic or nondomestic markets, there may be special problems involved in the implementation of marketing programs in nondomestic markets. These problems often arise because of the environmental differences that exist among and within many nations. This is not to say that a firm does not operate in a cultural, political, and economic environment in its domestic market. What makes the task more difficult in international marketing is that the environment often is composed of elements unfamiliar to the marketing executive.

In this chapter marketing management in an international context will be examined and several potential marketing strategies for a multinational firm will be discussed. In examining each of these areas, the reader will find that a common thread—knowledge of the local cultural environment—appears to be a major prerequisite for success in each area.

ORGANIZING FOR INTERNATIONAL MARKETING

When compared with the tasks it faces at home, a firm attempting to establish an international marketing organization faces a much higher degree of risk and uncertainty. In a foreign market, management is often less familiar with the cultural, political, and economic situation, the institutional structure of the distribution network, potential competitors and their actions, and the reliability and validity of media and market data. Many of these problems are the result of conditions external to the firm while others arise as the result of internal management situations.

Problem Conditions: External

While numerous problems could be cited, attention here will focus on the ones U.S. firms most often face when entering foreign markets.

Cultural Misunderstanding. Differences in the cultural environment of foreign countries may be misunderstood or not even recognized because of the tendency for marketing managers to use their own cultural values as as frame of reference.[2] This tendency to rely on one's own cultural values has been called the major cause of many international marketing problems.[3]

---

[2] In a study of 30 companies, one researcher found that executives tended to find cultural concepts too fuzzy for day-to-day use, although many admitted that such concepts were important. See S. Watson Dunn, "The Case Study Approach in Cross-Cultural Research," *Journal of Marketing Research* 3 (February 1966), pp. 26–31.

[3] James A. Lee, "Cultural Analysis in Overseas Operations," *Harvard Business Review* 44 (March–April 1966), pp. 106–14.

Political Uncertainty. Governments are unstable in many countries and social unrest and even armed conflict must sometimes be reckoned with. Other nations are newly emerging and anxious to exert their independence. These and similar problems can greatly hinder a firm seeking to establish its position in a foreign market.

Import Restrictions. Tariffs, import quotas, and other types of import restrictions hinder international business. These are usually established to promote national self-sufficiency and can be a huge roadblock for the multinational firm.

Exchange Controls. Often a nation will establish limits on the amount of earned and invested funds that can be withdrawn from that nation. These exchange controls are usually established by nations that are experiencing balance-of-payment problems. Nevertheless, these and other types of currency regulations are important considerations in the decision to expand into a foreign market.

Ownership and Personnel Restrictions. In many nations, the governments have established requirements that the majority ownership of a company operating in that nation be held by nationals of the country. Other nations require that the majority of the personnel of a foreign firm be local citizens. Each of these restrictions can act as obstacles to foreign expansion.

Problem Conditions: Internal

Given the types of external problems just discussed, the reader can see that the external roadblocks to success in a foreign market are substantial. However, an early study conducted by the management consulting firm of Booz, Allen, and Hamilton revealed that firms also experience greater internal problems in the management of a multinational firm.[4] The study cited several major internal management problems.

Coordination. The firms studied reported problems in getting management to view the firm as a single integrated unit rather than viewing it in terms of a domestic organization with a separate international division. This was seen as a problem in the orientation of top executives.

Organization. As a result of the first problem, the firms reported organizational difficulties when the international division was established as a separate unit. This occurred because the international operation tended to become isolated and to be treated as a stepchild.

Control. Problems with organization and coordination will ultimately result in problems with control. Controlling the multinational

---

[4] *The Emerging World Enterprise* (New York: Booz, Allen, and Hamilton, Inc., 1962), pp. 12–15.

firm has probably received more attention than any other management problem in international business. This is because it encompasses (or is the result of) all of the other management problems. The question that arises is: should managerial control be *centralized* at corporate headquarters or should it be vested in *decentralized* foreign locations?

This important management question has been explored from many viewpoints. For example, one viewpoint states that local personnel employed by a multinational firm may prefer authoritarian control, because of their cultural background and environment. For this reason it is suggested that the firm centralize its overseas activities as much as possible. Support for a centralized organization was also recommended by two writers who studied the changes that took place in organizational patterns when a firm became a world enterprise. They comment that:

> The really decisive point in the transition to world enterprise is top management recognition that to function effectively, the ultimate control of strategic planning and policy decisions must shift from decentralized subsidiaries or division locations to corporate headquarters . . .[5]

However, when examining the marketing organization of the multinational firm, other writers have suggested that these particular operations must be decentralized. The common rationale appears to be that the need for specific knowledge of local customs, buying habits, traditions, and mores, and the general need to adapt to a variety of foreign cultures and market environments make decentralized control of advertising and marketing decisions necessary.[6] Yet, even within the area of marketing one can find much disagreement. In an address before the New York Chapter of the International Advertising Association, one executive commented that because of their overconcern with cultural factors, the managements of many United States' parent corporations too frequently leave important advertising and marketing decisions in the hands of inexperienced nationals. As a result, the overseas affiliates do not realize their potential in marketing. Thus, greater centralization of advertising and marketing decisions was called for.

The crux of the disagreement regarding the type of marketing organization appears to be the extent to which cultural differences exist among peoples of the world and the importance of these differences in international marketing decisions. In one study, it was found that there

---

[5] Gilbert H. Clee and Wilbur M. Sachtjen, "Organizing a World-Wide Business," *Harvard Business Review* 42 (November–December 1964), p. 67.

[6] See Charles R. Williams, "Regional Management Overseas," *Harvard Business Review* 45 (January–February 1967), pp. 87–91; and Alberta R. Edwards, "Organizing for International Marketing Information," in S. Watson Dunn, *International Handbook of Advertising* (New York: McGraw-Hill, Inc., 1964), pp. 79–81.

was a relationship between management's attitude toward the importance of culture and whether the firm's marketing organization was centralized or decentralized. In the majority of firms in which foreign market decisions were decentralized, management felt that cultural differences were significant and should weigh heavily in a firm's international marketing decisions. In the remaining firms which had centralized marketing and advertising decisions, management placed significantly less importance on cultural differences among people.[7] In general, there seems to be a tendency to centralize financial and research activities, while permitting much local control of marketing, production, personnel, and purchasing decisions.[8]

PROGRAMMING FOR INTERNATIONAL MARKETING

In this section of the chapter the major areas in developing an international marketing program will be examined. As was mentioned at the outset, marketing managers must organize the same controllable decision variables that exist in domestic markets. However, many firms that have been extremely successful in marketing in the United States have not been able to duplicate their success in foreign markets.

International Marketing Research

Because the risks and uncertainties are so high, marketing research is equally important, and probably more so, in foreign markets than in domestic markets. In attempting to analyze foreign consumers and industrial markets, at least three important dimensions must be considered.

Population Characteristics. Obviously, population is one of the major components of a market, and significant differences exist between and within foreign countries. The marketing manager must not only be familiar with the total population, but also the regional, urban, rural, and interurban distribution. Other demographic variables such as the number and size of families, education, occupation, and religion are also

---

[7] James H. Donnelly, Jr., "Attitudes toward Culture and Approach to International Advertising," *Journal of Marketing* 34 (July 1970), pp. 60–63.

[8] *The Emerging World Enterprise*, p. 15. For additional discussion of the internal problems in multinational firms, see R. J. Aylmer, "Who Makes Marketing Decisions in the Multinational Firm?" *Journal of Marketing* 34 (October 1970), pp. 25–30; David Gestetner, "Strategy in Managing International Sales," *Harvard Business Review* 52 (September–October 1974), pp. 103–8; J. William Widing, Jr., "Reorganizing Your Worldwide Business," *Harvard Business Review* 51 (May–June 1973), pp. 153–60; Howard V. Perlmutter and David A. Heenan, "How Multinational Should Your Top Managers Be?" *Harvard Business Review* 52 (November–December 1974), pp. 121–32.

important. In many markets, these variables can have a significant impact on the success of a firm's marketing program. For example, in the United States a cosmetics firm can be reasonably sure of the desire to use cosmetics being almost universal among women of all income classes. However, in Latin America the same firm may be forced to segment its market by upper-, middle-, and lower-income groups, as well as by urban and rural areas. This is because upper-income women want high-quality cosmetics promoted in prestige media and sold through exclusive outlets. In some rural and less prosperous areas, the cosmetics must be inexpensive while in other rural areas, women do not accept cosmetics. Even in markets that are small in geographical area, consumers may differ in many of the variables mentioned. Any one or set of such differences may have a strong bearing on consumers' ability and willingness to buy.

Ability to Buy. In attempting to assess the ability of consumers in a foreign market to buy, four broad measures should be examined: (1) gross national product or per capita national income, (2) distribution of income, (3) rate of growth in buying power, and (4) extent of available financing.[9] Since each of these vary in different areas of the world, the marketing opportunities available must be examined closely.

Willingness to Buy. The cultural framework of consumer motives and behavior is integral to the understanding of the foreign consumer. Cultural values and attitudes toward the material culture, social organizations, the supernatural, aesthetics, and language should be analyzed for their possible influence on each of the elements in the firm's marketing program. It is easy to see that such factors as the group's values concerning acquisition of material goods, the role of the family, the positions of men and women in society, as well as the various age groups and social classes will all have an effect on marketing because each influences consumer behavior, values, and the overall pattern of life.

In some areas there appears to be a convergence of tastes and habits, with different cultures becoming more and more integrated into one homogeneous culture although still separated by national boundaries. This appears to be the case in Western Europe where there are encouraging signs that European consumers are developing into a mass market.[10] This obviously will simplify the task for a marketer in this region.

---

[9] John Fayerweather, *International Marketing*, 2d ed. (Englewood Cliffs, N.J.: Prentice-Hall, Inc., 1970).

[10] For representative views of this point, see Arthur C. Fatt, "The Danger of Local International Advertising," *Journal of Marketing* 31 (January 1967), pp. 60–62; and Ilmar Roostal, "Standardization of Advertising for Western Europe," *Journal of Marketing* 26 (October 1963), pp. 15–20. Also see John K. Ryans and Claudia Fry, "Some European Attitudes on the Advertising Transference Question: A Research Note," *Journal of Advertising* 5 (Spring 1976), pp. 11–13.

However, cultural differences still prevail among most areas of the world and strongly influence consumer behavior.

HIGHLIGHT 12–1

Behavioral Differences

He (the American businessman) should understand that the various peoples around the world have worked out and integrated into their subconscious literally thousands of behavior patterns that they take for granted in each other. Then when the stranger enters, and behaves differently from the local norm he often quite unintentionally insults, annoys, or amuses the native with whom he is attempting to do business.

Source: Edward T. Hall, "The Silent Language in Overseas Business," *Harvard Business Review* 38 (May–June 1960), p. 87.

Product Planning for International Markets

Before a firm can market a product, there must be something to sell —a product or a service. From this standpoint, product planning is the starting point for the entire marketing program. Once this is accomplished, management can then determine whether there is an adequate market for the product and can decide how the product should be marketed. Most firms would not think of entering a domestic market without extensive product planning. Unfortunately, this is often not the case with foreign markets. Often firms will enter foreign markets with the same product sold in the United States or at best one with only minor changes. In many cases, these firms have encountered serious problems. An example of such a problem occurred after World War II when American manufacturers began to export refrigerators to Europe. The firms exported essentially the same models sold in the United States. However, the refrigerators were the wrong size, shape, and temperature range for some areas and had weak appeal in others, thus failing miserably.[11] Although adaptation of the product to local conditions may have eliminated this failure, this adaptation is easier said than done. For example, even in the domestic market, overproliferation of product varieties and options can dilute economies of scale. This dilution result in high production costs, which may make the price of serving each market segment with an "adapted" product prohibitive. The answer to this question is not easy. In some cases, changes can be made

---

[11] See E. J. Tangerman, "Where Mass Design Failed," *Product Engineering* (December 1965), pp. 78–82.

HIGHLIGHT 12–2

Opportunities for Product Planning

Although potential opportunities for invention in international marketing are legion, the number of instances where companies have responded is disappointedly small. For example, there are an estimated 600 million women in the world who still scrub their clothes by hand. The women have been served by soap and detergent companies for decades, yet only last year did one of these companies attempt to develop an inexpensive *manual* washing machine.

The effort was launched by the vice president of Marketing-Worldwide of Colgate Palmolive who asked the leading inventor of modern mechanical washing processes to consider "inventing backwards . . ." The device developed by the inventor is an inexpensive (price under $10), all plastic hand-power washer . . . and is reported to have been very favorably received in Mexican test markets.

Source: Warren J. Keegan, "Five Strategies for Multinational Marketing," *European Business*, January 1970, p. 38.

---

rather inexpensively, while in others the sales potential of the particular market may not warrant extensive product changes. In any case, management must examine these problems carefully to avoid foreign marketing failures.

International Distribution System

The role of the distribution network in facilitating the transfer of goods and titles and in the demand stimulation process is as important in foreign markets as it is at home. Figure 12–1 illustrates some of the most common channel arrangements in international marketing. The continuum ranges from no control to almost complete control of the distribution system by manufacturers.

The channel arrangement where manufacturers have the least control is shown at the left of Figure 12–1. These are the most indirect channels of distribution. Here manufacturers sell to resident buyers, export agents, or export merchants located in the United States. In reality these are similar to domestic sales since all of the marketing functions are assumed by the middlemen.[12]

---

[12] The manufacturer does have slightly more control over the export agent than the resident buyer or export merchant, since the export agent does not take title to the goods.

FIGURE 12–1
Common Distribution Channels for International Marketing

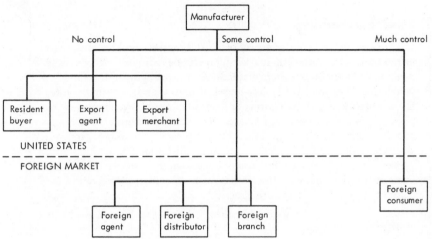

Manufacturers become more directly involved and hence have greater control over distribution when agents and distributors located in foreign markets are selected. Both perform similar functions except that agents do not assume title to the manufacturers' products while distributors do. If manufacturers should assume the functions of foreign agents or distributors and establish their own foreign branch, they greatly increase control over their international distribution system. Manufacturers' effectiveness will then depend on their own administrative organization rather than independent intermediaries. If the foreign branch sells to other intermediaries such as wholesalers and retailers, as is the case with most consumer goods, manufacturers again relinquish some control. However, since the manufacturers are located in the market area, they have greater potential to influence these intermediaries.

The channel arrangement that enables manufacturers to exercise a great deal of control is shown at the right of Figure 12–1. Here manufacturers sell directly to industrial users or ultimate consumers. This arrangement is most common in the sale of industrial goods.

Pricing for International Marketing

In domestic markets pricing is an extremely complex task often involving a great deal of trial and error. The basic approaches used in price determination in foreign markets are the same as those discussed earlier in the chapter on pricing. However, the pricing task is often more

---

HIGHLIGHT 12–3

Retailing in Australia

One somewhat singular aspect of Australian retailing lends support to the thesis that American marketing methods will work effectively in Australia. At times, the transplanted American might be forgiven for wondering if he had really left home. Woolworth and Penney stores stand close by on the main street of Brisbane. In Sydney, shoppers may patronize Macy's where "It's smart to be thrifty." There are many opportunities in other parts of Australia for housewives to buy groceries at Big Bear, Food Fair, Safeway, and Stop-and-Shop.

Yet, none of these retailers has any connection or ever has had with firms of the same name in the United States . . . Australian retailers are convinced that such names are effective.

Source: John S. Ewing, "Marketing in Australia," *Journal of Marketing* 26 (April 1962), pp. 54–58.

---

complicated in foreign markets because of additional problems with tariffs, taxes, and currency conversion.

Import duties are probably the major constraint for foreign marketers and will undoubtedly be encountered in all markets. Management must decide whether import duties will be paid by the firm, by the foreign consumer, or shared by both. This and similar constraints may force the firm to abandon an otherwise desirable pricing strategy or may force the firm out of a market altogether.

Another pricing problem arises because of the rigidity in price structures found in many foreign markets. The fact is that many foreign middlemen are not aggressive in their pricing policies. They often prefer to maintain high unit margins at the expense of low sales volume, rather than develop large sales volume by means of lower prices and smaller margins per unit. Many times this rigidity is engendered by legislation that prevents retailers from cutting prices substantially at their own discretion.[13] These are only a few of the pricing problems encountered by foreign marketers. Clearly, the marketer must be aware of such constraints prior to entering the market area.

International Advertising

Probably no other element in the marketing program has received more attention in recent years than international advertising. In 1963,

---

[13] William J. Stanton, *Fundamentals of Marketing*, 5th ed. (New York: McGraw-Hill, Inc., 1978), p. 511.

approximately one fourth of the international billings of U.S. advertising agencies were in areas other than Europe. By 1967, this figure increased to approximately 45 percent.[14] This indicates that United States firms are advertising in more areas of the world and attempting to communicate in a greater variety of cultures. In addition, total advertising expenditures by American firms in foreign countries doubled from 1957 to 1967 to over one billion dollars per year.[15]

When expanding their operations into the world marketplace, most firms are aware of the language barriers that exist and realize the importance of translating their messages into the proper idiom. However, there are numerous other issues that must be resolved such as (1) selecting media in foreign markets, (2) the selection of advertising agencies, and (3) the question of whether or not to use standardized advertisements multinationally.

The more countries and regions in which the firm advertises, the more complex media selection becomes when local or regional media are used. Since only 10 percent of U.S. advertising agency billings for foreign ads are in international editions of U.S. publications, such as Reader's Digest, it appears that the greatest proportion of foreign advertising expenditures of U.S. firms are in foreign media.[16] Often the media that are traditionally used in the domestic market are not available in foreign markets. If they are available, they may be so on a limited basis only or they may not reach the potential buyers. For example, one firm was forced to use sound trucks or roving movie vans to reach potential buyers in the Sub-Sahara area of Africa.[17] In addition to the problem of availability, other difficulties arise because of the lack of accurate media information. There is no rate and data service or media directory that covers all the media available throughout the world. Where data is available, its accuracy is often questionable.

Another important promotion decision that must be made is the type of agency used to prepare and place the firm's advertisements. There are two major approaches. The first is to use a local agency in each area where the advertisement is to appear. The rationale for this approach is that a local agency employing local nationals can better adapt the firm's message to the local culture. The other approach is to use a U.S. based international agency with overseas branches in the general area where the advertisement is to appear. Much discussion has developed over which approach is best, and one study of the na-

---

[14] Gorden E. Miracle, "International Billings of U.S. Agencies," The International Advertiser 8 (May–June 1967), p. 13.

[15] Dan Smith, "The Mixed-Up World of Advertising," International Management 22 (July 1967), p. 46.

[16] Miracle, "International Billings," p. 13.

[17] Charles J. Omana, "Advertising to the African Market," The International Advertiser 5 (October 1964), p. 8.

tion's largest firms found almost equal numbers using each approach.[18]

A controversy has also developed over the possible effectiveness of using identical advertisements (except for translation) on a worldwide basis. This controversy intensified since the success several years ago of the ESSO "Put a tiger in your tank" worldwide campaign. The disagreement appears to center around the extent to which cultural differences exist among peoples of the world and the importance of these differences in international marketing decisions. One group feels that people around the globe are basically the same and that traditional advertising appeals can be effective in any market.[19] Another group is strongly opposed to the use of standardized advertising because they believe that the cultural barriers are insurmountable.[20] A study among large firms found that the majority of the firms did not make extensive use of standardized advertisements.[21]

HIGHLIGHT 12–4

Culture and International Advertising

Maxwell House's advertising appeal, "America's Finest Coffee," worked well in Germany, but flopped in the Netherlands since the Dutch have been roasting coffee for three centuries and considered Americans amteurs at it.

An advertising director in Chile was irritated by the number of ads prepared outside of Chile showing palm trees, men wearing big hats, and Indians riding burros. Such scenes are not found in Chile.

A leading cosmetics manufacturer from the United States was stopped just before entering the Near East market with finely illustrated folders in Arabic showing the Venus de Milo. He was unaware that in Arab countries cut-off hands denote a convicted thief.

In Latin America, it is the hen and not the goose which lays the golden egg and a cat has only seven lives, not nine.

Source: Cited in Franklin R. Root, *Strategic Planning for Export Marketing* (Scranton: International Textbook Co., 1966), p. 93.

---

[18] Donnelly, "Attitudes toward Culture," p. 61.

[19] For examples see Fatt, "The Danger of Local International Advertising," p. 62; and Norton B. Leo, "Creative Strategy for International Advertising," in S. Watson Dunn, *International Handbook of Advertising* (New York: McGraw-Hill, Inc., 1964), pp. 181–82.

[20] See J. M. Lenormand, "Is Europe Ripe for the Integration of Advertising?" *The International Advertiser* 5 (March 1964), p. 14.

[21] James H. Donnelly, Jr. and John K. Ryans, Jr., "Standardized Global Advertising: A Call as yet Unanswered," *Journal of Marketing* 33 (April 1969), pp. 57–60. Further discussion of the standardization issue can be found in Robert D. Buzzell, "Can You Standardize Multinational Marketing" *Harvard Business Review* 46 (November–December 1968), pp. 102–13.

STRATEGIES FOR INTERNATIONAL MARKETING

Although the task of international marketing is similar to that at home, there are areas where significant differences arise which can have an important influence on the outcome of a marketing program. These differences must be considered when developing alternative marketing strategies for foreign markets. One approach to this problem involves five alternative strategies for marketing abroad.[22] Each of these strategies is based on the idea of adapting either the product or the communications appeal, or both, to the particular market.

Strategy One: Same Product, Same Message Worldwide

This approach involves a uniform strategy for each market, offering the same product and same advertising appeals. Obviously, this approach has numerous advantages. It is simple, demands on management time are minimal, and it requires no original analysis or data generation. The product is unchanged, so there are opportunities for economies of scale in production as well as marketing. In sum, it is the lowest cost strategy.

Unfortunately, the uniform strategy does not work for all products, although some firms such as Pepsi-Cola and Coca-Cola have been successful using this strategy. Other firms such as Chrysler and some food product manufacturers have not been successful with the uniform approach. These firms have been forced to adapt their marketing mix.

Strategy Two: Same Product, Different Communications

This strategy becomes necessary when the product fills a different need or is used differently but under conditions similar to those in the domestic market. Thus, the only adjustment necessary is in marketing communications. Examples of products where this strategy can be used are bicycles and motorcycles. In the United States they fill a recreation need, while in many parts of the world they serve as basic transportation.

Since the product remains unchanged, this strategy is also a relatively low-cost alternative. Additional costs would be incurred in identifying

---

[22] This section is based upon Warren J. Keegan, "Five Strategies for Multinational Marketing," *European Business* (January 1970), pp. 35–40. Also see Warren J. Keegan, "Multinational Product Planning: Strategic Alternatives," *Journal of Marketing* 33 (January 1969), pp. 58–62; William V. Rapp, "Strategy Formulation and International Competition," *Columbia Journal of World Business* (Summer 1973), pp. 98–112; Yoram Wind, Susan P. Douglas, and Howard V. Perlmutter, "Guidelines for Developing International Marketing Strategies," *Journal of Marketing* 37 (April 1973), pp. 14–23.

different product functions and reformulating the advertising and other communications.

Strategy Three: Different Product, Same Communications

This strategy involves a uniform approach to communications with the product being adapted to local conditions. This strategy assumes that the product will serve the same function in the foreign market but under different use conditions.

Esso used this strategy when it adapted its gasoline formulations to meet specific weather conditions prevailing in different markets. However, its standardized global campaign used the same basic message, "Put a tiger in your tank."

Strategy Four: Different Product, Different Communications

This strategy involves adapting both the product and the communications to local conditions. This is necessary because of different market conditions or because the product serves different functions.

Nescafe was forced to use this strategy in England when its instant coffee, which sold well in Europe, did poorly in England. Thus, a special blend was developed for England. When marketing the new blend, it was found that coffee was viewed as a nontraditional drink since tea was the traditional drink. The firm was thus forced to develop special advertisements emphasizing that coffee was for the young person looking for something different.

Strategy Five: Product Invention

When customer needs and conditions under which the product is used are in no way similar to the domestic market, then this strategy may be necessary. This involves the invention or development of an entirely new product designed to satisfy specific customer needs at a price within reach of the consumer. This strategy may be necessary in the less developed areas of the world. While it is often costly to pursue this strategy, it may be a rewarding one for the mass markets in the less developed nations of the world. The discussion of the hand-powered, plastic washing machine cited earlier in the chapter is an example of this strategy. Figure 12–2 summarizes the five strategies.

The choice of a particular strategy will, of course, depend upon the specific product-market-company mix. Depending on the area of the world under consideration and the particular product, different degrees of adaptation of the product and/or communications may be necessary. Some markets may require little change if similar to the home market.

FIGURE 12–2
Multinational Product-Communication Mix: Strategic Alternatives

Product Strategy	Communications Strategy	Product Examples	Product Function or Need Satisfied	Conditions of Product Use
1. Same	Same	Soft drinks, automobiles	Same	Same
2. Same	Different	Bicycles, recreation, transportation	Different	Same
3. Different	Same	Gasoline, detergents	Same	Different
4. Different	Different	Clothing, greeting cards	Different	Different
5. Invention	Develop new communications	Hand-powered washing machine	Same	Different

Others may require some adaptation of both product and/or communications while still others may require a specially made product. Whatever the case, each decision should be based on a complete product-market analysis.

CONCLUSION

The future of international marketing looks bright. In fact, many people see the day when there will be truly a "world market." While this day may be far into the future, the trends all appear to aim in that direction. This is why American firms are becoming more internationally minded and are in agreement that many marketing opportunities and challenges of the future lie in international marketing.

ADDITIONAL READINGS

Arensberg, Conrad M., and Niehoff, Arthur H.   *Introducing Social Change.* Chicago: Aldine Publishing Co., 1964.

Cunningham, William H.; Moore, Russell M.; and Cunningham, Isabella C. M.   "Urban Markets in Industrializing Countries: The Sao Paulo Experience." *Journal of Marketing* 38 (April 1974), pp. 2–12.

Hall, Edward T.   *The Silent Language.* New York: Doubleday and Co., 1959.

Lauter, G. Peter, and Dickie, Paul M.   "Multinational Corporations in Eastern European Socialist Economies." *Journal of Marketing* 39 (October 1975), pp. 40–46.

Miracle, Gordon E., and Albaum, Gerald S.   *International Marketing Management.* Homewood, Ill.: Richard D. Irwin, Inc., 1970.

Walker, Bruce J., Etzel, Michael J.   "The Internationalization of U.S. Franchise Systems: Progress and Procedures." *Journal of Marketing* 37 (April 1973), pp. 38–46.

Walters, J. Hart, Jr.   "Marketing in Poland in the 1970s: Significant Progress," *Journal of Marketing* 39 (October 1975), pp. 47–51.

Marketing Response to a Changing Society

Chapter 13
Marketing and Society

13

MARKETING AND SOCIETY

The primary concern of this chapter is the role of marketing in society. Basically, there are two issues involved. The first issue deals with the responsibility marketing and marketers have to society. In examining this issue, three subtopics will be discussed: (1) the societal concept of marketing; (2) marketing ethics; and (3) consumerism. The second issue deals with the boundaries of marketing and is concerned with the extent to which marketing is involved in our society.

MARKETING'S SOCIAL RESPONSIBILITY

Because business is essentially a social activity, marketing has a very critical social responsibility. Fulfilling this responsibility is both an ethical and practical matter. As an ethical matter, business and marketing have a responsibility to abide by society's laws, whether written or unwritten. As a practical matter, attracting and keeping a profitable customer franchise is a difficult task and failure to fulfill social responsibilities can result in the loss of corporate image as well as customers. Of all the business functions, marketing is most often criticized for failing to fulfill social responsibilities.[1]

The turbulent decade of the 1960s witnessed an articulate generation of young people attacking the so-called establishment. A large share of

---

[1] For an insightful discussion of the source of much of this criticism of marketing, see Robert L. Steiner, "The Prejudice against Marketing," *Journal of Marketing* 40 (July 1976), pp. 2–9.

this attack was directed at big business. These criticisms cut across an entire spectrum of issues—economic, social, political, and ethical. Neil Jacoby has studied the problem and provided a meaningful summary of the criticisms leveled at contemporary big business in America.[2]

Thesis 1. Big business corporations exercise concentrated economic power contrary to the public interest.

Thesis 2. Big business corporations exercise concentrated political power contrary to the public interest.

Thesis 3. Big businesses are controlled by a self-perpetuating, irresponsible power-elite.

Thesis 4. Big corporate businesses exploit and dehumanize workers and customers.

Thesis 5. Big corporate businesses degrade the environment and the quality of life.

A careful review of the above five propositions will reveal that their scope is very broad and societal in nature; also no one thesis is exclusively an attack on marketing practices. Nevertheless, each thesis, if analyzed carefully, can be said to have some marketing dimension to it, either directly or indirectly. Thus, it is not so much the issue as to whether big business and marketing are being maligned by critics; the critical issue is what should marketers do to get their "house in order" as a means of better serving not only individual consumers, but society as a whole.

Societal Concept

The 1960s might be designated as the decade of the marketing concept and it is likely that future historians will view the 1970s as the beginning of another orientation to marketing called the "societal concept of marketing."[3] "Like the marketing concept, the societal concept of marketing recognizes profit as a major business motive and counsels the firm to market goods and services that will satisfy consumers under circumstances that are fair to consumers and that enable them to make intelligent purchase decisions, and counsels firms to avoid marketing practices that have negative consequences for society."[4] It should be pointed out that many business firms are resisting the societal concept

---

[2] Neil Jacoby, *Corporate Power and Social Responsibility* (New York: Macmillan Publishing Co., Inc., 1973), chap. 1.

[3] George Schwartz, "Marketing: The Societal Concept," *University of Washington Business Review*, Autumn 1971, pp. 31–33.

[4] Ibid., p. 32.

because it requires changes in business conduct and marketing strategies that involve costs without yielding visible incremental profits.

It should also be mentioned that the societal concept of marketing is, to some extent, at odds with the so-called laissez faire business ethic, which is still the guiding philosophy of many business executives. Unfortunately, these executives have not recognized that our "free enterprise system" can no longer be equated with laissez faire capitalism. Instead large and small corporations alike must manage their affairs in a politico-economic environment that is not only subject to the pressures of competition but is also highly constrained by antitrust laws, trade regulations, governmental agencies, consumer groups, and so forth. One might describe this situation as "managed capitalism."

HIGHLIGHT 13–1

The Profit Concept?

It is high time to dispel the ancient notion that business is concerned solely with profits, and the modern accusation that our large corporations are pursuing the maximization of profits at the actual expense of social progress and reform.

Adam Smith made the point well when he said some 200 years ago that "The wise and virtuous man is at all times willing that his private interests should be sacrificed to the public interest."

Source: Anthony G. DeLorenzo, vice president, General Motors, Speech at University of Notre Dame, November 5, 1970.

The societal concept of marketing is closely related to another concept, namely "social marketing." This term in the present context has at least two meanings. Here it can be defined as "that branch of marketing concerned with the uses of marketing knowledge, concepts and techniques to enhance social ends as well as the social consequences of marketing policies, decisions and actions."[5] The term *social marketing* is also used in another and closely related sense where the focus is on the marketing of social goods, ideas, or causes. For example, "Social marketing is the design, implementation, and control of programs calculated to influence the acceptability of social ideas and involving consideration of

---

[5] William Lazer and Eugene Kelley, *"Social Marketing: Perspectives and Viewpoints* (Homewood, Ill.: Richard D. Irwin, Inc., 1973), pp. 4–5: Also see David J. Luck, "Social Marketing: Confusion Compounded," *Journal of Marketing* 38 (October 1974), pp. 70–72.

product planning, pricing, communication, distribution and marketing research."[6] Although there is clearly some ambiguity in these definitions, the point to be made is that marketing is now viewed as something more than a business activity. As such, it is considered to have more involvement with and greater responsibility to society.

Marketing Ethics

There are many definitions of ethics and there are many viewpoints of what constitutes ethical behavior. In an organizational framework, it is reasonable to define ethics as a discipline of standards and practical judgment and questions relative to those standards.[7] Marketing managers are confronted with a set of ethical standards imposed on them by society through legislation. They are also constrained by policies established by top-level planners in their own organizations. Aside from these two major constraints, however, marketing managers have a good deal of freedom to operate according to a wide range of ethical codes. Behavior in most cases is guided by so-called "situation ethics," where moral decisions are made in the context of a particular set of facts. In other words, marketing managers apply their own ethical principles or rules to each particular situation.

This general discussion of ethical viewpoints is not intended to provide the reader with solutions. If anything, the objective is to raise questions which must be faced by marketers. Perhaps if the reader understands the questions, then the problem is well on its way to being resolved. With this in mind, a few key questions that all marketing managers have to face are listed below.

1. What are the goals of the marketing program and do they conflict with the goals of society?
2. What is the morality of a product strategy such as planned obsolescence?
3. What is the morality of using deceptive advertising techniques to manipulate consumer groups such as children or the uneducated poor?
4. Should ethical criteria be established for salespeople and then pressure exerted to tempt salespeople to violate these standards?
5. Should the company's ethical standards for its product be no higher than the law requires even though this legal minimum does not eliminate all the known dangers connected with product use?

---

[6] Philip Kotler and Gerald Zaltman, "Social Marketing: An Approach to Planned Social Change," *Journal of Marketing* 35 (July 1971), pp. 5–12.

[7] Robert Bartels, "A Model for Ethics in Marketing," *Journal of Marketing* 31 (January 1967), p. 20.

Consumerism

One result of the perceived social irresponsibility of corporations is consumerism. Although no one definition will suffice, it is important to first clarify the concept in the form of a working definition. The following is offered: Consumerism is a political, economic, and social movement aimed at promoting and protecting the rights of buyers and the consuming public.

This definition implies several things. First, that the consumerism movement is not merely an economic or marketing issue. Second, that buyers and the consuming public have some basic rights which originate in various laws, systems of ethics, and the American tradition. Finally it implies that sellers or producers have significant market power along with obligations to use that power wisely. The power referred to here includes many things. For example:

1. Sellers have the right to introduce any product in any size, style, color, et cetera, so long as it meets minimum requirements of health and safety.
2. Sellers have the right to price the product as they please as long as they avoid discriminations which are harmful to competition.
3. Sellers have the right to promote the product using any amount of resources, media, or message so long as no deception or fraud is involved.
4. Sellers have the right to introduce any buying incentive schemes they wish so long as they are not discriminatory.
5. Sellers have the right to alter the product offerings at any time.
6. Sellers have the right to distribute the product in any reasonable manner.
7. Sellers have the right to limit the product guarantee or post-sale services.[8]

The above list is not exhaustive but it serves to illustrate the relatively greater power of sellers and the need to balance the rights and power of buyers and sellers. Consumerism in this context can be understood best if it is thought of as consumer welfare actions reflecting a mood of dissatisfaction on the buyer's side of the marketing equation.

The broad scope of consumerism is evidenced by the Consumer Advisory Council's list of the ten major fields of interest to consumers. The ten original fields are:

1. Consumer standards, grades, and labels.

---

[8] Philip Kotler, "What Consumerism Means for Marketers," *Harvard Business Review* 50 (May–June 1972), pp. 48–57.

HIGHLIGHT 13-2

The Consumer Bill of Rights

The right—to safety
to be informed
to choose
to be heard

Source: President John F. Kennedy, *The Consumer Bill of Rights*, 1962.

---

2. Two-way flow of information and opinion between government and the consumer.

3. Effective consumer representation in government.

4. To study the consumer credit situation and improve it if necessary.

5. To improve the administration, enforcement and scope of programs in federal agencies.

6. To accelerate economic growth.

7. Improvement of levels of consumption of low-income groups.

8. Antitrust action and prevention of price-fixing.

9. Provision of adequate housing for the nation's families.

10. Adequate medical care for all citizens.[9]

From all of the above, it is clear that the scope of consumerism is quite broad. However, there is a high probability that consumerism will eventually become part of two other areas of social concern: distortions and inequalities in the economic environment and the declining quality of the physical environment.[10] Concern over the economic environment has manifested itself in antitrust laws and other forms of public policy regulations. In addition, the establishment of such government agencies as the Small Business Administration and the Minority Enterprise Small Business Investment Company are further indications of public concern with inequalities in the economic environment.

Consumerism has also been identified with the widespread concern of the physical environment—pollution in particular. For example, man-

---

[9] Consumer Advisory Council, First Report" (Washington, D.C.: U.S. Government Printing Office, October 1963), pp. 5–8.

[10] David Aaker and George S. Day, "A Guide to Consumerism," *Journal of Marketing* 54 (July 1970), pp. 12–19.

ufacturers of soap products have in some cases altered the chemical composition of their laundry products to avoid pollution, and auto manufacturers are still working on better devices to eliminate certain unwanted gas emissions from car engines.

Recent Efforts

The social responsibility of corporations is a key issue today and it is slowly being resolved. A recent study of the National Industrial Conference Board covering over 1,000 companies clearly showed that the vast majority of chief executives feel that public affairs is a primary concern of top management. There is little question today that most managers recognize that society takes a serious interest in their affairs and expects them to act in a socially responsible manner. Citizen organizations such as The Project on Corporate Responsibility have attacked such giants as GM in order to force GM to accept the basic principle that "the corporation should undertake no activity which is inconsistent with the public interest." Both the federal and state governments are enacting laws and establishing agencies to protect consumers as well as the environment.

One of the most forceful and articulate statements on this issue can be found in the Council of Economic Development's statement, *Social Responsibilities of Business Corporations*. CED's policy statement starts with the basic proposition that business functions by public consent, and that the basic purpose of it is to serve constructively the needs of society, to the satisfaction of society. Three generations ago the idea that business is party to a contract with society would have provoked an indignant snort from many business people. The real impact of the CED's report is that it represents the thinking of top management persons who have arrived at a concerted opinion of the corporate stake in a good society. Indeed, this policy report is a useful benchmark as to what some of the *Fortune 500* top corporations think about business and marketing's social responsibility.

BROADENING THE CONCEPT OF MARKETING

Up to this point, the focus of this text primarily has been on marketing in the business firm. Basically, the text has taken a microview of marketing management dealing with planning and decision making primarily in the business firms and exchanges between business firms and consumers or industrial users. However, in recent years, marketing scholars have increasingly emphasized an expanded concept of what marketing entails.

A broadened or generic concept of marketing views marketing as consisting of much more than simply business transactions.[11] In this broadened context, marketing is defined as "human activity directed at satisfying needs and wants through exchange processes,"[12] and a product is defined as "something that is viewed as capable of satisfying a want."[13] Thus, the arena for marketing activities and application of marketing principles has been expanded to include nonbusiness areas in society, including the marketing of persons, places, organizations, and ideas. Figure 13–1 illustrates some examples.[14]

FIGURE 13–1
Some Organizations and Their Products and Customer Groups

Organization	Product	Customer group
Museum	Cultural appreciation	General public
National Safety Council	Safer driving	Driving public
Political candidate	Honest government	Voting public
Family Planning Foundation	Birth control	Fertile public
Police department	Safety	General public
Church	Religious experience	Church members
University	Education	Students

A distinction between many of these types of organizations and the business firm is that these organizations generally are not profit oriented. However, the basic goal of survival, which requires income, is common to both these types of organizations and business firms, and both must perform marketing functions to accomplish this goal. In fact, nonprofit organizations have three primary marketing tasks: resource attraction, resource allocation, and persuasion, and the concept of the

---

[11] For excellent articles dealing with this topic, see Philip Kotler and Sidney J. Levy, "Broadening the Concept of Marketing," *Journal of Marketing* 33 (January 1969), pp. 10–15; Philip Kotler, "A Generic Concept of Marketing," *Journal of Marketing* 36 (April 1972), pp. 46–54; Richard P. Bagozzi, "Marketing as an Organized Behavioral System of Exchange," *Journal of Marketing* 48 (October 1974), pp. 77–81; Richard P. Bagozzi, "Marketing as Exchange," *Journal of Marketing* 39 (October 1975), pp. 32–39.

[12] Philip Kotler, *Marketing Management: Analysis Planning and Control*, 3d ed. (Englewood Cliffs, N.J.: Prentice-Hall, Inc., 1976), p. 5.

[13] Ibid.

[14] This figure is taken from Philip Kotler, "A Generic Concept of Marketing," p. 47.

marketing mix—communication, distribution, pricing and product—are indeed applicable to these organizations.[15]

In summary, it appears that the main thrust of the broadened concept of marketing is that realistic marketing planning can in some cases enable nonbusiness organizations to improve their operations. However, it will be some time before the exact boundaries of marketing will be agreed upon by all marketers.[16]

CONCLUSION

This chapter was concerned with the role of marketing in society. The two basic issues discussed were social responsibility and the boundaries of the marketing discipline. It was suggested that marketing managers should pay close attention to the needs of society and that marketing principles can be useful for bringing about nonbusiness exchanges.

ADDITIONAL READINGS

Bell, Martin L., and Emory, William C.   "The Faltering Marketing Concept." *Journal of Marketing* 35 (October 1971), pp. 37–42.

Berry, Leonard L. "Marketing Challenges and the Age of the People." *MSU Business Topics* (Winter 1972), pp. 7–10.

El-Ansary, Adel L., and Kramer, Oscar E., Jr.   "Social Marketing: The Family Planning Experience." *Journal of Marketing* 37 (July 1975), pp. 1–7.

Feldman, Laurence P.   "Societal Adaptation: A New Challenge for Marketing." *Journal of Marketing* 55 (July 1971), pp. 54–60.

Gaedeke, Ralph M., and Etcheson, Warren W.   *Consumerism: Viewpoints from Business, Government, and the Public Interest.* San Francisco: Canfield Press, 1972.

Kangun, Norman; Cox, Keith K.; Higginbotham, James; and Burton, John. "Consumerism and Marketing Management." *Journal of Marketing* 39 (April 1975), pp. 3–10.

Kangun, Norman.   *Society and Marketing: An Unconventional View.* New York: Harper and Row, Inc., 1972.

---

[15] For a full discussion, see Benson P. Shapiro, "Marketing for Nonprofit Organizations," *Harvard Business Review* 53 (September–October 1975), pp. 123–32. Also see Philip Kotler, *Marketing for Nonprofit Organizations* (Englewood Cliffs, N.J.: Prentice-Hall, Inc., 1975).

[16] For discussion, see David J. Luck, "Broadening the Concept of Marketing—Too Far," *Journal of Marketing* 33 (July 1969), pp. 53–55; Ben M. Enis, "Deepening the Concept of Marketing," *Journal of Marketing* 37 (October 1973), pp. 57–62; F. Kelly Shuptrine and Frank A. Oshauski, "Marketing's Changing Role: Expanding or Contracting?" *Journal of Marketing* 39 (April 1975), pp. 53–66.

Pruden, Henry O., and Longman, Douglas S.   "Race, Alienation, and Consumerism." *Journal of Marketing* 36 (July 1972), pp. 58–63.

Root, W. Paul.   "Should Product Differentiation Be Restricted?" *Journal of Marketing* 36 (July 1972), pp. 3–9.

Varble, Dale L.   "Social and Environmental Considerations in New Product Development." *Journal of Marketing* 36 (October 1972), pp. 11–15.

Section II

ANALYZING MARKETING PROBLEMS AND CASES

The use of business cases was developed by faculty members of the Harvard Graduate School of Business Administration in the 1920s.[1] Case studies have been widely accepted as one effective way of exposing students to the decision-making process.[2]

Basically, cases represent detailed descriptions or reports of business problems. They are usually written by a trained observer who actually had been involved in the firm or organization and had some dealings with the problems under consideration. Cases generally entail both qualitative and quantitative data which the student must analyze and determine appropriate alternatives and solutions.

The primary purpose of the case method is to introduce a measure of realism into management education. Rather than emphasizing the teaching of concepts, the case method focuses on application of concepts and sound logic to real world business problems. In this way the student learns to bridge the gap between abstraction and application and appreciate the value of both.

The primary purpose of this chapter is to offer a logical format for the analysis of case problems. Although there is no one format that can be successfully applied to all cases, the following framework is intended to be a logical sequence from which to develop sound analyses.

---

[1] Ram Charan, "Classroom Techniques in Teaching by the Case Method," *Academy of Management Review* 1 (July 1976), pp. 116–23.

[2] For example, see William F. O'Dell, "And Once Again . . . The Case Method Revisited," *Collegiate News and Views* 29 (Winter 1975–76), pp. 17–21.

This framework is presented for analysis of comprehensive marketing cases; however, the process should also be useful for shorter marketing cases, incidents, and problems.

A CASE ANALYSIS FRAMEWORK

A basic approach to case analyses involves a four-step process. First, the problem is defined. Second, alternative courses of action are formulated to solve the problem. Third, the alternatives are analyzed in terms of their strengths and weaknesses, and fourth, an alternative is accepted and a course of action is recommended. This basic approach is quite useful for the student well versed in case analysis, particularly for shorter cases or incidents. However, for the newcomer this framework may well be inadequate and oversimplified. Thus, the following expanded framework and checklists are intended to aid the student in becoming proficient at case and problem analysis.

1.   Analyze and Record the Current Situation

Whether the analysis of a firm's problems is done by a manager, student, or paid business consultant, the first step is to analyze the current situation.[3] This does not mean writing up a history of the firm but entails the type of analysis described below. This approach is useful not only for getting a better grip on the situation, but also for discovering both real and potential problems—the central concern of any case analysis.

Phase 1: The Environment.   The first phase in analyzing a marketing problem or case is to consider the environment in which the firm is operating. The economic environment can have a decided effect on an industry, firm, and marketing program. For example, a depressed economy with high unemployment may not be an ideal situation for implementing a large price increase. The social and cultural environment can also have considerable effect on both multinational and domestic firms. For example, the advent of men's hairstyling could be considered an appropriate reaction to today's longer hairstyles, whereas a price reduction to stimulate demand for haircuts could well be inappropriate.

Phase 2: The Industry.   The second phase involves analysis of the industry in which the firm operates. This phase can be critical, particularly in terms of how the firm's product is defined. A too-narrow definition of the industry and competitive environment can be disastrous not

---

[3] See Frank F. Gilmore, "Formulating Strategy in Smaller Companies," *Harvard Business Review* 49 (May–June 1971), pp. 71–81.

only for the firm but also for the individual analyzing the case. In appraising the industry, it is useful to first categorize it by the Standard Industrial Classification (SIC) and in terms of the accompanying list.[4]

Class	*Possible Implications*

1. A few giants (oligopolistic).
 Examples:
   Aluminum producers
   Cigarette manufacturers
	Price cutting is fruitless.
	 Antitrust action is a hazard.
	 Concerned action leads to a monopolistic situation facing the customers.
	 Very high capital costs to enter the industry.

2. A few giants and a relatively small number of "independents."
 Examples:
   Auto industry
   Oil industry
   Tire industry
   Meat processors
	Price cutting by smaller companies may bring strong retaliation by giants.
	 Follow-the-leader pricing.
	 Antitrust action against the giants is a hazard.
	 Monopolistic prices.
	 Squeeze on the independents.
	 High capital costs to enter the industry.

3. Many small independent firms.
 Examples:
   Food brokers
   Sales reps
   Auto supply parts
   Kitchen cabinet manufacturers
   Real estate firms
   Tanneries
	Cost of entry is low.
	 Special services.
	 Usual local market.
	 Threat of regional or national linking into a major competitor.
	 Sophisticated business practices often lacking.

4. Professional service firms.
 Examples:
   CPA firms
   Management consultants
   Marketing research firms
   Advertising agencies
	Confusion of standards.
	 Easy entry (and exit).
	 Secretive pricing, often based on what the traffic will bear.

5. Government regulated to a great degree.
 Examples:
   Banking
   Stock brokerages
   Rail industry
   Communications industry
	Entry is usually difficult.
	 Government provides a semimonopoly which may lead to high profits or inability to survive in a changing world.

After initial definition and classification, attention should be paid to such factors as:

---

[4] Murdick, Robert G., Richard H. Eckhouse, R. Carl Moore, Thomas W. Zimmer, *Business Policy: A Framework for Analysis*, 2d ed. (Columbus, Ohio: Grid, Inc., 1976), p. 250.

1. Technology
    a. Level
    b. Rate of change
    c. Technological threats to the industry
2. Political-Legal-Social Influences
    a. Trends in government controls
    b. Specific regulations
    c. Social responsibility pressure
    d. Consumer perceptions of industry
3. Industrial Guidelines and Trends
    a. Pricing policies
    b. Promotion
    c. Product lines
    d. Channels of distribution
    e. Geographic concentration
    f. Increases or declines in firms or profitability
4. Financial Indicators
    a. Current ratio
    b. Working capital required
    c. Capital structure
    d. Sources and uses of funds
    e. Sales
    f. Profitability[5]

Sources for this information are contained in Section III of this book.

Phase 3: The Firm. The third phase involves analysis of the firm itself not only in comparison with the industry and industry averages but also internally in terms of both quantitative and qualitative data. Key areas of concern at this stage are such factors as objectives, constraints, management philosophy, strengths, weaknesses, and structure of the firm.

Phase 4: The Marketing Program. Although there may be internal personnel or structural problems in the marketing department itself that need examination, typically an analysis of the current marketing strategy is the next phase. In this phase the objectives of the marketing department are analyzed in comparison with those of the firm in terms of agreement, soundness, and attainability. Each element of the marketing mix as well as other areas such as marketing research and information systems is analyzed in terms of whether it is internally consistent and synchronized with the goals of the department and firm. Although cases are often labeled in terms of their primary emphasis, such as "Pricing" or "Advertising," it is important for the student to analyze the

---

[5] This list was partially adapted from Murdick et al., *Business Policy*, p. 253.

marketing strategy and entire marketing mix, since a change in one element will affect the entire marketing program.

In performing the analysis of the current situation, the student should analyze the data carefully to extract the relevant from the superfluous. Many cases contain information that is not relevant to the problem; it is the student's job to discard this information in order to get a clearer picture of the current situation. As the analysis proceeds, a watchful eye must be kept on each phase to determine (1) symptoms of problems, (2) current problems, and (3) potential problems. Symptoms of problems are indicators of a problem but are not problems in and of themselves. For example, a symptom of a problem may be a decline in sales in a particular sales territory. However, the problem is the root cause of the decline in sales—perhaps the field representative quit making sales calls and is relying on phone orders only.

The following is a checklist of the types of questions that should be asked when performing the analysis of the current situation.

CHECKLIST FOR ANALYZING THE CURRENT SITUATION

Phase 1: The environment
1. Are there any trends in the environment that could have an effect on the industry, firm, or marketing program?
2. What is the state of the economy? Inflation? Stagflation? Depression?
3. What is the cultural, social, and political atmosphere?
4. Are there trends or changes in the environment that could be advantageous or disadvantageous to the industry, firm, or marketing program? Can the marketing program be restructured to take advantage of these trends or changes?

Phase 2: The industry
1. What industry is the firm in? What class of industry? Are there other industries the firm is competing with?
2. What is the size of the firm relative to the industry?
3. How does the firm compare in terms of market share, sales, and profitability with the rest of the industry?
4. How does the firm compare with other firms in the industry in terms of a financial ratio analysis?
5. What is the firm's major competition?
6. Are there any trends in terms of government control, political, or public atmosphere that could affect the industry?

Phase 3: The firm
1. What are the objectives of the firm? Are they clearly stated? Attainable?
2. What are the strengths of the firm? Managerial expertise? Financial? Copyrights or patents?
3. What are the constraints and weaknesses of the firm?

4. Are there any real or potential sources of dysfunctional conflict in the structure of the firm?

5. How is the marketing department structured in the firm?

Phase 4: The marketing program

1. What are the objectives of the marketing program? Are they clearly stated? Are they consistent with the objectives of the firm? Is the entire marketing mix structured to meet these objectives?

2. What marketing concepts are at issue in the program? Is the marketing program well planned and laid out? Is the program consistent with sound marketing principles? If the program takes exception to marketing principles, is there a good reason for it?

3. What target market is the program directed to? Is it well defined? Is the market large enough to be profitably served? Does the market have long-run potential?

4. What competitive advantage does the marketing program offer? If none, what can be done to gain a competitive advantage in the market place?

5. What products are being sold? What is the width, depth, and consistency of the firm's product lines? Does the firm need new products to fill out its product line? Should any product be deleted? What is the profitability of the various products?

6. What promotion mix is being used? Is promotion consistent with the products and product images? What could be done to improve the promotion mix?

7. What channels of distribution are being used? Do they deliver the product at the right time and right place to meet consumer needs? Are the channels typical of those used in the industry? Could channels be made more efficient?

8. What pricing strategies are being used? How do prices compare with similar products of other firms? How are prices determined?

9. Are marketing research and information systematically integrated into the marketing program? Is the overall marketing program internally consistent?

The relevant information from this preliminary analysis is now formalized and recorded. At this point the analyst must be mindful of the difference between facts and opinions. Facts are objective statements such as financial data, whereas opinions are subjective interpretations of facts or situations. The analyst must make certain not to place too much emphasis on opinions and carefully consider any variables that may bias such opinions.

Regardless of how much information is contained in the case or how much additional information is collected, the analyst usually finds that it is impossible to specify a complete framework for the current situation. It is at this point that assumptions must be made. Clearly, since each analyst may make different assumptions, it is critical that assumptions be explicitly stated. One authority suggests that when presenting a case the analyst should distribute copies of the assumption list to all class members. In this way confusion is avoided in terms of how the analyst perceives the current situation and others can evaluate the reasonableness and necessity of the assumptions.[6]

2. Analyze and Record Problems and Their Core Elements

After careful analysis, problems and their core elements should be explicitly stated and listed in order of importance. Finding and recording problems and their core elements can be difficult. It is not uncommon upon reading a case for the first time for the student to view the case as a description of a situation in which there are no problems. However, careful analysis should reveal symptoms, which lead to problem recognition.

Recognizing and recording problems and their core elements is most critical for a meaningful case analysis. Obviously, if the root problems are not explicitly stated and understood, the remainder of the case analysis has little merit since the true issues are not being dealt with. The following checklist of questions is designed to assist the student in performing this step of the analysis.

CHECKLIST FOR ANALYZING PROBLEMS AND THEIR CORE ELEMENTS

1. What is the primary problem in the case? What are the secondary problems?
2. What proof exists that these are the central issues? How much of this proof is based on facts? On opinions? On assumptions?
3. What symptoms are there that suggest these are the real problems in the case?
4. How are the problems, as defined, related? Are they independent or are they the result of a deeper problem?
5. What are the ramifications of these problems in the short run? In the long run?

3. Formulate, Evaluate, and Record Alternative Courses of Action

This step is concerned with the question of what can be done to resolve the problem defined in the previous step. Generally, a number of alternative courses of action are available which could potentially help

---

[6] John K. Harris, "A Teaching Note on the Use of Assumptions in Case Study," *Decision Sciences* 6 (January 1975), pp. 184–85.

alleviate the problem condition. One authority suggests three to seven alternatives as a reasonable number of alternatives to work with.[7] Another approach is to brainstorm as many alternatives as possible initially and then reduce the list to a workable number.

Sound logic and reasoning are particularly important in this step. It is critical to avoid alternatives that could potentially alleviate the problem but that at the same time create a greater new problem or require greater resources than the firm has at its disposal.

After serious analysis and listing of a number of alternatives, the next task is to evaluate them in terms of their costs and benefits. Costs are any output or effort the firm must exert in order to implement the alternative. Benefits are any input or value received by the firm. Costs to be considered are time, money, other resources and opportunity costs, while benefits are such things as sales, profits, goodwill, and customer satisfaction. The following checklist provides a guideline of questions to be used when performing this phase of the analysis.

CHECKLIST FOR FORMULATING AND EVALUATING ALTERNATIVE COURSES OF ACTION

1. What possible alternatives exist for solving the firm's problems?
2. What limits are there on the possible alternatives? Competence? Resources? Management preference? Social responsibility? Legal restrictions?
3. What major alternatives are now available to the firm? What marketing concepts are involved that affect these alternatives?
4. Are the listed alternatives reasonable given the firm's situation? Are they logical? Are the alternatives consistent with the goals of the marketing program? Are they consistent with the firm's objectives?
5. What are the costs of each alternative? What are the benefits? What are the advantages and disadvantages of each alternative?
6. Which alternative best solves the problem and minimizes the creation of new problems given the above constraints?

4. Select, Implement, and Record the Chosen Alternative Course of Action

In light of the previous analysis, the alternative is now selected that best solves the problem with a minimal creation of new problems. It is important to record the logic and reasoning that precipitated the selection of a particular alternative. This includes articulating not only why the alternative was selected, but also why the other alternatives were not selected.

---

[7] Kenneth E. Schnelle, *Case Analysis and Business Problem Solving* (New York: McGraw-Hill, Inc., 1967), p. 215.

No analysis is complete without an action-oriented decision and plan for implementing the decision. The accompanying checklist indicates the type of questions that should be answered in this stage of the analysis.

CHECKLIST FOR SELECTING AND IMPLEMENTING THE CHOSEN ALTERNATIVE

1. What must be done to implement the alternative?
2. What personnel will be involved? What are the responsibilities of each?
3. When and where will the alternative be implemented?
4. What will be the probable outcome?
5. How will the success or failure of the alternative be measured?

HIGHLIGHT 14–1

An Operational Approach to Case and Problem Analysis

1. Read the case quickly to get an overview of the situation.
2. Read the case again thoroughly. Underline relevant information and take notes on potential areas of concern.
3. Review outside sources of information on the environment and the industry. Record relevant information and the source of this information.
4. Perform comparative analysis of the firm with the industry and industry averages.
5. Analyze the firm.
6. Analyze the marketing program.
7. Record the current situation in terms of relevant environmental, industry, firm, and marketing program parameters.
8. Make and record necessary assumptions to complete the situational framework.
9. Determine and record the major issues, problems, and their core elements.
10. Record proof that these are the major topics.
11. Record potential courses of actions.
12. Evaluate each initially to determine constraints that preclude acceptability.
13. Evaluate remaining alternatives in terms of costs and benefits.
14. Record analysis of alternatives.
15. Select an alternative.
16. Record alternative and defense of its selection.
17. Record the who, what, when, where, how, and why of the alternative and its implementation.

PITFALLS TO AVOID IN CASE ANALYSIS

Below is a summary of some of the most common errors analysts make when analyzing cases. When evaluating your analysis or those of others, this list provides a useful guide for spotting potential shortcomings.[8]

1. *Inadequate definition of the problem.* By far the most common error made in case analysis is attempting to recommend a course of action without first adequately defining or understanding the problem. Whether presented orally or in a written report, a case analysis must begin with a focus on the central issues and problems represented in the case situation. Closely related is the error of analyzing symptoms without determining the root problem.

2. *The search for "the answer."* In case analysis there are no clear-cut solutions. Keep in mind that the objective of case studies is learning through discussion and exploration. There is no one "official" or "correct" answer to a case. Rather, there are usually several reasonable alternative solutions.

3. *Not enough information.* Analysts often complain that there is not enough information in some cases to make a good decision. However, there is justification for not presenting "all" of the information in a case. As in real life, a marketing manager or consultant seldom has all the information necessary to make an optimal decision. Thus, reasonable assumptions have to be made and the challenge is to find intelligent solutions in spite of the limited information.

4. *Use of generalities.* In analyzing cases, specific recommendations are necessarily not generalities. For example, a suggestion to increase the price is a generality; a suggestion to increase the price by $1.07 is a specific.

5. *A different situation.* Considerable time and effort are sometimes exerted by students contending that "If the situation were different, I'd know what course of action to take" or "If the marketing manager hadn't already fouled things up so badly, the firm wouldn't have a problem." Such reasoning ignores the fact that the events in the case have already happened and cannot be changed. Even though analysis or criticism of past events is necessary in diagnosing the problem, in the end, the present situation must be addressed and decisions must be made based on the given situation.

6. *Narrow vision analysis.* Although cases are often labeled as a specific type of case, such as "Pricing," "Product," and so forth, this does not mean that other marketing variables should be ignored. Too

---

[8] This list has been partially adopted from Ralph W. Reber and Gloria F. Terry, *Behavioral Insights for Supervision* (Englewood Cliffs, N.J.: Prentice-Hall, Inc., 1975), pp. 213–15.

often students ignore the effects that a change in one marketing element will have on the others.

7.   *Realism.* Too often analysts become so focused on solving a particular problem that their solutions become totally unrealistic. For example, suggesting a million-dollar advertising program for a firm with a capital structure of $50,000 is an unrealistic solution.

8.   *The marketing research solution.* A quite common but unsatisfactory solution to case problems is marketing research; for example, "The firm should do this or that type of marketing research to find a solution to their problem." Although marketing research may be helpful as an intermediary step in some cases, marketing research does not solve problems or make decisions. In cases where marketing research is recommended, the costs and potential benefits should be fully specified in the case analysis.

9.   *Rehashing the case material.* Analysts sometimes spend considerable effort rewriting a two- or three-page history of the firm as presented in the case. This is unnecessary since the instructor and other students are already familiar with this information.

10.   *Premature conclusions.* Analysts sometimes jump to premature conclusions instead of waiting until their analysis is completed. Too many analysts jump to conclusions upon first reading the case and then proceed to interpret everything in the case as justifying their conclusions, even factors that are logically against it.

COMMUNICATING CASE ANALYSES

The final concern in case analyses deals with communicating the results of the analysis. The most comprehensive analysis has little value if it cannot be communicated effectively. There are two primary media through which case analyses are communicated—the written report and the oral presentation.

The Written Report

Since the structure of the written report will vary by the type of case analyzed, the purpose of this section is not to present a "one and only" way of writing up a case. The purpose of this section is to present some useful generalizations to aid the student in case writeups.

First, a good written report generally starts with an outline. The purpose of the outline is to:

1.   Organize the case material in a sequence that makes it easy for the reader to follow.
2.   Highlight the major thoughts of the case and show the relationships among subsidiary ideas and major ideas.

3. Reinforce the student's memory of the case ideas and provide the framework for developing these ideas.
4. Serve to refresh the student's memory of the case when it has to be referred to weeks later.[9]

The outline format should avoid too fine a breakdown and there should be at least two subdivisions for any heading. The following is an example of typical outline headings:

I. Current Situation.
    A. Environment.
        1. Economic.
        2. Cultural and social.
        3. Political and legal
    B. Industry.
        1. Definition.
        2. Classification.
        3. Technology.
        4. Political-legal-social factors.
        5. Industrial guidelines and trends.
        6. Financial indicators.
    C. Firm.
        1. Objectives.
        2. Constraints.
        3. Management philosophy.
        4. Strengths.
        5. Weaknesses.
        6. Structure.
    D. Marketing program.
        1. Objectives.
        2. Constraints.
        3. Strengths.
        4. Weaknesses.
        5. Target market(s).
        6. Product considerations.
        7. Promotion considerations.
        8. Pricing considerations.
        9. Channel considerations.
        10. Information and research considerations.
    E. Assumptions about current situation.
II. Problems.
    A. Primary problem(s).
        1. Symptoms.
        2. Proof.

---

[9] Murdick et al., *Business Policy*, p. 261.

    B. Secondary problem(s).
       1. Symptoms.
       2. Proof.
III. Alternatives.
    A. Alternative 1.
       1. Strengths and benefits.
       2. Weaknesses and costs.
    B. Alternative 2.
       1. Strengths and benefits.
       2. Weaknesses and costs.
    C. Alternative 3.
       1. Strengths and benefits.
       2. Weaknesses and costs.
IV. Decision and Implementation.
    A. What.
    B. Who.
    C. When.
    D. Where.
    E. Why.
    F. How.
V. Technical Appendix.

Writing up the case report now entails filling out the details of the outline in prose form. Clearly, like any other skill, it takes practice to determine the best method for writing up a particular case. However, simplicity, clarity, and precision are prime objectives of the report.

The Oral Presentation

Case analyses are often presented by an individual or team. As with the written report, a good outline is critical, and it is often preferable to hand out the outline to each class member. Although there is no one best way to present a case or to divide responsibility between team members, simply reading the written report is unacceptable, since it encourages boredom and interferes with all-important class discussion.

The use of visual aids can be quite helpful in presenting class analyses. However, simply presenting financial statements contained in the case is a poor use of visual media. On the other hand, graphs of sales and profit curves can be more easily interpreted and can be quite useful for making specific points.

Oral presentation of cases is particularly helpful to students for learning the skill of speaking to a group. In particular, the ability to handle objections and disagreements without antagonizing others is a skill worth developing.

CONCLUSION

From the discussion it should be obvious that good case analyses require a major commitment of time and effort. Individuals must be highly motivated and willing to get involved in the analysis and discussion if they expect to learn and succeed in a course where cases are utilized. Persons with only passive interest who perform "night before" analyses cheat themselves of valuable learning experiences which can aid them in their careers.

ADDITIONAL READINGS

Greer, Thomas V.   *Cases in Marketing: Orientation, Analysis and Problems.* New York: Macmillan Publishing Co., Inc., 1975, chap. 1.

McNair, Malcolm P.   *The Case Method of the Harvard Business School.* New York: McGraw-Hill, Inc., 1954.

O'Dell, William F.; Ruppel, Andrew C.; Trent, Robert H.   *Marketing Decision Making: Analytic Framework and Cases* (Cincinnati: South-Western Publishing Company, 1976), chaps. 1–5.

Ronstadt, Robert.   *The Art of Case Analysis.* Dober, Mass.: Lord Publishing, 1978.

Section III

SELECTED REFERENCE TOOLS FOR MARKETING MANAGEMENT

Marketing Sources
Financial Information Sources
Basic U.S. Statistical Sources
General Business and Industry Sources
Indexes and Abstracts

SECONDARY DATA SOURCES

In analyzing and presenting cases, it is often very useful for students to be able to find outside data sources as a means of supporting their recommendations or conclusions. The data referred to here is from secondary sources and located in most business libraries. The purpose of this section is to list and briefly describe some of the key data source books that are readily available to students. The references are listed under five specific headings: marketing sources, financial information sources, basic U.S. statistical sources, general business and industry sources, and indexes and abstracts.

MARKETING SOURCES

Britt, Stewart Henderson, and Shapiro, Irwin A., "Where to Find Marketing Facts." *Harvard Business Review* 40 (September–October 1962). For an updated article based on this work, see C. R. Goeldner and Laura M. Dirks, "Business Facts: Where to Find Them," *MSU Business Topics*, Summer 1976, pp. 23–36.

Commercial Atlas and Marketing Guide. Skokie, Ill.: Rand-McNally & Co. Statistics on population, principal cities, business centers, trading areas, sales and manufacturing units, transportation data, and so forth.

Current Sources of Marketing Information. Gunther, Edgar and F. A. Goldstein. A bibliography of primary marketing. Subjects include basic sources of information, the national market, regional data on the economy, and advertising and promotion.

Editor and Publisher "Market Guide." Market information for 1,500 American and Canadian cities. Data includes population, household, gas meters, climate, retailing, and newspaper information.

Industrial Marketing. "Guide to Special Issues." This directory is included in each issue. Publications are listed within primary market classifications and are listed for up to three months prior to advertising closing date.

Marketing Communications (January 1968 to January 1972, formerly *Printer's Ink,* 1914–1967). Pertinent market information on regional and local consumer markets as well as international markets to January 1972.

Marketing Information Guide. U.S. Business and Defense Services Administration. Annotations of selected current publications and reports with basic information and statistics on marketing and distribution.

Population and Its Distribution: The United States Markets. J. Walter Thompson Co. N.Y.: McGraw-Hill Book Co. A handbook of marketing facts selected from the U.S. *Census of Population* and the most recent census data on retail trade.

Sales and Marketing Management. (Formerly *Sales Management* to October 1975). This valuable journal is published twice monthly except December, for which there is one issue; *Survey of Buying Power* (July) is an excellent reference for buying income, buying power index, cash income, merchandise line, and retail sales.

FINANCIAL INFORMATION SOURCES

Blue Line Investment Survey. Quarterly ratings and reports on 1,000 stocks; analysis of 60 industries and special situations analysis (monthly); supplements on new developments and editorials on conditions affecting price trends.

Commercial and Financial Chronicle. Variety of articles and news reports on business, government, and finance. Monday's issue lists new securities, dividends, and called bonds. Thursday's issue is devoted to business articles.

Financial World. Articles on business activities of interest to investors including investment opportunities and pertinent data on firms such as earnings and dividend records.

Fairchild's Financial Manual of Retail Stores. Information about officers and directors, products, subsidiaries, sales, and earnings for apparel stores, mail order firms, variety chains, and supermarkets.

Moody's Bank and Finance Manual; Moody's Industrial Manual; Moody's Municipal & Government Manual; Moody's Public Utility Manual; Moody's Transportation Manual; Moody's Directors Service. Brief histories of companies and their operations, subsidiaries, officers and directors, products, and balance sheet and income statements over several years.

Moody's Bond Survey. Moody's Investors Service. Weekly data on stocks and bonds including recommendations for purchases or sale and discussions of industry trends and developments.

Moody's Handbook of Widely Held Common Stocks. Moody's Investors Service. Weekly data on stocks and bonds including recommendations for purchases or sale and discussions of industry trends and developments.

Security Owner's Stock Guide. Standard & Poor's Corp. Standard and Poor's rating, stock price range, and other helpful information for about 4,200 common and preferred stocks.

Security Price Index. Standard & Poor's Corp. Price indexes, bond prices, sales, yields, Dow-Jones averages, et cetera.

Standard Corporation Records. Standard & Poor's Corp. Published in loose-leaf form, offers information similar to Moody's Manuals. Use of this extensive service facilitates buying securities for both the individual and the institutional investor.

BASIC U.S. STATISTICAL SOURCES

Business Service Checklist. Department of Commerce. Weekly guide to Department of Commerce publications, plus key business indicators.

Business Statistics. Department of Commerce. (Supplement to *Survey of Current Business.*) History of the statistical series appearing in the *Survey.* Also included are source references and useful explanatory notes.

Census of Agriculture. Department of Commerce. Data by states and counties on livestock, farm characteristics, values.

Census of Manufacturers. Department of Commerce. Industry statistics, area statistics, subject reports, location of plants, industry descriptions arranged in Standard Industrial Classification, and a variety of ratios.

Census of Mineral Industries. Department of Commerce. Similar to *Census of Manufacturers.* Also includes capital expenditures and employment and payrolls.

Census of Retail Trade. Department of Commerce. Compiles data for states, SMSAs, counties, and cities with populations of 2,500 or more by kind of business. Data include number of establishments, sales, payroll, and personnel.

Census of Selected Services. Department of Commerce. Includes data on hotels, motels, beauty parlors, barber shops, and other retail service organizations.

Census of Transportation. First taken in 1964 covering 1963 statistics. Passenger Transportation Survey, Commodity Transportation Survey, Travel Inventory and Use Survey, Bus and Truck Carrier Survey.

Census Tract Reports. Department of Commerce, Bureau of Census. Detailed information on both population and housing subjects.

Census of Wholesale Trade. Department of Commerce. Similar to *Census of Retail Trade* except information is for wholesale establishment.

County and City Data Book. Department of Commerce. Summary statistics for small geographical areas.

Economic Almanac. National Industrial Conference Board. A handbook of useful facts about business, labor, and government. Also contains significant and trustworthy statistical data most helpful for persons concerned with current economic problems. Monthly update is entitled *Conference Board Business Record.*

Economic Report of the President. Transmitted to the Congress, January (each year) together with the *Annual Report* of the Council of Economic Advisers. Statistical tables relating to income, employment and production.

Handbook of Basic Economic Statistics. Economic Statistics Bureau of Washington, D.C. Current and historical statistics on industry, commerce, labor, and agriculture.

International Commerce. Department of Commerce. Current views on foreign countries, commodities, investment opportunities, etc.

Metropolitan Statistical Areas (Annual). Department of Commerce. Federal general standard data, representations, and codes for metropolitan statistical areas.

Special Current Business Reports. Department of Commerce. Reports monthly department store sales of selected items.

Statistical Abstract of the United States. Department of Commerce. Summary statistics in industrial, social, political, and economic fields in the United States. It is augmented by the *Cities Supplement, The County Data Book,* and *Historical Statistics of the United States.*

Statistics of Income: U.S. Business Tax Returns. Internal Revenue Service. Summarizes data for proprietorships, partnerships, and corporations.

Survey of Current Business. Department of Commerce. Facts on industrial and business activity in the United States and statistical summary of national income and product acounts. A weekly supplement provides an up to date summary of business.

GENERAL BUSINESS AND INDUSTRY SOURCES

Aerospace Facts and Figures. Aerospace Industries Association of America.

Annual Statistical Report. American Iron and Steel Institute.

Automobile Facts and Figures. Automobile Manufacturers Association.

Canner/Packer Yearbook. Acreage and prices of fruit and vegetables; amounts packaged for processed and manufactured foods over a period of years and/or by region.

Chain Store Age Executive. (Formerly *Chain Store Age* to January 1975). Special issues include January, "Outlook," a preview of the coming year for chain stores; March, "Annual Produce Merchandising Report," a report on trends for produce sections of chain store merchandising; July, "Annual States Manual," performance analysis of 35 products; November, "Annual Meat Study," article on trends in meat sales.

Computerworld. Computerworld, Inc. Last December issue includes "Review and Forecast," an analysis of computer industry's past year and the outlook for the next year.

The Discount Merchandiser. McFadden-Bartell Publishing Co. Special annual issue in May and June provide marketing and sales facts and figures on the discount store industry.

Discount Store News. Lebhar-Friedman Publications, Inc. September issue includes a statistical summary of discount store sales by product class.

Distribution Worldwide. Chilton Co. Special annual issue, *Distribution Guide,* compiles information on transportation methods and wage.

Drug and Cosmetic Industry. Drug Markets, Inc. Separate publication in July, *Drug and Cosmetic Catalog,* provides list of manufacturers of drugs and cosmetics and their respective products.

Drug Topics. Litton Publications Corporation. November *Red Book* lists all pharmaceutical products and their wholesale and retail prices.

Electrical World. January and February issues include two-part statistical report on expenditures, construction, and other categories by region; capacity; sales; and financial statistics for the electrical industry.

Encyclopedia of Business Information Sources. Paul Wasserman et al., eds., Gale Research Company. A detailed listing of primary subjects of interest to managerial personnel, with a record of sourcebooks, periodicals, organizations, directories, handbooks, bibliographies, and other sources of information on each topic. 2 vols., nearly 17,000 entries in over 1,600 subject areas.

Food and Beverage Industries: A Bibliography and Guidebook. Albert C. Vara, ed., Gale Research Company. A comprehensive guide to publications of local, national, and world governmental agencies, industry, trade association, and private research agencies for sources of information on organization and development, agriculture, marketing, market structure trends, store operations, and other subject areas.

Forest Industries. Miller Freeman Publications, Inc. March issue includes "Forest Industries Wood-Based Panel," a review of production and sales figures for selected wood products; extra issue in May includes a statistical review of the lumber industry.

Implement and Tractor. Intertec Publishing Corporation. January issue includes equipment specifications and operating data for farm and industrial equipment. November issue includes statistics and information on the farm industry.

Industry Surveys. Standard & Poor's Corp. Continuously revised analysis of leading industries (40 industries made up of 1,300 companies). Current analysis contains interim operating data of investment comment. Basic analysis features company ratio comparisons and balance sheet statistics.

Men's Wear. Fairchild Publications, Inc. July issue includes "MRA Annual Business Survey," which reviews trends in sales, markups, etc. by geographic region and for the total men's wear industry.

Merchandising Week. Billboard Publications, Inc. Last February issue includes "Annual Statistical and Marketing Report," which compiles ten-year reports on sales and usage of electrical products; May, "Annual Statistical and Marketing Forecast," provides estimates for the year's sales and performance of electrical products.

Modern Brewery Age. Business Journals, Inc. February issue includes a review of sales and production figures for the brewery industry. A separate publication, *The Blue Book,* issued in May, compiles sales and consumption figures by state for the brewery industry.

Middle Market Directory. Dun & Bradstreet. Inventories approximately 18,000 U.S. companies with an indicated worth of $500,000 to $999,999, giving officers, products, standard industrial classification, approximate sales, and number of employees.

National Petroleum News. McGraw-Hill, Inc. May issue includes statistics on sales and consumption of fuel oils, gasoline, and related products. Some figures are for ten years along with ten-year projections.

Operating Results of Department and Specialty Stores. National Retail Merchants Association.

Petroleum Facts and Figures. American Petroleum Institute.

Poor's Register of Corporations, Directors, and Executives of the United States and Canada. Standard & Poor's Corp. Divided into two sections. The first gives officers, products, sales range, and number of employees for about 30,000 corporations. The second gives brief information on executives and directors.

Product Management. (Formerly *Drug Trade News*) July issue includes "Advertising Expenditures for Health and Beauty Aids," an annual survey of advertising expenditures for the industry; quarterly, "Top Health and Beauty Aids Promotions" reviews marketing promotion of top drug and cosmetic companies.

Progressive Grocer. Progressive Grocer, Inc. April issue includes annual report on sales in grocery industry by size and type of store, industry trends and issues, etc.

Quick-Frozen Foods. Harcourt, Brace, Jovanovich Publications. October issue includes "Frozen Food Almanac" providing statistics on the frozen food industry by product.

Sources of Business Information. Edwin T. Coman, ed., Berkeley: University of California Press, 2d ed., 1964. Guide to reference material in statistics, finance, real estate, insurance, accounting, management, marketing, advertising, and other areas. Lists for each field the principal bibliographies, periodicals, sources of statistics, business or professional associations, and handbooks.

Statistics Sources. Paul Wasserman et al., eds. Gale Research Corp., 4th ed., 1974. A subject guide to industrial, business, social, educational, financial data and other related topics.

The Super Market Industry Speaks. Super Market Institute.

Vending Times. February issue includes "The Buyers Guide," a special issue providing information on the vending industry; June issue includes "The Census of the Industry," a special issue containing statistics on the vending industry.

INDEXES AND ABSTRACTS

Accountants Digest. L. L. Briggs. A digest of articles appearing currently in accounting periodicals.

Accountants Index. American Institute of Certified Public Accountants. An index to books, pamphlets, and articles on accounting and finance.

Accounting Articles. Commerce Clearing House. Loose-leaf index to articles in accounting and business periodicals.

Advertising Age Editorial Index. Crain Communications, Inc. Index to articles in *Advertising Age.*

American Statistical Index. Congressional Information Service. A comprehensive two-part annual index to the statistical publications of the U.S. government.

Applied Science & Technology Index. (Formerly *Industrial Arts Index* to

1958). H. W. Wilson Co. Reviews over 200 periodicals relevant to the applied sciences, many of which pertain to business.

Battelle Library Review. (Formerly *Battelle Technical Review* to 1962). Battelle Memorial Institute. Annotated bibliography of books, reports, and articles on automation and automatic processes.

Bulletin of Public Affairs Information Service. Public Affairs Information Service, Inc. (Since 1915—annual index.) A selective list of the latest books, pamphlets, government publications, reports of public and private agencies, and periodicals relating to economic conditions, public administration, and international relations.

Business Education Index. McGraw-Hill Book Co. (Since 1940—annual index.) Annual author and subject index of books, articles, and theses on business education.

Business Periodicals Index. H. W. Wilson Co. A subject index to the disciplines of accounting, advertising, banking, general business, insurance, labor, management, and marketing.

Catalog of United States Census Publication. Washington, D.C.: Dept. of Commerce, Bureau of Census. Indexes all available Census Bureau Data. Main divisions are: agriculture, business, construction, foreign trade, government, guide to locating U.S. census information.

Computer and Information Systems. (Formerly *Information Processing Journal* to 1969). Cambridge Communications Corporation.

Computing Reviews. Association for Computing Machinery.

Cumulative Index of NICB Publications. The National Industrial Conferences Board. Annual index of NICB books, pamphlets, and articles in the area of management of personnel.

Funk & Scott Index of Corporations & Industries. Investment Index Company. Indexes articles on companies and industries that have appeared in related financial publications.

International Abstracts in Operations Research. Operations Research Society of America.

International Journal of Abstracts of Statistical Methods in Industry. The Hague, Netherlands: International Statistical Institute.

Journal of Economic Literature. (Formerly *Economic Abstracts* to 1969). The Hague, Netherlands: International Statistical Institute (semimonthly, not all in English).

Journal of Economic Abstracts. Harvard University.

Management Information Guides. Gale Research Company. Bibliographical references to information sources for various business subjects.

Management Review. American Management Association.

Monthly Checklist of State Publications. U.S. Library of Congress, Exchange and Gift Division. Record of state documents received by Library of Congress.

Personnel Management Abstracts. Wayne University.

Psychological Abstracts. American Psychological Association.

Public Affairs Information Service. Public Affairs Information Service, Inc. A selective subject list of books, pamphlets, and government publications covering business, banking, and economics as well as subjects in the area of public affairs.

Reader's Guide to Periodical Literature. H. W. Wilson Co. Index by author and subject to selected U.S. general and nontechnical periodicals.

Sociological Abstracts. American Sociological Association.

Social Sciences and Humanities Index. (Formerly *International Index* to June 1965.) H. W. Wilson Co.

The Wall Street Journal Index. Dow Jones Company, Inc. An index of all articles in the *WSJ* grouped in two sections: corporate news and general news.

NAME INDEX

A

A & P, 85
Aaker, David A., 123, 125, 204
Adams, J. S., 48
Adler, Lee, 15, 95
Albaum, Gerald S., 24, 26, 129, 196
Alexander, Ralph S., 83, 91, 124
Alexis, Marcus, 64
American Institute of Certified Public Accountants, 232
American Management Association, 233
American Marketing Association, 170
American Petroleum Institute, 232
American Psychological Association, 233
American Sociological Association, 234
Angelman, Reinhard, 7
Ansoff, H. Igor, 15, 96
Arensberg, Conrad M., 196
Aronson, E., 48
Aspinwall, L., 78
Assmus, Gert, 107
Association for Computing Machinery, 233
Ayer, N. W., Agency, 29
Aylmer, R. J., 185

B

Baer, Earl A., 140
Bagozzi, Richard P., 206

Bailey, Earl L., 94
Banks, Seymour, 125
Baranoff, Seymour, 169
Barban, A. M., 116
Barksdale, Hiram C., 174
Barnes, Jim D., 166
Bartels, Robert, 202
Beach, Frank H., 141
Becherer, Richard C., 178
Belk, Russell W., 54–55
Bell, Martin L., 207
Berenson, Conrad, 22
Berry, Leonard L., 120, 179, 207
Bettman, James R., 156
Bird, Monroe M., 140
Blackwell, Roger D., 13, 50, 53
Block, Carl E., 55
Bonfield, E. H., 45
Boone, Louis E., 51, 64, 154
Booz, Allen, and Hamilton, Inc., 74, 94, 183
Bowersox, Donald J., 154
Boyd, Harper W., Jr., 38
Brien, Richard H., 20, 39
Briggs, L. L., 232
Britt, Stewart Henderson, 227
Brooks, Douglas G., 159
Brown, Rex V., 39
Bucklin, Louis P., 78, 149, 154
Buell, Victor P., 73, 87, 169
Burley, James R., 148
Burton, John, 207

Buskirk, Richard H., 141
Buzzell, Robert D., 15, 39, 192

C

Callom, Frank L., 64
Campbell Soup Company, 95
Capaldini, L. A., 179
Cardozo, Richard N., 107
Carvey, Davis W., 37
Catry, Bernard, 81
Cayley, Murray A., 84
Chaffray, Jean-Marie, 68
Charan, Ram, 211
Chase, Richard B., 129
Chestnut, Robert W., 45
Chevalier, Michel, 81
Churchill, Gilbert A., Jr., 39, 68, 129
Claycamp, Henry J., 83, 93
Clayton, Edward R., 140
Clee, Gilbert H., 184
Cleland, David I., 24
Clewett, R. L., 52
Coca-Cola, 193
Cohen, Dorothy, 125
Cohen, J. Kalman, 15
Coman, Edwin T., 232
Comer, James B., 134
Connor, Richard A., Jr., 180
Copley, Thomas P., 64
Corey, Raymond E., 62
Council of Economic Advisors, 229
Cox, Donald F., 39
Cox, Keith K., 207
Cravens, David W., 136
Crissey, William J. E., 129, 138
Cummings, William H., 47
Cunningham, Isabella C. M., 196
Cunningham, William H., 140, 196
Cyert, Richard M., 15

D

Dalrymple, Douglas J., 157
Darden, Bill R., 165
Darman, Rene Y., 140
Davenport, J. William, Jr., 129
Davis, Harry L., 52
Day, George S., 35, 204
Day, Robert L., 35
Dean, Joel, 165
Deardon, John, 39
DeLorenzo, Anthony G., 201
Dhalla, Nariman K., 81
Dickie, Paul M., 196
Dirks, Laura M., 227
Dodge, Robert H., 141
Dommermuth, William P., 124
Donnelly, James H., Jr., 49, 96, 120, 129,
    169, 175, 180, 185, 192

Douglas, Susan P., 193
Doyle, Peter, 123
Drucker, Peter, 107
Dun and Bradstreet, 21, 231
Duncan, Delbert F., 63
Dunn, Albert H., 140
Dunn, S. Watson, 116, 182, 184, 192
Dupont Company, 29, 87
Durand, Richard M., 180
Dussenbury, Warren, 107

E

Eckhouse, Richard H., 213
Eckrich, Donald W., 180
Edwards, Alberta R., 184
El-Ansary, Adel I., 149, 154, 207
Emory, William C., 39, 207
Engel, James E., 50, 53
Engel, James F., 84
English, Wilke D., 140
Enis, Ben M., 118, 207
Ernest, John W., 140
Esso, 194
Etcheson, Warren W., 207
Etzel, Michael J., 96, 170, 196
Evans, G. H., 90
Evans, Marshall K., 39
Ewing, John S., 190

F

Faris, Charles W., 69
Fatt, Arthur C., 186, 192
Fayerweather, John, 186
Feldman, Laurence P., 207
Fenwick, Ian, 123
Ferber, Robert, 36
Festinger, Leon, 47
Fildes, Robert, 81
Fiorillo, Henry F., 84
Fisher, Paul M., 138
Fitzpatrick, Albert A., 165
Fogg, C. Davis, 133
Forbes magazine, 119
Ford, Neil M., 129
Fortune 500, 205
Frank, Ronald E., 78, 84
Frey, Albert F., 111
Fry, Claudia, 186
Fryburger, Vernon, 125

G

Gaedeke, Ralph M., 207
Gardner, Daniel M., 64
Gardner, David M., 27
General Electric Company, 87
General Foods, 95
General Motors, 205
Gensch, Dennis H., 123

George, William R., 174
Gestetner, David, 185
Gibson, Lawrence D., 39
Gilmore, Frank F., 212
Gitlow, Howard S., 180
Goeldner, C. R., 227
Goldstein, F. A., 227
Goldstucker, Jac L., 57
Goslin, Lewis N., 93
Greelick, M. R., 177
Green, Paul E., 28, 69, 78
Green, Paul G., 107, 165
Greer, Thomas V., 224
Greif, Edwin C., 140
Grikscheit, Gary M., 129
Guiltinan, Joseph P., 160
Gunther, Edgar, 227
Gwinner, Robert F., 129

H

Haas, Kenneth B., 140
Haas, Robert W., 60–61, 178
Hague, Lou R., 39
Hall, Edward T., 187, 196
Halterman, Jean C., 111
Hamelman, P. W., 91
Hancock, Robert S., 64
Hansen, Flemming, 55
Harper, Donald V., 165
Harper, Paul C., Jr., 107
Harris, John K., 217
Hartley, Robert J., 28
Hasty, R. W., 95
Harvard Graduate School of Business
    Administration, 211
Haug, Arne F., 52
Hawkins, Del L., 39
Haynes, Joel B., 154
Heany, Donald F., 15
Heenan, David A., 185
Henry, Walter A., 49
Higginbotham, James, 207
Hills Brothers Company, 95
Hise, Richard T., 180
Hollingsworth, A. Thomas, 154
Holloway, Robert J., 64
Hopkins, David S., 94
Howard, John A., 54
Hunt, Shelby D., 49

I

Internal Revenue Service, 230
International Advertising Association,
    184
Ivancevich, John M., 49, 129

J

Jacoby, Jacob, 45

Jacoby, Neil, 200
Jadicke, Robert K., 136
Jain, Arun K., 52
James, Don L., 170
Johnson, Eugene M., 140, 169, 174
Johnson, James C., 154
Johnson, Richard A., 39
Jolson, Marvin A., 130, 141
Judd, Robert C., 180

K

Kangun, Norman, 207
Kast, Fremont E., 39
Keegan, Warren J., 188, 193–94
Kelley, Eugene, 201
Kelley, G. T., 78
Kelley, William T., 21, 25
Kennedy, John F., 204
Kerby, Joe Kent, 55
Kernan, Jerome B., 64–65, 124–25
King, Robert L., 6
King, William R., 24
Kingman, Merle, 110
Klompmaker, Jay E., 141
K-Mart, 85
Kollat, David T., 13, 50, 53
Kotler, Philip, 7, 15, 19–21, 23, 25, 45,
    50, 73, 75, 91, 107, 125, 129, 147,
    151–52, 155, 157, 159, 162, 169, 180,
    202–3, 206–7
Kramer, Oscar E., Jr., 207
Kurtz, David L., 51, 140–41

L

Lambert, Zarrel V., 156
Lauter, G. Peter, 196
Lazer, William, 78, 201
LeBreque, Roger J., 27
Lee, James A., 182
Lehmann, Donald R., 58
Leighton, David S. R., 181
Lenormand, J. M., 192
Leo, Norton B., 192
Levitt, Theodore, 69, 75, 80, 107, 174,
    180
Levy, Sydney J., 206
Lilien, Gary L., 68
Lodish, Leonard M., 136
Lofthouse, Stephen, 81
Longman, Douglas S., 208
Luck, David J., 39, 93, 201, 207
Lynn, Robert A., 165

M

McCarthy, E. Jerome, 86, 153
McCaskey, Michael B., 15
McGrath, Joseph E., 39
McGuire, W. J., 48

McNair, Malcolm P., 224
McNeal, James V., 125
McVey, Phillip, 146
Mallen, Bruce, 154
Marketing Worldwide of Colgate Palm-
    olive, 188
Markin, Ron J., Jr., 55
Martilla, John A., 37
Martineau, P., 52
Maring, Elizabeth, 107
Maslow, A. H., 41–42, 44
Mayer, Charles S., 39
Mazze, Edward M., 91, 93
Melville, Donald R., 93
Messy, William F., 84
Michman, Ronald, 154
Miller, Bill R., 115
Miller, David, 166
Mills, J., 48
Mintzberg, Henry, 15
Miracle, Gordon E., 78, 191, 196
Moller, William G., Jr., 154
Monroe, Kent B., 156
Montgomery, David B., 39
Montgomery Ward, 152
Moore, Carl L., 136
Moore, Laurence J., 140
Moore, R. Carl, 213
Moore, Russell M., 196
Mossman, Frank H., 138
Mulrichell, Donald F., 166
Murdick, Robert G., 213–14, 222
Myers, James H., 52
Myers, John G., 125

N

National Industrial Conferences Board,
    135, 205, 233
National Retail Merchants Association,
    232
Nugent, Christopher E., 39
Nylen, David W., 125

O

O'Dell, William F., 211, 224
Oliver, Richard L., 129, 140
Omana, Charles J., 191
Operations Research Society of Amer-
    ica, 233
O'Shaughnessy, John, 58
Oshauski, Frank A., 207
Oxenfeldt, Alfred R., 158, 165
Ozanne, Urban B., 68

P

Palda, Kristian S., 166
Parker, Donald D., 169
Parsons, Leonard J., 157

Pepsi-Cola, 193
Perlmutter, Howard V., 185, 193
Pessemier, Edgar A., 45, 107
Peter, J. Paul, 46
Phelps, Maynard D., 93
Pinson, Christian, 7
Playboy magazine, 119
Pooler, Victor H., 69
Procter and Gamble, 84, 87
Progressive Grocer, Inc., 232
Pruden, Henry O., 140, 208

R

Rao, Murlidhar, 68
Rapp, William V., 193
Rathmell, John R., 169, 171–72
Reader's Digest, 119, 191
Reber, Ralph W., 220
Regan, William J., 180
Reid, David M., 125
Reinmuth, James E., 166
Reynolds, Fred D., 55
Richie, J. R. Brent, 27
Riordan, Edward A., 129
Robertson, Dan H., 141
Robertson, George M., 64
Robertson, Thomas S., 129
Robeson, James F., 13
Robicheaux, Robert A., 149
Robinson, H., 48
Robinson, Patrick J., 69
Robinson, William A., 124
Roering, Kenneth J., 55
Rokus, Josef W., 133
Roostal, Ilmar, 186
Root, Franklin R., 192
Root, H. Paul, 107
Root, W. Paul, 208
Rosenberg, Larry J., 29
Rosenbloom, Bert, 154
Ross, Ivan, 46, 107
Rothenburg, Aaron M., 150
Rotzoll, Kim, 125
Rosenzweig, James E., 39
Rudelius, William, 107
Runkel, Philip J., 39
Runyon, Kenneth E., 42
Ruppel, Andrew C., 224
Russell, Frederic A., 141
Ryan, Michael J., 45–46
Ryans, John K., Jr., 186, 192

S

Sachtjen, Wilbur M., 184
Sandage, C. H., 125
Scheibelhut, John H., 129
Scheving, Eberhard E., 81
Schlinger, Mary Jane, 46–47

Schnelle, Kenneth E., 218
Schoeffler, Sidney, 15
Schwartz, George, 200
Sears, Roebuck Company, 85, 152
Sederberg, Kathryn, 110
Semon, Thomas T., 58
Shapiro, Benson P., 207
Shapiro, Irwin A., 227
Sheth, Jagdish N., 61
Shrawder, J. Edward, 57
Shuckman, Abraham, 166
Shuptrine, F. Kelly, 207
Silk, Alvin J., 68
Small, Robert J., 29
Smallwood, John E., 81
Smith, Adam, 201
Smith, Dan, 191
Smith, Samuel V., 39
Smith, Wendell R., 83–84
Smith & Wesson, 96
Sommers, Montrose S., 64–65, 124
Spitz, Edward A., 93
Sports Illustrated magazine, 119
Sprecher, C. Ronald, 180
Stafford, James E., 20, 39
Standard & Poor's Corporation, 228, 232
Stanton, Roger R., 52
Stanton, William J., 62, 78, 169, 171, 190
Stardt, Thomas A., 81
Stasch, Stanley F., 38
Staudt, Thomas A., 93
Steiner, Robert L., 199
Stern, Louis W., 151, 154
Stevens, Robert E., 64
Stobough, Robert B., 166
Strain, Charles E., 115
Strauss, George, 69
Super Market Institute, 232

T

Tangerman, E. J., 187
Tarpey, Lawrence X., 46
Tauber, Edward M., 99, 107
Taylor, Donald A., 39, 81
Terry, Gloria F., 220
Thompson, Joseph W., 141
Time magazine, 119
Townsend, Phillip L., 166
Trent, Robert H., 224
Trombetta, William L., 93
Tucker, Spencer A., 166

Tull, Donald S., 28, 39
Twedt, Dik Warren, 93
Tybout, Alice M., 35

U

Uhl, Kenneth P., 25
Ulman, David B., 89
Urban, Glen L., 39

V

Van Horne, James C., 102
Vara, Albert C., 231
Varble, Dale L., 208
Ven Katesan, M., 47
Verdoorn, P. J., 36
Vertinsky, Ilan, 180
Vogue magazine, 119
Vollmann, Thomas E., 39

W

Wales, Hugh G., 39
Walker, Bruce J., 154, 170, 196
Walker, Orville C., Jr., 129
Walters, C. Glenn, 55
Walters, J. Hart, Jr., 196
Wasserman, Paul, 231–32
Wasson, Chester R., 55, 81, 83, 96
Weber, John A., 107
Webster, Frederick E., Jr., 66–67, 69, 129,
    143–44, 149, 165
Weigand, Robert E., 66
Wells, William D., 55
Westfall, Ralph, 38
Widing, J. William, Jr., 185
Wilemon, David L., 154
Wilkie, William L., 27, 45
Will, R. T., 95
Williams, Charles R., 184
Wilson, David T., 62
Wilson, Timothy L., 93
Wind, Yoram, 66, 69, 83–84, 93, 193
Winer, Leon, 15, 141
Winick, Charles, 166
Woodruff, Robert B., 136
Woodside, Arch G., 125, 129
Wright, John S., 57

Y–Z

Yuspeh, Sonia, 81
Zaltman, Gerald, 35, 180, 202
Zimmer, Thomas W., 213

SUBJECT INDEX

A

Abstracting, 26
Abstracts, 232–34
Accountants Digest, 232
Accountants Index, 232
Accounting Articles, 232
Accounting information system, 20
Action-oriented decision in case analysis, 219
Advertising, 109–23
   budgets, 114
   information source for consumer, 45
   in international marketing, 190–92
   research process in, 31
   sales management, 131
Advertising Age Editorial Index, 232
Aerospace Facts and Figures, 230
Agents, 143, 145
   services, 172
"Age of Information," 19
AIDAS formula in personal selling, 128
Aids in marketing management, 20
Allocation of funds in advertising programs, 116
Alternative action courses, 217
Alternative evaluation in consumer purchase decisions, 45–46
Alternative search in purchase decisions, 44–45
Alternative strategies for foreign markets, 193–95

American Statistical Index, 232
Analysis strategies for international marketing, 193–96
Ann Page label, 85
Annual cash flow payback, 103
Annual reports in marketing information system, 22
Annual Statistical Report, 230
Applied Science and Technology Index, 232
Attitude modeling in consumer evaluations, 45–46
Audio-visual message in advertising campaigns, 116–17
Auditing of sales force, 132
Automobile Facts and Figures, 230
Availability of middlemen in distribution strategy, 147

B

Balance-of-payments problems in international marketing, 183
Basing-point pricing, 163
Battelle Library Review, 233
Battle of the brands, 152
Behavioral science
   in consumer purchasing, 49
   distribution system as a social system, 151
   industrial buyers, 56, 62
   personal selling, 126
Better Business Bureau, 10

"Black-box" selling process, 128
Blue Book, The, 231
Blue Line Investment Survey, 228
Bonus payments in sales compensation plan, 139
Boycotting of market research, 35
Brands
    advantages in, 86
    images, 42, 164
    loyalty, 47
Brokers, 143
Bulletin of Public Affairs Information Service, 233
Business and industry sources, general, 230–32
Business Education Index, 233
Business Periodicals Index, 233
Business Service Checklist, 229
Business Statistics, 229
Buying process, 40–49
    advertising, 118
    operational view of, 61
    stages, 66–68
Buying risks reduced in personal selling, 127

C

Canner-Packer Yearbook, 230
Capital investments in international marketing, 181
Capital outlays in industrial buying, 58
Capitalism and laissez-faire ethic, 201
Case analyses, 212
Cash flow, 102–4, 106
Catalog of United States Census Publication, 233
Ceiling effect in advertising budget, 121
Census of Agriculture, 229
Census of Manufacturers, 229
Census of Mineral Industries, 229
Census of Retail Trade, 229
Census of Selected Services, 229
Census of Transportation, 229
Census of Wholesale Trade, 229
Census Tract Reports, 229
Centralized versus decentralized control, 184
Chain Store Age Executive, 230
Channels of distribution, 144–53
    advertising, 110
    cooperative advertising, 113
    fluctuating demand for services, 172
    in foreign markets, 188–89
    inseparability of services, effects of, 172
    intangibility of services, effects of, 171
    market research part in, 31

Channels of distribution—*Cont.*
    marketing function in, 144
    marketing mix, 12
    in new product failure, 104
    packaging in, 85–86
    service innovations, 175
Checklist for case analyses, 215
Checklist for chosen alternative, 218
Checklist for problem analysis, 217
Child Protection and Toy Safety Act (1969), 11
Child Safety Act (1966), 10
Cigarette Labeling Act (1966), 10
Classification
    classes of firms, 213, 215
    consumer goods, 78
    consumers' family life cycle, 53
    industrial products, 77
    industry, 212, 215
    intermediaries, 143
    of motivation in industrial buying, 62–64
    of product in marketing planning, 75
    product influences in purchase decisions, 58
Clayton Act, 163
Client relationship in services, 173
"Cognitive dissonance," 47–49
Commercial Atlas and Marketing Guide, 227
Commercial and Financial Chronicle, 228
Commissions on sales, 139
Communication
    advertising media, 122
    personal selling, 126
    process, elements of, 116–18
    product use in foreign markets, 193–95
    use of intermediaries, 178
Compensation
    sales force, 138
    sales management, 131
Competition
    effect on pricing decisions, 162
    lack in service marketing, 174
    pricing objectives, 159
Competitive environment, 9
Competitive parity, 115
Competitive pricing, 115
Computer and Information Systems, 233
Computers
    industrial goods, 145
    sales forecasting, 134–35
    storage of information, 20, 27
Computerworld, 230
Computing Reviews, 233

Conference Board Business Record, 229
Consumer Advisory Council on consumers' interests, 203–4
Consumer behavior
  advertising, 117
  felt need, 41–44
  foreign markets, 186–87
  selling process, 128
Consumer credit, improvements in, 204
Consumer Credit Protecting Act (1968), 10
Consumer goods
  product classification, 76
  channels of distribution, 144–45
Consumer needs, 127
Consumer Product Warranty Act (1975), 11
Consumer reaction to price decisions, 155
Consumer relations in product management, 87
Consumer Reports, 45
Consumerism, 203–5
Consumption rate, effect on pricing decisions, 156
Contests in sales promotion, 124
Control
  of brand quality, 152
  of channels of distribution, 148–49
  of distribution in foreign markets, 189
  in marketing plan, 14
  in multinational corporations, 183–85
  sales management function, 132–33
Convenience goods, 76, 126–27
Conventions as sales promotion, 124
Cooperative environment, 9
Coordination problems in international marketing, 183
Core values, changes in, 50
Corporate responsibility, 205
Correlation analyses in sales forecasting, 135
Cost accountants, 24
Cost accounting system, 138
Cost-oriented pricing, 159–60
Cost-plus pricing, 159
Costs
  appraisal in channel selection, 31
  of capital in new product development, 101–2
  of distribution, 149
  estimates in research process, 34
  evaluation in case analysis, 218
  marketing, analysis of, 138
  marketing, in foreign markets, 193–94
  overhead, reduction of, 98
  of production, 159
  reduction by research, 28

Costs—*Cont.*
  selling, 138
  unprofitable product development, 95
Council of Economic Development, 205
Council on Environmental Quality (1970), 11
County and City Data Book, 229
County Data Book, 230
Coupons in sales promotion, 124
Creative marketing services, 173
Credit cards, 176, 179
Credit distribution, 176
Cultural environment
  advertising in foreign markets, 192
  effect on marketing, 212
  international marketing, 182–83
Cultural misunderstanding in international marketing, 182
Cumulative Index of NICB Publications, 233
Current Sources of Marketing Information, 227
Customer expectations method of sales forecasting, 135
Customer needs identified for target market, 11–12
Customer relations, 136

D

Data bank, computer, 21
Data collection and analysis in research process, 32–34
Data processing
  market research process, 35
  systems in retail banking services, 177
Dealer, 143
Deception, avoidance of in selling, 203
Deceptive advertising, 202
Deceptive pricing practices, 163
Decision making
  information for, 19
  research in, 27
Demand
  influence on pricing, 155
  stimulation process in foreign markets, 188
Demographic factors in price decision, 155–56
Demographic variables in foreign marketing, 185–86
Department of Commerce guides for secondary sources, 229–30
Direct channels
  distribution in foreign markets, 188–89
  for industrial goods, 145, 149
"Direct pay deposit" banking services, 177

Direct sale
  distribution of services, 176
  inseparable services, 172
Discount Merchandiser, The, 230
Discount Store News, 230
Discounted cash flow, 101
Dissemination, processing information
  for, 27
Dissonance, postpurchase consumer be-
  havior, 47–49
Distribution coverage for products, 148
Distribution in foreign markets, 188–89
Distribution Worldwide, 230
Distributor, 143, 145
Drawing accounts in compensation
  plans, 139
Drug Abuse Control Amendments
  (1965), 10
Drug and Cosmetic Catalog, 230
Drug and Cosmetic Industry, 230
Drug Topics, 231
Dun's Market Identifiers (DMI), 21

E

Economic Almanac, 229
Economic environment, 9–10
  case analysis, 212, 215
  inequalities in, 204
Economic Report of the President, 229
Economies of scale
  in foreign markets, 187–88
  products for international markets,
    193
Editor and Publisher "Market Guide,"
  227
Edsel automobile, 28
Education
  business school graduates, 89
  consumer behavior, 49
Eight-M formula, the, 112
Electrical World, 231
Electronic media, 119
Elements of product strategy, 74
Encoding in advertising, 117
*Encyclopedia of Business Information
  Sources,* 231
Environment
  declining quality and consumerism,
    204
  influences on pricing decisions, 162
  a managed capitalism, 201
  marketing analysis, 9–11
  problems in international marketing,
    182
Ethics
  research surveys, 34–35
  standards, 202–5
Evaluation of products in industrial buy-
  ing, 67–68

Evaluation of research reports, 37
Exchange controls in international mar-
  keting, 183
Exclusive distribution of products for
  specialized selling, 148
Expense control as a function of sales
  management, 137
External information flows, 21–24

F

Fair Credit Reporting Act (1968), 11
Fair Packing and Labeling Act (1965),
  10
*Fairchild's Financial Manual of Retail
  Stores,* 228
Family life cycle in buying process, 52–
  53
Federal Boat Safety Act (1971), 11
Federal Trade Commission, 163
Federal Trade Commission Act, 163
Felt need in consumer behavior, 41–44
Financial activities centralized in multi-
  national firms, 185
Financial Information Sources, 228–29
Financial information system, 20, 22
Financial World, 228
Financing availability to consumers in
  foreign markets, 186
Five Ps of research process, 30–38
Flexibility
  in channels of distribution, 148, 150
  in product definition, 75
Fluctuating demand for services, 172
"Followership" technique in advertis-
  ing, 115
*Food and Beverage Industries: A Bibli-
  ography and Guidebook,* 231
Forecasting
  information systems, 22
  marketing research role in, 28
  product managers' responsibility, 89
  sales, 133–35
Foreign media advertising by U.S. firms,
  191–92
Forest Industries, 231
Formal marketing information system,
  21
Franchises, 150
Fringe benefits in sales compensation
  plans, 140
Fundamentals of selling, 129–30
*Funk and Scott Index of Corporations
  and Industries,* 233

G

General business and industry sources,
  230–32
Geographic flexibility in advertising
  media, 120

Geographic markets expanded by credit cards, 179
Geographic regions
  sales management, 132
  sales territories, 135–37
"Going rate pricing," 162
Goods distribution process, 142
Government regulations
  on advertising, 110
  on prices, 162
Government representation of consumers, 204
Gross national product effect in foreign markets, 186
Group influences on consumer behavior, 44, 49–55
Growth functions technique of sales forecasting, 135
Growth vectors, 96

H

Handbook of Basic Economic Statistics, 230
Hazardous Radiation Act (1968), 11
Health care services as intermediaries, 177
Health maintenance organization (HMO), 177
Hierarchy of needs, 43–44
Historical Statistics of the United States, 230
Horizontal communication flow, 24
Horizontal market for industrial goods, 76
How-to approach to selling, 128

I

Idea generation in product planning, 98–99
Implement and Tractor, 231
Import duties in foreign markets, 190
Import restrictions in international marketing, 183
Income, information flow on consumer, 24
Indexes, 232–34
Indirect channels of retail goods distribution, 145, 149
Industrial buyer behavior, 56–69
Industrial goods
  channels of distribution, 145
  product classification, 76
Industrial Marketing, 228
Industrial markets, buyer behavior in, 56–66
Industry Surveys, 231
Information
  flows in marketing system, 21–25

Information—*Cont.*
  sources, 24
"Information Era," 19
Information systems, 19–27
  marketing, 20
  place in marketing decisions, 15
  sales forecasting, 134
Input in product planning, 105
Input-output system in selling process, 128–29
Inseparability of services, 171–72
Insurance, use of intermediaries in, 178
Intangibility of services, 171
Intelligence information, 21
Intensive distribution of convenience goods, 148
Intermediaries in service industries, 176–78
Internal information flows, 24–25
International agency advertising in foreign markets, 191
International Abstracts in Operations Research, 233
International Commerce, 230
International Journal of Abstracts of Statistical Methods in Industry, 233
Interview surveys for market research, 34–35
Inventory
  costs, 149
  product development, 101
Investment outlay, 105–6
Invoice in information system, 22

J–K

Jobber, 143
Joint decision making in buying process, 59–61
Journal of Economic Literature, 233
Jury of executive opinion method of sales forecasting, 135
Kenmore label, 85

L

Laissez-faire ethic, 201
Law of diminishing returns in advertising, 112
Leadership in distribution strategy, 151
Legal environment, 10–11
Legal standards vesus ethical standards, 202
Legislation as constraint on business behavior, 11
Life cycle in industrial products, 79–81
Limited decision making by consumers, 53–54
Lobbying for restriction of market research, 35
Long-run strategic planning, 24

M

Magazine media for advertising, 119
Magnuson-Moss Warranty—Federal Trade Commission Act (1974), 11
"Managed capitalism" societal concept, 201
Management education, 211
Management Information Guides, 233
Management philosophy in case analyses, 214
Management Review, 233
Manpower, sales force, 131, 133, 138
Manufacturer's representative, 143
Marginal analysis of economic theory, 111
Market profiles, 21
Market segmentation
  product planning, 84–85
  sales territories, 136
  social class role in, 51–52
Marketing
  activities, 124
  communication, 21
  decisions in multinational companies, 184
  ethical standards in, 202
  information, 144
  intermediaries, 142–43
  skill in advertising, 117–18
Marketing Communications, 228
Marketing concepts, 5
  basic elements, 6
  broadened view, 205–7
  development of, 73
  responsibility of management, 81–83
  sales management, 131
  social role of marketing, 200
Marketing Information Guide, 228
Marketing management defined, 7–8
Marketing mix, 11
  services marketing, 178–79
  variables, 74
"Marketing nerve center," 25
Marketing objectives
  determine pricing decision, 158
  distinctiveness of product, 161
  in planning, 11
Marketing plan
  advertising budgets, 110
  place of advertising campaign in, 116
Marketing-program approach in advertising, 116
Marketing program in case analyses, 214–15
Marketing research, 27–38
  activities centralized in multinational firms, 185

Marketing research—*Cont.*
  analysis of foreign markets, 185–86
  case analysis, 214
  lack in service marketing, 174
  for price decisions, 156
  sales forecasting, 134
Marketing sources, 227–28
Marketing strategy, 88
  case analyses, 215
  for international markets, 193–96
  in pricing, 165
  product life-cycle, 82
  service marketing, 179
  variables in services, 169
Marketing studies by sales management, 132
Marketing systems in service marketing, 173
Marketing team, 130
Mark-up pricing, 159
Mass markets
  European development of, 186
  pricing policy, 161
  products for underdeveloped countries, 194
Mass selling, 108
Material goods and consumer values in foreign markets, 186
Media
  communication channels, 117
  selection in advertising, 118–23
  selection factors, 123
  selection in foreign markets, 191
Men's Wear, 231
Merchandising Week, 231
Metropolitan Statistical Areas, 230
Middle management, 131
Middle Market Directory, 231
Middlemen, 143, 146–47
  advertising, 113
  distribution control, 85
  in foreign markets, 188–89
  pricing in foreign markets, 190
  services, 172, 176
Minority Enterprise Small Business Investment Company, 204
Models
  advertising, 123
  advertising process, 113
  industrial buying process, 57
  planning, 12
  pricing decision, 164
  selling process, 128
Modern Brewery Age, 231
Monthly Checklist of State Publications, 233
Moody's Bank and Finance Manual, 228
Moody's Bond Survey, 228
Moody's Directors Service, 228

Moody's Handbook of Widely Held Common Stocks, 228
Moody's Industrial Manual, 228
Moody's Municipal and Government Manual, 228
Moody's Public Utility Manual, 228
Moody's Transportation Manual, 228
Morale of sales personnel, 138
Motivational forces in industrial buying, 62–66
Motor Vehicle Information and Cost Savings Act (1974), 11
Multinational corporations, 181

N

National Commission on Product Safety Act (1967), 10
National Industrial Conference Board, 135, 205, 233
National Petroleum News, 231
National Traffic and Motor Vehicle Safety Act (1966), 10
Neilson Index, 112
"Net percent value analysis" of investment profitability, 101
New product development, 94–106
Nonbusiness organizations, 206
Nondiscriminatory practices, 203
Nonpersonal selling, defined, 108
Nonprofit organizations, marketing tasks in, 206

O

Operating Results of Department and Specialty Stores, 232
Opportunity costs, 95
Oral presentation of case analyses, 223
Order processing as a distribution cost, 149
Organization
  centralized information system, 26
  influences on industrial buying, 59–61
  international marketing, 182–85
  new product changes, 97
  new product department, 106
  objectives, 8–9
  problems in international marketing, 183–85
  in product development, 100–101
  product management, 89, 91
  role playing in, 65
  sales management, 131–40
Ownership requirements in international marketing, 183

P

Packaging, 85
  design, 126

Patent search, 24
"Payback method" in cash flow, 103, 106
Penetration policy in pricing decisions, 161
Per capita national income, effect in foreign marketing, 186
Percent of sales as advertising budget, 114
Performance evaluation, 136
  advantage of sales territories, 136
  of media, 122
  rewards for results, 138
  sales management function, 131
Perishability of services, 172
Personal motives in buying process, 62–65
Personal selling, 126–40
Personnel
  information system, 20
  in marketing plan, 14
  research process, 34
  restrictions in international marketing, 183
Personnel Management Abstracts, 233
Per unit expenditure method of advertising budgeting, 114–15
Petroleum Facts and Figures, 232
"Phantom freight," illegal pricing of, 163
Piggyback service in freight transport, 175
Pilot plant operations, 24
Pitfalls in case analysis, 220–21
Planned obsolescence, 202
Planning
  advertising, 109–18
  channels of distribution, 147
  compensation for sales force, 138
  decision implementation, 219
  and development, 24
  foreign markets, 187–88
  long-range view of marketing, 80
  market segmentation, 84–85
  marketing tasks, 12
  product, 81–86
  research process, 30–35
  sales management, 131–37
Point-of-purchase displays in sales promotion, 124
Policy guidelines in new product development, 98
Pollution, consumer concerns in, 204–5
Poor's Register of Corporations, Directors and Executives of the United States and Canada, 232
Population distribution in foreign markets, 185
Population growth factor in sales growth, 174

Population and Its Distribution: The United States Markets, 228
Premiums in sales promotion, 124
Price
  discrimination, 163
  elasticity, 155, 157
  fixing, 163
  system, 155
Price-quality relationships, 157
Pricing
  without discrimination, 203
  for international marketing, 189–90
  objectives, 158
Primary data in research process, 32–33, 35
Private brands, 85
Prizes in sales compensation plans, 139
Problem analysis approach, 219
Problem recognition, 217
Product
  audit technique of marketing management, 90–92
  characteristics effect on pricing, 160
  class in purchase decisions, 53–54
  committees, 106
  consumption rate in relation to pricing, 161
  development, 95–96
  development concept, 73
  development in distribution of services, 179
  distinctiveness, 161
  failure, 29, 94, 104–6, 187
  influences on industrial buyers, 56–59
  information, 131
  invention for foreign markets, 188, 194
  life cycle, 92, 161
  line, 83
  management concept, 87
  manager, 87–90
  mix, 83, 97
  overlap, 84
  perishability, 161
  planning, 81–86, 94–105, 187–88
  quality evaluation, 45
  specialization in sales territories, 136
  strategy, 73–83
Product Management, 232
"Product provincialism," 75
Profit contribution of product, 92
Profit sharing in sales compensation, 139
Profitability
  new product development measured, 101–4
  product importance in, 74–75
  of target market, 12

Profits
  advertising goals, 111–12
  introduction phase of product, 79–80
  marketing objectives, 11
  multinational corporations, 181
  new product effects, 98
  organization objectives, 8–9
  purchasing motive, 76
  and social concepts, 200–201
Progressive Grocer, 232
Project on Corporate Responsibility, The, 205
Project planning, 100ff.
Promotion
  mix defined, 108–9
  place of sales forecasting in, 134
Promotional pricing, 163
Psychological Abstracts, 233
Psychological factors in price decision, 156
Psychological information system, 27
Public Affairs Information Service, 233
Public Health Smoking Cigarette Act (1969), 11
Publicity; *see* Advertising
Pulling products through channels, 153
Purchase decision, 46–47
  consumer behavior, 53–54
Purchase response to price decisions, 156
Purchasing agents
  buying functions, 60
  purchase responsibility, 65
  study of in buying process, 58–59
Pushing products through channels, 153
"Put a tiger in your tank" campaign, 192, 194

Q

Quality control, 152
  importance in industrial buying, 77
  product development, 101
  product failure, 94, 104, 187
  Teflon case, 29
Quality related to price, 156
Quantity discounts, price differentials in, 163
Questionnaires in research process, 34
Quick-Frozen Foods, 232
Quotas, 134–37
  imports, in foreign marketing, 183

R

Railroads
  product provincialism, 75
  services, 175
Rate-of-return pricing, 159
Raw materials
  buying motives, 63

Raw materials—*Cont.*
  limited life, pricing relationship, 161
  product classification, 76
Reader's Guide to Periodic Literature, 234
Red Book, 231
Reference groups and consumer behavior, 52–53
Reinforcement, consumer behavior, 47
Rental services, 10
Requisition forms in buying process, 61
Research; *see also* Marketing research
  advertising budget, 115–16
  inputs in information system, 22
  in new product planning, 105
  process, 30–38
Responsibility
  in buying process, 66–67
  of management in product planning, 81–83
  of purchasing agents, 65
Retail banking services, 177
Retailer, 143–44
Retailing in Australia, 190
Retrieval of information
  computer storage, 25–26
  indexing, 26
Return on investment
  advertising, 112
  marketing research, 28
  new product development, 101–2
  pricing objectives, 159
Rights of consumers, 203–4
Risks
  assumed by middlemen, 175–76
  in foreign markets, 182–85
  industrial buying, 62–64
  marketing functions, 144
  new product development, 98
  perceived by consumers, 46
  reduction by research, 28
Robinson-Patman Act, 85, 163
Role of product manager, 90
Role performing in buying process, 64–65
Routinized decision making by consumers, 54

S

Safety of products, 203
Salaries of sales force, 139
Sales
  advertising goals, 111–12
  agents, 143
  compensation plans, 138–40
  management, 130–40
  quotas, 134–37
  reports for product improvement, 92
  territories, 135–37

Sales—*Cont.*
  trends, 91
  volume in target market, 12
Sales force
  defined, 133
  composite method of sales forecasting, 135
Sales and Marketing Management, 228
Sales promotion
  defined, 124
  information source for consumer, 45
  packaging, 85–86
  personal selling, 126–40
  research process in, 31
Salesperson in selling process, 129
Sample design and selection, 33–34
Scanning for information in trade journals, 25
Sealed-bid pricing, 162
Search activity, 25
  research process, 30–35
Secondary data in research process, 32
Security Owner's Stock Guide, 228
Security Price Index, 229
Selection of channels of distribution, 146
Selective distribution, middleman limited in, 148
Self-service stores, 126
Selling process, 127–30
Service establishments, 170
Service marketing, 169, 173
Services
  defined, 171
  in marketing concept, 73
Sherman Antitrust Act, 163
Shopping centers, 151
Shopping goods, classified, 76
Short-run tactical decisions, 24
Simulation models in sales forecasting, 135
Situation analysis, 9
Situational influences on consumer behavior, 54–55
Skimming policy in pricing decisions, 161
Small Business Administration, 204
Social behavior in selling process, 129
Social class
  attitudinal differences, 52
  consumer behavior, 50–52
Social environment, 10
  advertising opportunity, 111
  consumer attitudes in foreign markets, 186
  effect on marketing, 212
  information on developments in, 24
  political uncertainty in foreign marketing, 183

Social marketing defined, 201
Social irresponsibility in corporations versus consumers, 203
Social Responsibilities of Business Corporations, 205
Social responsibility, 7, 214
    role of marketing, 199–202
Social Sciences and Humanities Index, 234
Social system, 151
Societal concept of marketing, 200
Sociological Abstracts, 234
Sources of Business Information, 232
Sources of information on consumer behavior, 44–45
Special Current Business Reports, 233
Specialty goods defined, 76
Spending patterns, information on, 24
Standard Corporation Records, 229
Standard Industrial Classification (SIC), 213
Standard of living effect on services, 174
Standards of ethics in marketing, 202
Standards of performance
    marketing objectives, 11
    quotas, 136
Starch Reports, 112, 115
Statistical Abstract of the United States, 230
Statistical analysis in marketing research, 28
Statistical sources, basic U.S., 229–30
Statistics of Income: U.S. Business Tax Returns, 230
Statistics Sources, 232
Statistics specialists in information system, 27
Subcultures, 50
Super Market Industry Speaks, 232
Supply and demand, role of intermediaries, 143
Supply influences on pricing decisions, 158
Support services, information evaluation, 26
Survey of Current Business, 230
Systems theory of channels of distribution, 149

T

Target markets, 11–12
    advertising, 119

Target markets—*Cont.*
    influences on pricing, 155
    international markets, 181ff.
    media selection, 123
Tariffs in international marketing, 183
Task approach in advertising program budgets, 116
Taxes as carrying costs, 149
Teflon case, 29
Test marketing
    advertising, 115–16
    market research, 29
    new product planning, 100
    research process, 37–38
Threshold effect in advertising budget, 121
Time and place utility of services, 172
Time series analyses in sales forecasting, 135
Trading stamps in sales promotion, 124–25
Training programs, 129
    lack in service marketing, 174
    manuals, 129
    research, place of, 31
    of sales people, 127
Transportation
    distribution costs, 149
    market function, 144
Transportation Safety Act (1974), 11

U–V

"Used apple policy," 80
Values
    constraints of social, 10
    of consumers in foreign markets, 186
    cultural, changes in, 49–50
    index used in buying, 68
Variables of marketing mix, 12
Vending machines, 126
Vending Times, 232
Vertical information flow, 24
Vertical market in industrial goods, 76

W

Wall Street Journal Index, The, 234
Warner social class hierarchy, 51
Wholesale Meat Act (1967), 10
Wholesaler, 143
Wholesome Poultry Products Act (1968), 11
Written report, 221

This book has been set in 10 and 9 point Palatino, leaded 2 points. Section and chapter numbers are 54 point Palatino italic. Section titles are 24 point Palatino and chapter titles are 20 point Palatino. The size of the type page is 26 by 45½ picas.